Provocative reading that calls for a response. You'll have a number of reactions as you work through these pages, but rest assured, Wendy's transparent and engaging style brings you safely to a clear and developed understanding that rings with truth.

[Match] is a refreshing read that wrestles with important issues from the full scope of the Bible and theology. A delightful departure from the usual complaints and proof-texting and an immensely practical read from someone who knows and loves the church.

—DAVE LAMB
Senior Pastor, Highland Hills Baptist Church, Grand Rapids, Mich.

A Match Made in Heaven is a must read for pastors because it is not just about singles issues . . . it's about the Church. It is a biblically based theology of singleness in the church. More than a surface treatment of the issues, it is stimulating reading with depth and simplicity.

—CHIP BERNHARD
Senior Pastor, Spring Creek Church, Pewaukee, Wisc.

This book says about singles and the church what no seminary class or workshop I have ever attended has said. Wendy's insights on ministry to and by singles in the church are profound and cannot be ignored. These are the *ABC*s of singles ministry in today's multidimensional society.

—DAVID W. LOFTIS
Associate Pastor, Colonial Baptist Church, Cary, N.C.

Too often the contemporary church has marginalized singles. Wendy Widder's balanced, insightful book provides a remedy. Equipped with biblical perspectives and practical ideas, she envisions the church as the Family of God that includes and affirms single and married people alike. Essential reading for singles looking for their place in the church and for church leaders wanting to welcome them.

—ALBERT Y. HSU
author of *Singles at the Crossroads*

This candid and warm book is a very helpful diagnosis for healing for the marriage of the church and its singles. Wendy has obviously heard both sides of the story and wants them to live together in a healthier way.

It's a courageous call for the church to love its singles and view their calling with more respect, and for the singles to learn to honor the church better and really be one with it.

—KNUTE LARSON
Senior Pastor, The Chapel, Akron and Green, Ohio

An insightful, thought-provoking, and, at times, a very challenging read. As a single, I can relate to many specific issues that Wendy tactfully addresses. A good book for anyone who desires to increase their understanding of the "singles culture."

—GLORIA A. BAKER, PH.D.
Associate Professor of Kinesiology, Cornerstone University

This book identifies missed opportunities and mistakes on all sides and provides a blueprint for building a stronger, richer, more Christlike church family—one that embraces and celebrates the distinct plan God has for each of us.

—JEANINE HILL
PR professional and single adult church member

In the growing body of Christian literature for singles, it is refreshing to find a book that looks beyond dating or personal contentment, and considers Christian stewardship of singleness and how it fits into God's larger plan.

Armed with plenty of true stories (funny, sad, and sometimes both), *A Match Made in Heaven* presents an honest assessment and helpful prescription for how singles and the Church should relate to one another and truly picture the Family of God. As a result, this book has value for singles, church leaders, and all Christians seeking a biblical perspective on singleness.

Those who are expecting a book that is primarily about the single life will be surprised by the broad theological themes and richness of background that shape the book's message. Wendy Widder is one of the first evangelical authors to begin developing a "theology of singleness" and to evaluate the Church's rising singles demographic through the Reformed worldview of Creation-Fall-Redemption. Her work will likely spark additional thought and reflection on this often misunderstood but very important topic.

—DAVID K. "KELLY" FATH JR.
Singles Leader, Calvary Church, Fruitport, Mich.

Much writing about singles ministries boils down to "how-to" programmatic manuals, but *Match* engages in a thoughtful, provoking, and far-ranging analysis of culture, Church, and the socio-developmental needs of singles. This book is a must read, and must subsequently be discussed by church leaders and singles alike, even together. These overdue conversations may well result in healing and growth.

—MARK A. LAMPORT, PH.D.
Professor of Educational Ministries,
Grand Rapids Theological Seminary

Speaking the truth in love, Wendy has provided a valuable tool for the Body of Christ. In highlighting the metaphor of family, Wendy has put her finger on the pulse of solution. The context and security of a family provide an appropriate backdrop for loving one another regardless of marital status.

—DOUG CRAWFORD
Senior Pastor, West Cannon Baptist Church, Belmont, Mich.

a match made *in* heaven

a match made *in* heaven

HOW SINGLES AND THE CHURCH CAN LIVE HAPPILY EVER AFTER

wendy widder

Kregel
Publications

A Match Made in Heaven: How Singles and the Church Can Live Happily Ever After

Published by Kregel Publications, a division of Kregel, Inc., P.O. Box 2607, Grand Rapids, MI 49501.

Scripture quotations are from *The New King James Version.* © 1979, 1980, 1982, Thomas Nelson, Inc., Publishers. Portions of Scripture that are italicized indicate emphasis added by the author.

The names of many people in this book have been changed to protect their privacy.

Cover design: John M. Lucas

Library of Congress Cataloging-in-Publication Data
Widder, Wendy.
A match made in heaven: how singles and the church can live happily ever after / by Wendy Widder.
      p. cm.
Includes bibliographical references.
     1. Church work with single people. 2. Single people—
Religious life. I. Title.
BV639.S5W53
248.8'4—dc21   2003014275

ISBN 0-8254-4112-9

Printed in the United States of America

1 2 3 4 5 / 07 06 05 04 03

To the memory of
Dr. "Joe" Crawford
who affirmed my singleness
the first time he met me
and then went on to leave
a larger than life legacy that continues
to shape the way I read the "Story"
—and hopefully the way I tell it to others.

To Mike Wittmer
who learned well from Dr. Crawford.
Thanks for being willing to
step into his shoes—
too big for anyone to fill—
and provide me with advice, encouragement,
and friendship for so many steps
along the way.
You've helped me
pick up the pace.

Contents

Preface

I've been single my whole life and I've been associated with the church my whole life. I know, along with many of you—singles and church leaders—that being single in the church is a little like being a dill pickle in a fruit salad. In a Christian culture that idealizes marriage and focuses on families, singles are oddballs. It doesn't matter how many times well-meaning churchgoers (or leaders) have tried saying otherwise; nobody is really fooled.

For my single friends, I understand why some of us have just given up. The frustrations are too many and the hurts too great. We've either quit going to church altogether, or we've resigned ourselves to second-class citizenship in the Family of God. Others of us have switched churches looking for more active singles ministries—places we can belong, have fun, and hopefully even find a spouse . . . so we can get out of singles ministries altogether!

On the surface, each of these responses to the discomforts and even denigration of being single in the church makes sense. I empathize with the singles who choose them. I'm pretty tempted myself sometimes. But if you think about it, these responses just make us *feel* more comfortable about our place in the church, rather than really *changing* our place in the church. These responses tell the church it's okay that they're mostly about families and singles don't fit.

And I suppose even the hardiest of singles could live with this misaligned focus if the church was just a place we *go*—or don't go—on Sundays. But it's not. In fact, the church isn't a place we *go* at all. As gifted author Marva Dawn loves to say, "church" is not where we *go*, it's what we *are*. The redeemed community of God knit together in

Christ, we—not the buildings—are the Church. When we stay home, sneak out, or switch churches, we may provide temporary solutions for our individual feelings, but we do nothing to make *us, the church,* better. I hope this book provides a tool for us to do our part as singles to make the church better.

However, this issue has two sides. If pastors and church leaders don't understand what it's like to be single in the church, things will not get better. That's why I have written this book for church leaders as well.

Some of my best friends are pastors. When they heard I was writing a book about singles and the church, they were a little nervous—and perhaps with good reason. In a recent Ellison Research survey, more than half the church leaders surveyed ranked their church's ministry to singles as poor. Another 34 percent said ministry to singles in their church is only fair. Easily the lowest-rated of all fifteen areas surveyed, singles ministry can understandably make church leaders uncomfortable.

These statistics, however, don't tell the whole story. As pastors and singles leaders, you have good reason for not excelling when it comes to singleness in the church. You've been set up to fail. You've been asked to do the impossible. The truth is that singles don't fit in the church—at least the church we know. In a Christian culture where marriage has long been the ideal and families the primary focus, singles *can't* fit.

Something in the church is broken, and the fact that you've picked up this book suggests you want to help fix it. You love the church—disfigured as she is by flaws, quirks, and even sin—and you are investing the best of your life's energy to see her become more and more the glorious bride of Christ.

I love the church, too. And like you, I want to see it become better. You are the ones who, by your faithful teaching and leading, initiate change. You are the ones who shape the beliefs and perspectives of your congregations. What they think about singles in the church will reflect what you think about singles in the church. What they do with singles in the church will mirror what you do with singles in the church. Today's church is broken when it comes to singleness, and you are the ones who, by heeding God's call to ministry, bear the responsibility to fix it—or at least to try.

My pastor friends were also nervous when they heard about this book because I wrote it as a seminary student—and most pastors know what seminary students are like. We specialize in identifying everything that's wrong with the church. We view the flaws in ministry from our high and mighty pedestals of idealism. We want to start our own churches because it seems infinitely easier than reforming the ones we know.

Let me assure you, this is not a book to bash the church. It's not a book to cast stones at church leaders, the ones who give their blood, sweat, and tears for the ministry. Although my seminary experiences certainly shaped my thinking, the heart of this book didn't come from an ivory tower classroom. It came from sitting in a pew as a single adult in a family church. It came from hearing about many in the singles community who have given up on the church. It came from loving the church too much to let it stay the way it is.

What does it mean for the church to be the Family of God? Can singles really fit? I believe they can—and if we are to be what God has called us to be, I believe they must.

Thank you for joining me for this journey. I pray you will read with a willingness to look hard in the mirror, as I have had to while writing. And I pray that you will come away with a better understanding of and appreciation for the amazing story God continues to write through His people, the Church.

Acknowledgments

These are both my favorite and my least favorite pages to write. On one hand, they represent the lifeblood of a project—the people whose faces nudge closest to the surface of my memories as I reflect on the process of writing this book. I am overwhelmed with gratitude for their roles in helping me complete it. On the other hand, I will inevitably omit people who are dear to me, people who have prayed for me, people who have cheered me on. To these dear unnamed friends, may the One who never overlooks, forgets, or runs out of space richly reward you.

Rodney Clapp *(Families at the Crossroads)* and **Albert Hsu** *(Singles at the Crossroads)* whose provocative books have contributed much to my thinking in this whole area. Add them to your reading list.

Kregel friends—Thanks for providing a place for me in your company and in your hearts. You were a place to belong when I needed it most.

Ray and Danielle—Thanks for endearing yourselves to me by warmly welcoming me into your sweet little family. Your friendship has been enriching and encouraging, and I hope I've given a little something to you in return. And besides all that, it's been nice to have a fellow Packer fan in Lions territory!

Geoff and Ruth—Your initiative and persistence in becoming my friends gave me hope when I was losing hope. Thank you for doggedly trying to wear my shoes and work for change, while sharing yourselves and reminding me that these issues belong to the entire church—not just singles. You've made the load lighter.

Norma—Thanks for putting up with an absent roommate as I spent an entire year in captivity to my computer. Your patience and willingness to process ideas out of the blue provided the first safety net for potential heresy—a new fear we acquired as seminary students.

Tammy—Your friendship continues to be one of the brightest spots in my life. Thank you for genuine interest in whatever I'm learning, enthusiastic endorsement of whatever I'm writing, and unfailing love through whatever God is taking us.

Jeff and Julie—I liked it better when we were in the same time zone . . . okay, in the same country . . . okay, in the same hemisphere. Thank you for your commitment to our friendship, no matter the distance. Thank you for sharing your lives, your wisdom, and your humor with me. God be with you 'til we meet again.

Kelly—I'm thankful that providence left you in Michigan at the same time it brought me here. Through you God provided an avid supporter of these ideas and a solid sounding board for refining them— and all that in addition to just being good company. You are a faithful friend.

Becky C.—Your passion to serve God with the best of who you are and what you have are constant challenges to those who call you friend. Thanks for your example and thanks for contributing so many insightful comments on the issues in this book.

Mom and Dad—Your unwavering commitment to each other has illustrated for your children how a perfect match works. Thanks, too, for your involvement in and commitment to the local church for decades—you've made it nearly impossible for me not to love it as well. A deep love for the Family of God is truly one of the best things I've inherited from you.

Suzy—Thank you for the sacrifices you made to comb through this manuscript, helping me make it as clear and clean as possible. I'm glad God made us sisters, but even more thankful that He's behind our commitment to remain friends.

David and Carol—Since the day we met, you have welcomed singles into *your* family and into *the* Family. Thanks for letting me be one of them. Your friendship is a much-treasured gift, a gift I wish I could enjoy from not quite so far away.

My professors at GRTS—Thanks for loving the Lord, the Book, the Church, and those who represent its future.

The nearly two dozen friends who gave me the invaluable gift of time and input to read this book in process. I am grateful for your insights and suggestions—thanks for going the extra miles to make these pages better.

My silver-haired friends at Spring Creek—No one has friends more faithful than you. You have both whetted my appetite and helped satisfy my longing for intergenerational relationships—the backbone of the church community. I pray that when my steps shuffle as some of yours do, I'll be able to keep up with the model you've set.

Spring Creek Family—I recognize the dangers of writing this book. It is possible that you will interpret my impassioned words about the church's need to rethink and "re-act" in relation to singles as an indictment against you. They are not. You have loved me much and loved me well . . . just the way I am, for as long as I've been. You have shaped me. Anything valuable and true in these pages is to God's glory in large part because of the work He's accomplished *in* me *through* you. Anything erroneous or hurtful in these pages is because of my failure to learn well. It is my earnest prayer that the things I have said will only help you grow ever more beautiful as the Bride of Christ. I love you back . . . just the way you are.

West Cannon Family—Thank you for being the kind of family that anyone in their right mind would want to be part of. Your faithfulness to the Word of God and to the body of Christ radiates His beauty in a thousand ways. You have urged me forward in this process because what you have is too good for singles *not* to be an integral part of it. I pray that these words will encourage you to grow as you have helped me grow, to reach out of comfort zones as you have forced me to reach out of my comfort zone, and to spur you on to become an even more beautiful extension of the Family of God.

Introduction

Daniel Thomas Horton made a name for himself—although it didn't happen with all the grandeur he'd imagined. It was the last out of the last game of the last season in the well-worn home stadium of the Milwaukee Brewers baseball team. Far behind his seat in the bleachers he could see the retractable roof of the new Miller Park towering over the parking lot of a tired Milwaukee County Stadium. Within weeks, his team's home would be imploded into a pile of twisted metal and concrete rubble.

Daniel, with all the insane fervor of a "fan"-atic, had planned the perfect celebration to mark the end of an era. At just the right moment, he got up from his not-so-comfortable seat in the left field bleachers, jumped the fence, and rushed on to the field, confident that a wave of nostalgic fans would swell behind him in triumphant baseball glory. They didn't. Bleacher bums who had promised allegiance chickened out at the last minute, and even Daniel's friends were too afraid to join him. Instead of leading a jubilant crowd, a disappointed Daniel followed the sheriff's deputies off the field to receive his $518.50 citation. His rush had ended in a riot of one.

Although I'm not looking for glory or a spot on the evening news, I have to confess that in the writing of this book, I have entertained some of the same hopes that Daniel Thomas Horton had when he rushed the baseball field. Like most authors (at least, I *hope* I'm not alone), I have grand illusions (or delusions) that my writing will capture you after the first page, and you won't rest until you've finished the book and enthusiastically recruited all your friends to join the throng of loyal readers.

Lest you think me unusually arrogant, I really do know better ... even my mother doesn't read my books in one sitting (although she does a fine job of recruiting). And while I *do* hope you are interested enough to read and recommend what I write, what I really long for is a groundswell of God-fearing people to catch a vision of what we, the Church of Jesus Christ, can—and *must*—become together for the glory of God.* I pray that God will override *my* feeble attempt to communicate and then grip your heart with *His* life-changing truths, causing you to leap over the fence in a daring statement of loyalty to Christ and His Bride.

> *We have expended much energy to formulate ministries for singles in the church, but we have been slower to discover that there exists a relationship between singles and the church.*

Singleness is a not a new topic in the church. In fact, the issue has been around for as long as the Church has. In the New Testament era, singleness was just one way for a person to fulfill his or her role in God's plan—neither singleness nor marriage was better. During the time of the church fathers, singleness was elevated as a superior way to achieve greater spirituality. Marriage was good, but those—like monks and nuns—who chose celibacy, sacrificing marriage and sex for the purpose of serving God, were perceived as the most religious. It wasn't until Martin Luther emerged in the religious turbulence of the sixteenth century and confronted both the Roman Catholic view that celibacy was superior to marriage and the hypocrisy of a sexually corrupt "celibate" clergy, that the goodness of marriage reasserted itself and, in fact, overtook singleness. A reformed monk, Luther married at the age of forty-two and although he intended to bring balance

---

* I choose to capitalize the word "Church" when I am referring to the ideal that Christ established for His followers. Someday as Christ's bride, the Church will stand before Him spotless. Until then, we are groups of people often in need of much reform. I will not capitalize "church" when I am referring more specifically to these groups of people with which we're much more familiar!

to the church's perspective of marriage and singleness, such statements as "before God a married woman is better than a virgin"[1] are the ones that shaped the beliefs of his religious descendents. The general view of Protestants today is that singles are "crippled people [whose] best hope [is] to endure their hardship."[2]

In recent years, the evangelical church has taken a closer look at the issue of singleness, but it has generally addressed the topic in virtual isolation from the rest of the body of Christ. We have made great strides in drawing singles into the church and plugging them into a thriving (or surviving) singles ministry where we hopefully deal with some of their unique needs. We have expended much energy to formulate ministries for singles *in* the church, but we have been slower to discover that there exists a relationship between singles *and* the church—a vital relationship, a symbiotic relationship. The primary relationship between them has been one of the married members who have "arrived," waiting for the others to catch up.

At best, singleness has been a slowly accepted but little understood lifestyle that some poor souls have to settle for when they can't seem to find anyone to marry. At worst, singles have been perceived—if not treated—as the "odd men out" in the Family of God, marginalized into second-class citizenship in His kingdom.* In either case, the body of Christ has often been guilty of misunderstanding, misjudging, and mismanaging a significant and growing percentage of the evangelical population.

But the church is not alone in her need for improvement. I'll be the first to say that singles could use a little reforming, too. (Personal experience tells me so!) We singles have migrated by the score to ministries designed (and funded) for us, taken what was offered, and then moved on to the next singles activity in town. Many twenty-something singles, especially, have reveled in lingering adolescent luxuries afforded to young unmarried adults, and then wondered why the church perceives singles as uncommitted. Clustered in our section

---

* Similarly, I choose to capitalize the word "Family" when I refer to the Family of God because it represents, as we will discuss throughout this book, the primary familial relationships we have since Jesus came.

of the sanctuary week after week or tucked away in our singles class, we erect a formidable front that dares couples or families to approach us with any attempt at true community.

> *This is not something singles can fix, and it's not something the church can fix. It's something we must fix. If you are part of the Family of God— single or married—you are part of the solution.*

For those of us not in a singles group, we've often arrived late for the services, sat in the back, snuck out after the closing prayers, and then moaned about the fact that no one knows our names. We've come to church with inappropriate or unrealistic expectations—and we've left when met with disappointment. We've often believed the lie, without even realizing it, that "it's all about me"—even in the church.

Perhaps the greatest problem for singles is that we have wrestled, and not very successfully, with a culturally induced identity crisis. We have not understood ourselves very well in light of God's revelation and Christ's redemption, so we have not been good teachers in our churches. If *we* don't know who we are, how can *they?*

Please do not misunderstand me. I am not unappreciative of the tireless efforts made by faithful men and women on behalf of singles during the last couple of decades. I am single and have been on the receiving end of their gifts to the kingdom. I applaud them. I thank them for having the vision and determination to make a difference.

But I don't think we've arrived yet. I don't think we've fully grasped the significance of this issue—both in the lives of the Church *and* of the singles. I don't pretend to know all the answers, but I hope that by helping to identify the problem we can find a solution together—as a Family. This is not something singles can fix, and it's not something the church can fix. It's something *we* must fix. If you are part of the Family of God—single or married—*you* are part of the solution. I urge you to look around and see an issue that won't go away just because you're busy with other ministries and responsibilities. I beg you to get out of the bleachers and jump—for the sake of the Family.

In this book we will follow the well-traveled path of relationships: gaining first impressions, getting to know each other, hanging out together, saying "I love you," and committing to each other 'til death do us part. The book may not take long to read, but building the relationship will. All relationships do. It will also take great effort. All relationships do. However, the rewards of a match truly made in heaven are indescribable.

Sound good? Then come with me. I have someone I'd like you to meet.

stage one

FIRST IMPRESSIONS

It was definitely not love at first sight. He was immature and ignorant, while I was mature and educated. He demanded constant attention ihn public, and I quietly took in my surroundings. He was wild and nearly uncontrollable, but I was responsible and restrained. If ever there was an unlikely pair, we were it. Of course, this might have something to do with the fact that he was five and I was thirteen.

Alex and I met—or more accurately, happened to be in the same place at the same time—on the legendary Bee Bus Route 666, sardonically named the Beast Bus by those of us who endured the year of tribulation with the "little kids" and Andy, the bus driver who should have turned in his license years earlier. Decked in his tweed Scotsman's cap, Andy once got up at a stoplight—on a hill—and started to hobble down the aisle. Somehow I don't think he was coming to congratulate anyone on good behavior. While he moved his gnarled, knobby hands from one tattered bus seat to the next, the yellow bus started to roll backward. Never ones to sit silently, we yelled. Andy didn't pay any attention—partially because he was mostly deaf and partially because he was used to our yelling. Fortunately, it didn't matter that Andy ignored us, because a snowplow idling behind us kept us from going too far back the way we'd come.

Alex was one of the "little kids"—and a generally obnoxious one at that—and didn't do much to earn my affection in those early days. I'm sure he didn't care—kindergartners have far more important things on their minds than wooing older women—and I didn't care either. All I know is I was happier when he got off the bus . . . and even happier when he didn't get on at all.

Without a doubt, the early days of our acquaintance gave no sign of what would come many years later. While I was busy with algebra, cheerleading, and locker combinations, Alex was stacking blocks, losing teeth, and trying to get his right foot in the right shoe. We had nothing in common— except Bus 666—and certainly no reason to think we'd ever consider exchanging rings and vows with each other.

Imagine the surprise (and not just ours . . .) when a grown-up Alex longingly cast his eyes on a kinder, gentler Wendy . . . and found her already looking at him. Imagine the delight when God turned unbelievable circumstances and unlikely people into unexpected gifts.

chapter one

An Unlikely Pair

Sunday, again. Sigh. With barely enough energy to go through the motions, I got ready for another morning of "churching," a weekly event I already hated with a holy passion after only a few weeks in town.

I had recently moved away from the church that had marked my attendance records since the day I'd entered its nursery. Teacher Joan from the "2s and 3s" department and Teacher Sally from the "4s and 5s" still gave me hugs in the hall. Dellamae, the former church secretary who had brightened my childhood with her candy jar, often stopped to squeeze my arm and see how things were going. Everyone knew me. And everyone loved me (and, of course, they are all reading these words). I belonged there. I found reasons to be there when there really weren't any reasons. Every time I walked in the doors, I knew I was home. It was my Family.

> *Singles already have a nagging sense that they don't fit in the church, and my visiting experiences didn't do anything to alleviate that feeling.*

Just a few weeks removed from those familiar surroundings, Sunday had plummeted from the highlight of my week to the worst day in my week. Every time I walked in the doors of an unfamiliar church, I was nobody. No one rushed to greet me. No one gave me hugs. No one had a clue how many people just a few hours away loved me. And worse yet, no one seemed to care.

I knew that finding a church home would be the worst part of relocating, and I was (for once) sorry to be right. My weekly Sunday morning ritual included a lot of "self-talk," psyching myself up for what was sure to be difficult and disappointing—as it is for all newcomers. It was, however, made more difficult by the fact that I had to do it alone. I had no one to help me think through my impressions. I had no one to laugh with me about the sadly funny visitor moments. I had no one to absorb my frustrations. I had no one to encourage me to keep going.

Singles already have a nagging sense that they don't fit in the church, and my visiting experiences didn't do anything to alleviate that feeling. As I sat alone in Sunday School classes—those smaller group settings that, according to every piece of church literature I read, encourage interaction and relationship building—I watched lots of people who genuinely enjoyed each other's company, but seemingly had no desire to enjoy mine. Weekly, as person after person walked past my chair, I wondered if I had unknowingly worn my invisible outfit. When I went to singles classes, I either felt like an invader in someone else's territory or I felt the once-over look of those who were *definitely* there for relationship building—with strings and rings attached. When I went to classes not specifically for singles, I put thoughts in the minds of the people who didn't talk to me: "Why is she alone?" "Who is she?" "Look at that outfit. No wonder she's alone." "Is she divorced?" "Maybe her husband isn't a Christian. Poor thing."

I wanted to stand up on my metal folding chair and shout, "I'm a perfectly normal human being who just happens to be single. Is that all right with you?!" (Of course, had I done this, I would have utterly disproved my statement . . .) Instead, I bit my lip (and my tongue) and fought the tears. I sat alone drinking bad church coffee because somehow it felt better to have something in my hand since people weren't shaking it.

As I write this, I've joined a church in my new town. It's filled with wonderful people and numerous opportunities for service. I'm grateful. It's characterized by solid Bible teaching and a forward vision. I'm thankful. But, I'd be lying if I said I *really* feel like I belong there as a single. Oh, I know they want me—at least the few people I've gotten to know. And I know they appreciate me—at least the ones who know me. And I know they don't want me to go anywhere else. But sometimes I still feel stuck outside, trying to find an unlocked door to get in to where the real Family is.

I know it takes awhile to fit into a new church, and I expect with time, things will only get better for me and my new church. They will understand me better as a single, and I will understand them better as a church family. But I'm concerned about those barriers that take so long to dismantle, because too many singles—members of the fastest growing household type in America—won't stick around to see it happen.[1]

During those especially difficult first six months in my new church, it often seemed as if no one would have cared if I had called it quits. I didn't, however, because I believe in the Church. I am convinced the Church is God's instrument to reach a lost world. I stuck it out because I was determined to find my place in another local extension of Christ's body. A less convinced and comimitted single wouldn't have bothered. There are many less painful ways to spend a string of Sundays.

And I'm concerned that even if singles do tough it out, the barriers might not really come down after all. If the church is going to minister to "the most unchurched population in America and one of the greatest mission fields in the world," it is going to have to figure out how singles fit in the Family.[2] And if singles are going to find a home in the church, they are going to have to learn what it means to be part of a family.

A Compatibility Test

Why does this tension exist between the church and the single? What causes such an awkward relationship—or no relationship at all? No one is going to suggest (I hope) that it's because singles don't belong in the church. We all know that the church is supposed to indiscriminately open her arms to everyone—regardless of race, economic status, or social position—and everyone who is in Christ should find full membership and genuine fellowship within the church community.

We also all know that this has been among the church's greatest struggles throughout her two thousand year existence.

Neither will anyone suggest (again, I hope) that the church lacks the resources to meet some of the unique needs of singles. Empowered by the Holy Spirit and commissioned by Jesus Christ Himself, the church has everything she needs for the life and godliness of her members. Nothing is outside the reaches of the saving grace of God. Yet again, many of us recognize that the church has drifted dangerously close to the cultural sirens of psychotherapy, professional counseling, and self-help programs—and has taken in some damaging water along the way.

Three Strikes and Someone's Out

I'd like to suggest three reasons behind the not-quite-right relationship between singles and the church—three reasons that they look, for all the world, to be an unlikely pair with dismal prospects for the future. The first is an indictment against the church, while the second focuses the blame on singles. The third is a shared responsibility.

> Today's evangelical community is so consumed with preserving and enhancing the traditional family that an accurate understanding of that other family, the Family of God, is virtually impossible.

The first reason is what Mary Jo Weaver calls "family idolatry,"[3] a misappropriated understanding of the biological family, especially in relation to the Christian community. Today's evangelical community is so consumed with preserving and enhancing the traditional family that an accurate understanding of that *other* family, the Family of God, is virtually impossible. Such an intense family focus has resulted in the denigration and dishonoring of singleness.[4] Singles have no choice but to believe they are not valued *just as they are*. In spite of stammering assurances to the contrary, singles aren't fooled. They *don't* belong. The stark truth is that the percentage of singles in the church (36%) doesn't match the percentage of singles in society (47%), because the real focus of most churches is the nuclear family.[5]

A second reason for the difficult dynamics between singles and the church is the consumer attitude we all bring to church. Enough finger walking through the Yellow Pages can deliver almost anything we want fixed exactly the way we like it. We know what we want, and we want it now. If one establishment can't come through for us, we'll go somewhere else without a backward glance. Why should church be any different? We expect satisfaction—instantly, of course—and if one church can't produce, we'll almost flippantly find another. A combination of this culturally engrained mentality and the "no strings attached" lifestyle of the single adult has bred a generation of singles who come and go as they please, with minimal commitment and an overriding sense that the church exists to meet their needs. With expectations like this, it's impossible for the church to measure up.

A final reason for the awkward relationship is an inadequate theology of singleness. Marriage is accepted as the norm for Christians, yet Jesus never married and Paul speaks of the single life in glowing terms. Still we have unconsciously bought into the belief that being single means being miserable—at least moderately—and leading a second-class life. We pat singles' hands and offer encouraging words that singleness—whether by choice, change, or chance[6]—is okay, but most of us don't really believe it. We say we think singleness is great, but truthfully speaking, most people conclude that marriage is better. However, according to the New Testament, both marriage and singleness—regardless of its varied circumstances—are *equally* valuable ways to serve God.

Better and Worse?

A misunderstanding of truly biblical teaching on marriage, family, singleness, and the church results in ideas like the one espoused by the editor of a conservative Baptist newsletter in response to a concerned reader who asked why none of the churches in the newsletter's directory advertised singles ministries. "It seems the independent Baptists couldn't care less about singles," challenged the single reader. The editor responded, "While recognizing fully the need for a strong position on the sanctity of marriage and the scriptural truth of monogamy, it is also time that we must reach out to people even if they have a lot of baggage from their past lives. Scriptural standards should be observed in this area, as in everything else. A singles ministry . . . should be a spiritual, scriptural ministry of the church, finding people as they are and leading them to where God says they should be."[7] Reading between these lines, I surmised what the editor (and lots of others in the evangelical community) thinks about the life of a single and the role of the church as it related to single adults: first, singleness is abnormal for Christians; second, if I am single, I must have a lot of baggage; third, the church's mission is to get me married.

> *God has uniquely equipped the individual members of His Church to fulfill particular ministries to the body and to the world. Some of us are best equipped as singles and some of us are best equipped with a spouse—and frankly, we don't always get to choose.*

Thankfully, I don't believe any of these things are true. I believe that God has uniquely equipped the individual members of His Church to fulfill particular ministries to the body and to the world. Some of us are best equipped as singles and some of us are best equipped with a spouse—and frankly, we don't always get to choose. But neither, *truly neither*, is better than the other. So why does the church have an insatiable drive to see everyone married? Why do we assume God has someone for everyone? Why are singles Sunday school classes laughingly labeled "successful" when they dissolve because the majority got married? Why does the unmarried remnant have to feel like unwanted leftovers, the scraps after a season of weddings?

We have erred. A married majority of churchgoers is determinedly marching its individual family units down the kingdom road, enjoying the camaraderie of other families and swapping life experiences, while smatterings of single people trail behind. We have erred. It's time we admit it—and figure out how to fix it.

"Tradition!"

Fiddler on the Roof is a memorable musical about the woes of Tevye, a penniless Jewish dairyman in a tiny Russian village who bears the responsibility of providing good dowries and husbands for his five daughters. The musical opens with a fiddler, balanced on a roof of course, playing his haunting melody while Tevye talks to the audience about how to maintain balance in a changing world. The secret, says the lumbering man, is tradition. Talking to his milk cow, to the gray sky, to us, to anyone who will listen, Tevye declares that it doesn't matter how tradition started. What matters is that "because of our tradition, everyone of us knows who he is and what God expects him to do."

Thus opens the story of a man whose world was rocked, shaken, and shattered in rapid succession by his three oldest daughters who dared to question "God's expectations" and then break centuries of tradition, forcing Tevye to as well. One by one, they chose their own husbands instead of meekly marrying whatever men the local matchmaker found. Such a thing was "unheard of! Absurd!" Matchmaking was the way things were done, the way things had *always* been done.

Prior to the heart-melting encounters with his first two daughters-in-love, Tzeitel and Hodel, Tevye would never have given a thought to changing tradition. After all, what good reason could there be to change the very thing that tells people who they are and what God expects them to do?

If Tevye was right about tradition, then he had a good point. Indeed, we should kick and scream against anything that threatens to change it! Only God has the right to change His expectations of us, and given the nature of His Word (unchanging) and the authority of His Word (absolute), I don't think we should anticipate any adjustments.

> Some things are unchangeable because they
> represent what God expects as clearly defined
> by Scripture. The struggle comes in discerning
> which behaviors and beliefs are merely tradition
> and which ones are truly biblical.

But was Tevye right? Does tradition define who we are and what God expects us to do? I'm quite sure you're shaking your head. Of course not, you say. Tradition provides helpful ways of doing things and creates nostalgic community bonds, but it is not authoritative. (That is what you just said, isn't it?) It is not the same as the Bible, where God *does* tell us who we are and what He expects from us. The Bible alone is the standard for the believer's faith and practice.

Before the story's end, even Tevye has figured out that perhaps tradition wasn't all he thought it was. Perhaps God's expectations of his daughters were not dictated by tradition. Tevye learned, albeit reluctantly, to weigh the importance of tradition against his love for his daughters. And he changed. He slowly removed the barriers and granted his daughters their freedom.

Except for Chava, daughter number three. When Chava met a Gentile stranger on the road, the stage was set for Tevye's toughest test. Warming their hands together over a fire, father and daughter had a less than warm conversation about her romantic interests outside the Jewish faith. "The world is changing, Papa," pled Chava. "No, Chava, no," Tevye brusquely responded. "Some things do not change for us. Some things will never change." Tevye didn't explain what made some things unchangeable, but I can tell you. Marrying outside the faith was an unchangeable tenet of the Jewish faith, and Tevye had no problem drawing the line. Chava hadn't challenged tradition; she had challenged the faith.

This time Tevye was right. There *are* some things that ought never to change. However, these "unchangeables" aren't merely based on tradition—a point that *Fiddler on the Roof* leaves the viewer to interpret. Some things are unchangeable because they represent what God expects as clearly defined by Scripture. The struggle comes in discerning which behaviors and beliefs are merely tradition and which ones are truly biblical.

Fiddler on the . . . Steeple?

You know, of course, that Christianity has its own traditions, much like the Jewish culture has traditions. Many of our traditions are good, and they help give continuity to our faith. My church has baby dedications for parents who want to commit publicly to raising their children in the Christian faith. This can be a good thing for parents who want to make themselves accountable to the body of Christ. Other churches have catechetical programs for their children, teaching them solid truths of the Scripture in a step-by-step format. This can be a good thing for children as they learn Scriptural truths when their minds are best able to receive them. These kinds of traditions can be very positive and build believers up in the faith. Good traditions are often grounded in centuries of Christian living, demonstrating a value and appreciation of those who, long before we came on the scene, wrestled with issues in their particular cultures while figuring out how to live Christianly in an unchristian world.

Some of our traditions, however, are not as good and need some reexamination. Some are matters of practice and some of belief. For example, the traditional practice of making visitors stand up in services and introduce themselves to a gawking congregation (especially in a larger church) can be an excellent way to scare newcomers out of ever coming back. Hopefully, your church has already reexamined this tradition, found it wanting, and scribbled it off the list of things to do on a Sunday morning. Most evangelical churches have a longstanding traditional belief that we will spend forever in heaven with Jesus. But if I read my Bible right, heaven is the temporary place we will live until the creation of the *new* heaven and *new* earth, where we *will* live forever with Jesus. The traditional belief of "heaven forever" has been accepted as gospel truth for so long that it is difficult to get people to rethink it, much less change it. (Just try telling the people in the pews around you on Sunday that they won't be living in heaven forever and see what happens.) The more deeply ingrained a tradition is, the harder it is to change. And, obviously, if we believe a tradition is biblically based, it's even harder to change.

> *One of our most difficult tasks as Christians is keeping up with the times while holding fast to the truth.*

The danger with traditions is that we get comfortable and don't bother ourselves with thinking, or *re*thinking, about them. I understand this as well as anyone. I am a multi-task, project-oriented person who likes to get things done. Finished. Checked off the list. When a project is done, I don't like to revisit it. As a high schooler, I did quite a bit of sewing for myself, and I got a lot of wear out of the outfits that turned out well—the first time. If I made a big mistake along the way, or if a completed garment needed altering, it died a slow death, buried in a mound of others like it in a remote corner of the spare room.

This "get it done and move on" attitude has its advantages, but its disadvantages are more dangerous than a towering pile of abandoned projects. People like me don't like to *re*think issues that have already been thought through and "figured out." We'd like to just move on to the next task. The world, however, is always reshaping old issues, changing and reinventing them for a new generation. One of our most difficult tasks as Christians is keeping up with the times while holding fast to the truth. We must be willing to scrutinize our traditional beliefs and behaviors—even the ones we *think* are rooted in God's Word—and make sure we've not missed the mark. We must go through the ongoing struggle of discerning which traditions are valuable (or not), and which are truly unchangeable. We need to think, rethink, and rethink again.

Finding a New Roof to Balance On

Rethinking our traditional beliefs and practices related to singleness, marriage, family, and the church is critical for the future of Chris-

tianity. Some of these traditions have resulted in singles believing they
don't belong in the body, a sad reality that Gilbert Bilezikian descrip-
tively calls self-mutilation of the body of Christ: "The church sustains
unfathomable damage when single adults are not accepted as full par-
ticipants," because it deprives itself of the precious resources and ministry gifts that God has given singles in the church, while limiting its
outreach to unsaved singles—after all, who wants to be part of a place
you can't really be part of after all?[8]

Belief always affects behavior, so if anything is going to change, we'll
have to be willing to examine what we believe—and why. We'll have to
take a look at some long held traditions—some of which *appear* to be
biblical. We'll have to examine them and see what to keep and what to
discard. Some of our traditions are purely cultural, and we'll have to
discern what is valuable and what is harmful. We'll have to think, and
rethink, and rethink again.

I believe there is an unlikely pair, a match of unbelievable beauty,
just waiting to get together. Singles and the church are perfectly suited
to one another—if only someone will introduce them and create a
healthy environment in which the relationship can grow.

GETTING TO KNOW YOU

Many years after the traumatic events aboard Bee Bus 666, Alex and I encountered another kind of passenger abuse aboard a different bus. We were teammates on a street evangelism team at the Atlanta Olympic Games—an experience that introduced us to each other as adults. He perhaps felt like he was meeting me for the first time altogether, but I remembered him all too well. I had to admit, however, that Alex had grown up quite nicely indeed. His shoes were on the right feet and his ready smile would make any dentist happy (but not rich). I was smart enough, though, to realize that appearance wasn't everything. The real test would come when we rode the bus together again.

After a particularly busy day on the streets of downtown Atlanta, our tired team of nine hopped a Marta public transportation bus with approximately 75,000 other people to go see the 9:30 P.M. laser light show at Stone Mountain, Georgia—the "Eighth Wonder of the World." The highly acclaimed, and definitely spectacular, laser beam show against the mammoth granite relief carving of Southern Civil War heroes Jefferson Davis, Robert E. Lee, and Thomas "Stonewall" Jackson on their horses, was well worth the uncomfortable trip, and when it ended we cheered with the crowd, picked up our gear, and headed for the bus. Knowing the distance we had to travel back to our home base, we wanted to be on the first bus. Nice thought.

The 75,000 people who had arrived with us headed for the same bus, along with the 175,000 other people who had spent their day enjoying the breathtaking scenery at the popular tourist attraction and were finally ready to go home. Apparently the Stone Mountain officials had not been informed that the Olympics were in town and their crowds might be larger than usual, so when I say we headed for "the bus," I mean it; I think there was only one bus running that night. In what well could have been the worst traffic jam of the Olympic Games, we stood smushed in a mob of people facing the bus stop. Except for an occasional and momentary shuffle forward, we were not going anywhere. When the bus finally pulled up without a fleet of busses behind it and we realized the direness of the situation, I looked around and said "There is no way all these people are going to fit on that bus."

Alex, squashed next to me, disagreed, "That's the sad thing. We will fit."

He was right. We moved toward the lone bus in the steamy wave of humanity, and when we finally boarded, we pushed and were shoved until we reached the back where we clung to an overhead bar to maintain balance in the surging, swaying throng of people. Sardines in a can breathe better than we did in that bus. And while it was exhausting to stand and hold the bar in the jostling crowd, it was preferable to sitting below the raised arms of hundreds of people who'd spent the day sweating in the Georgia sun.

Given the situation, however, we were relieved just to be on the bus and headed in the right direction. We consoled ourselves with the fact that we'd soon be at the Marta train station where we would catch a train that would take us back to our van so we could drive two more hours back to home base. As uncomfortable as we were, at least we were uncomfortable and in motion.

Forty-five grueling minutes later, we were treated to a second look at Stone Mountain—from the very spot where we'd boarded the bus nearly an hour before. Apparently the Stone Mountain officials failed to inform the Marta driver that our tour was over. While it may have felt like we were driving round and round and round, we didn't really believe it was true until that moment. We were stuck in a slow-motion, sweat-drenched nightmare, and there didn't seem to be any way to wake up.

Alex was unusually quiet as we left Stone Mountain—again. This was partly because he needed a restroom—an unfortunate problem he'd confessed an hour earlier as we inched our way toward the bus. No way could he have forfeited his spot "in line" for needed relief. But his quietness was also partly due to the fact that Alex had grown up. A bus ride was not nearly as exciting to him as it had been in kindergarten, and a crowd no longer formed his personal audience. He had also (thankfully) outgrown his penchant for leaping from seat to seat in crowded busses—an element of maturity that was particularly helpful on this trip. That Marta bus ride required the stamina and grit that only comes with age—although not automatically. Determination and discipline practiced over time produce the character to withstand adversity without complaint. Alex had been practicing in the years we'd been apart.

The initial thoughts I'd had about him were wrong—or at any rate, outdated. He was more than I'd given him credit for. Much more. What I thought I knew about him was just enough to reveal that I didn't really know him at all.

chapter two

Knowledge

Lannon Quarry is a perfect place for kids, summer days, and swimming. Located a short distance from my childhood home in Menomonee Falls, Wisconsin, its cool waters provided relief on sultry days. My dad would pack up the family in our white VW Squareback and head parkward. (Only later did I realize that these trips were probably as much for my parents' sanity as their kids' enjoyment. Nails scratching on a chalkboard can sometimes be a preferable sound to overheated siblings in the doldrums of summer vacation.)

Rocky crags and trees surrounded the lake, and one stretch of its shoreline was designated as the beach. This entire swimming area was cordoned off from the deeper fishing waters by a bobbing rope, and then was itself sectioned into regions for mere "splashers" and real swimmers. Just beyond the deeper swimming waters floated a raft for divers—a destination I never reached. A beginner swimmer, I stayed close to the beach, played in the sand, and splashed (and quite possibly annoyed) my older sister in the shallow water. It was achievement enough to eventually be allowed out as far as the bobbing rope—a whole twenty-five feet from shore—where my tippiest of toes barely touched the bottom.

In my expert opinion, swimming couldn't get any better than Lannon Quarry. My experience (and my age) made me an authority on the matter. After all, the lake was huge (nobody I knew had ever been to the other side—I'm not sure it was even *possible* to get to the other side!), the water was wet, the sand was warm, and well, *we* went there! How could any place compete with that?

When I reached my last year of high school, my class took its senior trip to the East Coast where I saw the ocean for the first time. Whoa. This wasn't Kansas (or Wisconsin) anymore. There was no bobbing rope, no designated shallow area, no floating raft, and certainly no opposite shore. Water reached as far as my eyes could see, and beyond. The shoreline stretched to apparent infinity in either direction.

The late May afternoon was hot and the water was refreshingly cold, so I went swimming. Sorta. Actually, my attempt to swim in the ocean at Rehoboth Beach was a dismal failure. I waded into the water, moving slowly enough to let my legs adjust to the temperature before venturing far enough to *really* feel the cold. Another couple of steps took me to the "I'm serious about this" stage. Just then a wave knocked me off my feet. So much for the slow and easy approach. Sputtering bitter Atlantic water, I tried to stand up, but before I could recover my balance, another wave knocked me over. I had severely underestimated the power of ocean waves. Lannon Quarry only had ripples—and usually only because we made them. Every attempt I made to regain control was blown apart by foaming waves that carried the force of the unfathomable ocean behind them as they crashed into me—carried only by the force of my two seventeen-year-old legs. By the time a friend pulled me out of the water, those two seventeen-year-old legs were covered with scratches from too many encounters with the shell-covered ocean floor.

> *Neither singles nor the church comes to this relationship without some knowledge of each other. The question really is what kind of knowledge do we have?*

If I had never left my quaint swimming hole at Lannon Quarry, I would have never known there was such a place as Rehoboth Beach. I would have been content with my limited experience, never realizing that God's great earth has so much more to explore and understand. My perspective would have been stunted. Worse than that, however, I probably would have assumed I knew what I needed to know about bodies of water—and never stretched myself to learn more.

Few things in life stretch us more than relationships, and by definition, relationships are dependent upon knowledge. If I don't know you, we don't have a relationship. In fact, relationships require *mutual* knowledge and association. I "know" lots of people with whom I have no relationship. The President. Bill Gates. Oprah Winfrey. John Grisham. Elizabeth Taylor. There are hundreds of recognizable faces in my mental Rolodex, but if those people don't know I exist, I cannot accurately say I *know* them. I can only say I *know of* them. There is also an ever-increasing host of other people that I really have met, but for various reasons, we have never moved beyond a handshake and hello.

I'd like to suggest that we have a similar situation between today's church and its singles population. In extreme cases, there is *no* relationship between the church and its singles. One may have an awareness of the other, but the two have never even been formally introduced. In the majority of situations, however, the two have metaphorically shaken hands and said hello—and gone their separate ways. The relationship is filed in a fat stack of other casual relationships and put on a back shelf, only to be pulled out when it is convenient or advantageous. What we fail to recognize is that there is a dynamic relationship waiting to happen—a match of perfect proportions—if we will just take the time to know each other.

Neither singles nor the church come to this relationship without some knowledge of each other. The question really is what kind of knowledge do we have? How much do we really know about one another? I'm willing to bet that most of us are contentedly splashing along the shores of Lannon Quarry when there is an ocean waiting to be discovered. Exploring the expanse of that ocean requires that we work through three formidable adversaries of knowledge: apathy, arrogance, and assumptions.

Apathy: "I Don't Know and I Don't Care"

"Ignorance is bliss" is a flippant expression we use when we are glad to have been excused from a distasteful responsibility simply because we don't have the knowledge to do it. If all I know about copy machines, for example, is how to enter the number of needed copies and press start, I'm in luck when the machine jams on my last copy for the Sunday morning class I'm teaching. Ignorance is bliss! . . . Guess the next guy will have to figure out how to unjam the machine. I'll just take my copies and go. If, however, I *am* the next guy and all I know about copy machines is how to enter the number of needed copies and press start, ignorance is not such bliss. It's an unfortunate predicament. It's especially unfortunate if I previously had the opportunity to watch an expert (like the church secretary) surgically remove a troublesome piece of paper from the bowels of the machine.

Indifference to learning is not always as harmless as a jammed copy machine. I am a single woman, and I live five hours away from the person in my life who cares most about my car—my dad. My dear father is meticulously concerned about the condition of my little red 1996 Cavalier. I, sorry to say, am not. I drive it, and when the gauge gets close enough to "E," I fill it with gas and drive it some more. One weekend when I was home, my dad and I took my car to our trusty mechanic to get new tires and fresh oil. At the end of the day, the mechanic read me the check-off list before he'd take my money. As he explained the day's work to me, I listened well enough to be able to repeat his report to my dad, but really was thinking "Uh-huh. Great. The tires look nice. Here's my VISA card."

When I gave my dad the mechanic's report and mentioned the words "leak" and "gasket" in the same sentence, I got his attention. I really had no idea what I'd said, but his superior knowledge alerted him to the red flags (dare I say, red lights and sirens?!) in the mechanic's diagnosis. I drove merrily back to my apartment, five hours away from my very concerned father, who determined I should have the gasket checked again when I came home four weeks later. Okay, whatever. Make the appointment and I'll be there.

During the following weeks, I detected a slight odor around my car. Given what I've confessed to knowing about cars, you'll be surprised that I actually knew what the smell was. Antifreeze. It's an odor I only recognize because my dad has said a thousand times how much he hates the smell—just after we've walked past a car giving off the odor.

One fateful Wednesday shortly after the advent of the odor, I pulled into my parking spot and turned off the ignition. Before I could open the car door, the odious smell assaulted my nose. By the time I'd walked fifteen feet to my mailbox and turned around, a large orange puddle was already forming under my car—and growing larger from a steady stream of Dex-cool feeding it.

Indifference to the problem might have said, "I'm going home this weekend to get that fixed. I'll let the mechanic worry about it." Ignoring the smell and the puddle and trying to drive my car without caring about the available new knowledge would have been absolutely foolish—and the cause of even greater problems. Ignore-ance does not necessarily lead to bliss. Having your head in the sand is not always advisable—especially if the tide is coming in.

> *As a spiritual body, we often live in blissful oblivion, content in our own region of the body and with no concern for other parts.*

Apathy Applied

Both singles and the church are guilty of apathy. We are often content with what we know—and never venture into the worlds of those unlike us. We make little effort to understand the body of Christ to which we are joined at salvation. It's unthinkable to be unaware of parts of your physical body—if I stub my toe on the footstool, the rest of my body (along with everyone in the house) is fully aware of my pain. It is impossible for my hands, so far removed from the actual point of conflict, to ignore the injury. Instead, they rush in to help— or at least offer sympathy. Yet as a spiritual body, we often live in blissful oblivion, content in our own region of the body and with no concern for other parts. Many members of the church are unaware that an issue even exists between singles and the church. And many who do know don't really care. Many singles are oblivious to any greater purpose of the church beyond meeting their needs—and they make no attempt to find out.

Arrogance: "It's Just My Opinion . . . but It's Right"

Before I go to bed tonight, I will pull out tomorrow's clothes, pack my school bag, and decide what to eat for tomorrow's lunch. Do not be impressed; this is not the sign of a highly organized person. It is the sign of someone who loves to sleep. Every extra minute in Dreamland is precious.

I hate mornings. Oh, I don't hate *God's* mornings. God created gentle mornings. While the world rolls over in its sleep, He sprays a soft mist of dew on the darkened hemisphere. As the darkness steals away, He paints the soft watercolors of a sunrise on the horizon while slumbering neighborhoods rub the sleep out of their heavy eyes. I love the beauty and stillness of God's mornings.

God didn't set a big loud alarm clock in the sky to jar the world awake at 5 A.M. Alarm clock buzzers are a human invention, and they are not gentle. They are misfits in God's mornings. They are the blinding flash of a camera in a blackened room. They are a herd of elephants stampeding through a field of pastel tulips. They are raucous cymbals in a flute solo.

I am a slow and reluctant riser, so I intentionally set my alarm to go off forty-five minutes before the time I need to get up. Then I have five nine-minute snoozes to actually crawl out from between my snuggly sheets. This generally works pretty well for me, although it backfires on the days I'm especially comatose and try to sneak in a sixth snooze. My clock quits after forty-five minutes. It goes back to sleep for the day—and so do I.

When a college friend heard about my alarm clock routine, he commented, "That's silly. Why don't you just set it for the time you need to get up and then get up?"

I don't recall the exact look I gave him at this comment, but I'm pretty sure it wasn't one of my nicer ones. While it is true that I could possibly train myself to do this, that's not the point. My friend obviously had a way of doing things that was not only different from mine, but in his opinion, superior. Therefore I should just change my ways and do things his way.

The tendency to think my way of doing something is superior to anyone else's is a perversion of knowledge rooted in the prideful perspective that my knowledge—however limited—is right. After all, if something works for me, certainly it is right for everyone else too. I, like my pop-out-of-bed college friend, find myself unable to allow space for individual differences and preferences. Instead I pass judgment on your behavior based on my needs and preferences. This is nothing less than narrow-minded arrogance (and a great way to lose friends), and if carried even further, it becomes a means to manipulate you into behaving like I think you should. I perceive my knowledge to be authoritative.*

> Our personal experiences and opinions easily dictate what we think should be true for others. Everyone should be like us.

Arrogance Applied

Both singles and the church are also guilty of arrogance. Nothing breeds a sense of superior knowledge like experience, and since everyone in the church has personal experience *both* as a single and as a churchgoer, experts abound. A happily married mother of three who met her husband in college may think that what the post-college singles in her congregation really need is just to find the right person and settle down. Meanwhile, a never-married single sharing duties in the toddler room with parents of young children may get irritated

---

* By authoritative knowledge, I mean knowledge that can stand up to anything and always be right. I am not suggesting that authoritative knowledge does not exist at all, as is widely believed in our world today. "Truth" is not whatever I decide is best for myself. Truth is what God's Word says, and its authority must never be compromised. However, I am quite certain that some of my understanding about what the Bible says is not what it actually says. My judgment has gone awry, and I must be ever cautious about my conclusions—as well as the way I communicate these conclusions. The communication of God's truth is pictured in Scripture through the use of agricultural terms—we plant seeds. Flinging them in people's faces does no good. The riches of God's Word must be planted and tended with care and compassion—but I cannot force the ground to produce. Only God makes the seeds grow.

because they never get to church on time—after all, being on time is just a matter of organization and planning. Our personal experiences and opinions easily dictate what we think should be true for others. Everyone should be like us.

Assumptions: "I Don't Need You to Teach Me"

A third perversion of God's gift of knowledge is closely related to arrogance, but goes a significant step further. I have an opinion (which is right, thank you very much) *and* nothing you say will make me change my mind. From this dogmatic opinion, I make authoritative assumptions about you. I have subtly shifted from judging your behavior (like my alarm clock friend) to judging *you*.

One of the clearest biblical examples of unbending opinion, closemindedness, and subsequent judgment is found in the Jewish religious leaders of Jesus' day. If ever a group of people had an apparent monopoly on knowledge, they did. Entrusted with the very words of God, they specialized in interpreting what Scripture meant and how it applied to everyday life. They had rules for everything, and their rules were grounded, although loosely, in God's Word. What they determined to be true was accepted as such—and people conformed accordingly.

When Jesus, Truth Incarnate, appeared in their temple with a band of disciples trailing behind Him, they heard His words—words that didn't directly align with what they taught—and because He challenged their entire system of beliefs, they hated Him. They were unwilling to listen, learn, and change what they held to be true. Their stubborn refusal to learn truth from the Teacher led to an assumption about His character, a hatred of him, and an unfair judgment that ultimately resulted in His death.

Today, dramatized Pharisees and Sadducees make annual appearances in Easter musicals across America. Robed in black, the modern bevy of "bad guys" hides beneath prayer shawls and behind pasted-on beards. They slink through the throngs of enraptured peasants listening to Jesus and gather in small clusters along the edges of the crowd to formulate their sinister plot. The squints of their eyes and the furrows of their brows deepen as the drama unfolds. When Jesus unleashes His seven woes on the lot of them, no one is shocked. They deserve it!

> *"You're a nice girl. . . . Why aren't you married?"*
> *may be spoken in love by a kindhearted saint,*
> *but it reflects an assumption that normal, nice*
> *people get married.*

Certainly there is truth in these annual displays. Ultimately the religious leaders *were* the bad guys who plotted and carried out the death of Christ. But if we only perceive them as dark-robed evil conspirators, we miss an important part of the picture. I'm not sure the average first-century Jews would recognize their respected leaders in our annual parade of Pharisees and Sadducees. These "bad guys" were the esteemed voices of instruction. They were the pastors and Sunday school teachers of the day. They were the ones who could read in a culture of oral tradition. They were the ones who knew what the people like us needed to know and do in order to please God. In fact, the nation's standing before God was dependent on what they knew.

Don't exempt yourself too quickly from this company of "bad guys." Even those who are not pastors or teachers are probably closer to being a modern religious leader than the general Jewish populace was. In our highly literate and book-saturated culture, we each have access to the precious instructions in Scripture. Most Jews didn't. The role of our religious leaders is not as pronounced as theirs was because we can individually read God's Word and approach Him. With this in mind, I'm afraid that our hearts often match those that hid under the dark robes of religious prestige. We have an understanding of Scripture, and nothing will affect our thinking or change our minds. (One has to wonder about the purpose of going to church. . . .) We also have interpretations of life and people, and new information is an unwelcome intrusion and sometimes even a threat.

Assumptions Applied

You guessed it—both singles and the church are guilty of assumptions. Based on individual knowledge and experience, we have passed certain judgments on each other. Most church members (including singles) believe that marriage is the biblical norm and don't *really* believe Paul's statement that singleness can be "better." "You're a nice girl. . . . Why aren't you married?" may be spoken in love by a kind-hearted saint, but it reflects an assumption that normal, nice people get married. Others equate singleness with a lack of commitment and an abundance of time and money. On the other hand, some singles judge the entire church family based on the comments of a few. Others assume the church is only for families, therefore they don't belong. Or they believe the church exists primarily to meet their needs. While it is true that each of these assumptions may be valid in particular instances, it is nonetheless unfair to cast generalized judgments on either "singleness" or "the church."

Going Back to The Book and The Beginning

Given this understanding of ourselves, it seems likely that singles and the church have much to learn—and unlearn—about each other. At the risk of assuming my experiences capture everything there is to know about singles and the church, arrogantly telling you what you ought to believe, or presumptuously judging you for not believing the same as I do, I want to reintroduce both singles and the Church to you. Perhaps you will come to understand them in a fresh way, as I have. Perhaps you, like me, will see on your mental slate some erroneous ideas and misleading experiences that need to be erased so more accurate ones can take their place. The critical relationship between the Church of Jesus Christ and its singles will be dictated and driven by a knowledge that first recognizes how much it doesn't know and then pushes to keep growing.

God has much to say about singleness and the church, but some of it isn't explicitly written in a specific chapter and verse. His Story is bigger than that.* He took sixty-six books, forty men, and hundreds of years to put it all together—and sometimes we just want to take it apart and find a quick answer. To really understand who singles are and what the Church is, we have to back away and see the whole picture. God's Story to man starts in Genesis with creation.

---

* God's Story is the ultimate story—and that's why I capitalize it. It is the narrative that gives meaning to every other story throughout history, including our personal stories.

chapter three

Singles

After an elementary science unit that included the creation-versus-evolution discussion, I asked my fifth grade students to answer the question, "What would you say to someone to help them understand that evolution is not true?" When I read the answer Kris wrote in all sincerity, I began to wonder if I had misinterpreted the advice of everyone who told me I'd make a great teacher.

"Well," she penciled in response, "we were made in god's image. And that thair is no way we were born from animals. Beacus why would my mom have baby pitchers of me. And plus how could my mom go all to africa. To get four kids from grollis. Well I am glad I was not born from an animal."

> *Creation answers a lot of huge questions for us. It tells us who we are, where we came from, and where we're going.*

Obviously, I had missed a few points in my lessons on creation (and spelling, punctuation, capitalization, and sentence structure). It's not the first time, though. In fact, for most of my life I've missed a few points in the creation story. Not until recently have I begun to grasp the incredibly significant truth stuffed into the first few chapters of Genesis—and I feel like I'm wading into the shallow waters along the shore of Rehoboth Beach while the waves crash around me. Creation answers a lot of huge questions for us. It tells us who we are, where we came from, and where we're going. In it, we discover who we are in relationship to God, each other, and creation itself. It beautifully depicts the meaning of marriage and the origin of singleness, and it even lays the groundwork for the Church.

Creation

Man and Woman As Imago Dei

For six days God spoke into existence a world we can only imagine—and not even very well. By the end of that very first week, the Earth and all its surrounding galaxies dazzled with newness and perfection, unmarred by the effects of the Fall and sin that are all too familiar to us. During the first three days, God created empty regions that He would fill on the next three days. He formed territories of light and darkness, water and sky, and dry land in the midst of the seas. Then on days four, five, and six, He set about the task of filling each region with its appropriate inhabitants—sun, moon, and stars filled the regions of light and darkness; the waters and sky burst with fish and birds of every kind; and animals scampered, loped, and thundered across the foliaged land. The heavens sparkled with dazzling light from every angle, and the planet teemed with life in a million different forms.

But, even in all its splendor, this creative activity was just the prelude to God's greatest creation. On day six, the Story pauses after the creation of the animals, and the rhythm of the language changes. Instead of the "let there be . . . and there was" sequence that repeats itself throughout Genesis 1 up to the middle of day six, God said, "Let Us make man in Our image, according to Our likeness" (1:26). It's as if God put up His hand and called all of creation to attention for the grand finale. All eyes turned to a mound of fresh dirt as the Creator fashioned a human being *in His likeness,* the father of the human race, Adam.* Then from

---

* *Adam* means "dirt." Naming in the Bible always carries incredible significance, unlike the way we typically choose names. I assure you that God didn't pick this name for Adam just because it had a nice ring to it or because his uncle's middle name was Adam. Adam was formed from the dirt, and by naming him "dirt" God intended for Adam to remember that he was inextricably tied to the earth. Adam was made to live here. Perhaps, too, God chose this name for Adam just in case he was ever tempted to think too much of himself—it's hard to be too proud when your name is mud.

the body of the man, God shaped the woman whom Adam would later name Eve. The creation of this pair was unlike anything else in the catalog of created things. The author of Genesis tells us they were made in the *imago Dei*, the image of God.* And then, just in case you weren't paying attention to the narrative and you missed it the first time, it's repeated twice more in the next verse: "So God created man *in His own image; in the image of God* He created him; male and female He created them" (1:27). Adam and Eve, in their maleness and femaleness, were made in the image of God, and this was the feature that set them apart from the rest of the created order.

> God allowed Adam to experience the "problem" of aloneness before He created the solution.

Lots of really intelligent people are undecided as to what all the *imago Dei* entails, and I don't expect I'll solve the dispute, but I do believe one of the significant aspects of image-bearing is disclosed in Genesis's second telling of the creation story. While Genesis 1 and the beginning of chapter 2 sweep through the full seven days of creation, pausing for obvious effect at the origin of humanity, the latter part of Genesis 2 rewinds the tape and replays it frame by frame through these culminating creative events. This focused look at God's creation of man and woman expands on what's already been stated and reveals God's intentions for interconnectedness among His created likeness.

In this deliberate retelling, a different kind of "first" occurs than the kind we saw in the initial account. The overriding theme of the Genesis 1 telling is the recurring statement of God's approval. Six times the text says, "God saw that it was good." During the creation of humanity, however, God says—for the first and only time—that something was *not* good. After placing Adam in the Garden of Eden and

---

* I've only learned this Latin phrase since being in seminary, so for the rest of you who have real and normal lives, *imago Dei* rhymes with Chicago Fray-ee, which of course is an entirely fictional phrase, but every time I drive through Chicago, I think I get stuck in the middle of it.

assigning him to take care of it, God said (to Himself), "It is *not good* that man should be alone"(2:18). It wasn't that God had made something bad—He just hadn't completed the process yet. He happened to have the perfect remedy for this incompleteness within His creation plan, but don't miss the fact that He neither told Adam about it *nor* instantly fixed it.

Instead God allowed Adam to experience the "problem" of aloneness before He created the solution. Adam was too busy categorizing and naming the animals to notice that something wasn't quite right in his world, but when the job was done and he put his feet up on the broad back of Mr. Lion and stroked the silky ears of Mrs. Lion, the light began to dawn. Mr. and Mrs. Lion; Mr. and Mrs. Tiger; Mr. and Mrs. Bear. Oh my! They each had someone that *belonged* to them, someone that was *like* them. Adam had seen it all—phfff! he'd *named* it all—and he knew there was no one out there for him. Scripture puts it rather matter-of-factly: "But for Adam there was not found a helper comparable to him" (2:20). What God knew in verse eighteen, Adam knows by verse twenty. He's alone and it's not good.

Not only did God let Adam experience the "crisis," but He let him be part of the solution. God put Adam to sleep, performed surgery, and fashioned the man's perfect complement out of his own body. Eve entered the goodness of the Garden, Adam woke up, and God introduced them. It was love at first sight, and marriage became the crowning event of God's creation. The two became one.

Imago Dei is reflected in this marriage relationship. God intended man and woman to enjoy the intimacy of a perfect relationship forever—just like He does. God is One, but within that one Being are three Persons. One God—three Persons. He is Father, Son, and Holy Spirit. In my limited little brain, this doesn't compute (and I doubt it computes in yours, either). However, that doesn't diminish its truth in any way. Lots of things I *should* understand (like how people can drive down the highway for forty miles with their turn signal on, and where socks go when they get lost in the dryer) don't make sense to me; what makes me think that I should easily comprehend the attributes of the transcendent, eternal self-existent Creator of all things?

Not only does the *essence* of such a relationship not compute, but the *implications* of it don't come easily either. This is primarily because I have no concept of relationships without sin. Better stated, I have no concept of relationships without *myself*. There's great truth behind the tongue-in-cheek advice given to disgruntled church-goers looking for a new church: "If you find the perfect church, don't join it; you'll wreck it." Relationships are like that, too. Specifically, the problem with human relationships is not that they involve humans, but rather that they involve *fallen* humans. We are sinful people, and everywhere we go, we take the destructive forces of sin with us. Every friendship, association, and family connection is infected with our pride and selfishness, constantly threatening to drive wedges between us and those we claim to love.

But just imagine if it weren't so. Imagine what it would be like to give and give and give, and *never* give a thought to the recipient's ungratefulness or inability to repay you. Imagine what it would be like to *always* want and pursue the best for the other person, no matter the personal sacrifice. It's hard to put others first when every ounce of my sinful self rises to the top, like beads of oil, looking for attention and praise. Even in my circle of closest friends, those I love most, I'm sorry to admit that I see myself at the center. For these dearest of friends, I'm willing to make great sacrifices—but there are limits, even for friends.

Nothing I experience compares to the untainted love and perfect fellowship that the Triune God enjoys. Larry Crabb gives an excellent description of how wonderful this Tri-unity must be:

> Imagine the sheer delight of enjoying perfect relationships with two others with no fear of things turning sour, a community of three cut from the same fabric yet unmistakably distinct. Imagine three who, without a hint of competitiveness, are absolutely thrilled with the uniqueness of the other two. . . . Imagine a community without even the shadow of evil, with nothing but perfect goodness, where every member can be fully himself without fear of promoting rivalry or releasing something bad.[1]

Wow! Crabb rightly calls this kind of relationship pure "fun"—unhindered enjoyment of one another. *This* is what God had in mind when He brought Eve to Adam! As His image bearers, Adam and Eve—two distinct people—could enjoy perfect unity and equality just as Father, Son, and Holy Spirit—three distinct People—enjoy perfect unity with plurality and enriching diversity. The two would be one in a similar way that the Three are One, although obviously on a human level. While there are similarities between God and His image bearers, the differences between the Triune God and the Edenic couple can't be overstated. God is infinite and uncreated. People will *never* be either, but instead will *always* be dependent on God for their very existence—both here and hereafter. But being created in God's image means that human beings mirror something of what God is like, and in this case, their marriage was to be a mirror of the Triune God. They were created for unhindered intimacy of mind, emotion, and body—unlike Mr. and Mrs. Lion, Mr. and Mrs. Tiger, and Mr. and Mrs. Bear. Man and wife create a teeny, tiny picture of how incredible God is in His perfection.

> Instead of making His image bearers simultaneously, God incorporated singleness into the process of creation. He made Adam first and allowed him to experience what it was like to be alone.

It is obvious that the lone Adam could not mirror the three Persons of the Godhead. He needed Eve, his "comparable helper" perfectly suited to be one with him while at the same time maintaining her distinct identity. Only together could they adequately reflect the amazing relationships within the Godhead.

Singleness As Man in Process

It was not mere coincidence that God changed His creative pattern when it came time to make people. He certainly could have formed both man and woman at the same time, like He apparently did the rest of the creatures. But people *are* different from animals, regardless of what modern "science" says, and God made this clear even in the way He created them. Instead of making His image bearers simultaneously, God incorporated singleness into the process of creation. He made Adam first and allowed him to experience what it was like to be alone—even if only for a short time.

> *When God rested on the seventh day, singleness as a way of life was no longer in the picture.*

The fact that Adam recognized the deficiency of his condition so quickly is perhaps one of the most telling statements about the effect of sin on human relationships—and the incredible significance of community to the wholeness of people. There was Adam, appointed vice-regent (what power!) of a brand spankin' new creation filled with endless possibilities for exploration and adventure (imagine racing cheetahs, wrestling lions, and playing melon-ball with monkeys—what fun!)—and yet it didn't take him long to realize that something was not quite as it should be. God's first man was pretty incredible. God's first man was *imago Dei*, designed for intimacy with another human being and fully aware that he was not quite complete without her. Neither would Eve have been complete without Adam. While he needed her, she would not have even existed without him.

God changed the pattern of creation when it came time to make man and woman because He wanted to make it perfectly clear how integral the relationship of man and wife is to the image of God. God's presentation of the woman to the man only *after* Adam noticed the void intensified his appreciation for her presence and heightened his awareness of her value. God culminated and completed His "very good" work by establishing the monogamous relationship of absolute faithfulness, unlimited intimacy, and pure ecstasy between His image-bearing male and His image-bearing female. When God rested on the seventh day, singleness as a way of life was no longer in the picture.

The Fall

The Loss of "Very Good"

Regrettably, the story doesn't end on Day Seven. The way things were in the Garden was not the way they would stay. Just a few short verses—and an uncertain amount of time—after their discovery of each other in Eden's earthly paradise, Adam and Eve sacrificed their perfect life together for the alluring promise of something better. The irony of the serpent's declaration is inescapable: "For God knows that in the day you eat of it your eyes will be opened, and you will be like God, knowing good and evil" (3:5). Satan assured the very image of God that if they did as he advised, they would be like God, when in truth they sacrificed what perhaps made them most like God—the intimacy of fellowship.

With the taste of fruit still fresh on their lips, Adam and Eve realized that their newly acquired knowledge was not all Satan had cracked it up to be. In an instant, everything changed. Instead of being more like God, they hid from Him and from each other. Their intimacy shattered, they stood in shame and pointed fingers of accusation at each other. The one became two again—two people opposed to each other and thoroughly consumed by their need for self-preservation.

And they passed it on to us. Although we are all born into the same human race, children of the original created pair, we are born separated from each other because we are separated from God. We each stand alone against the world and are consumed by our needs for self-preservation and personal achievement. Peruse the library of books available on how to create community, build teams, and foster unity, and you'll get an idea of how difficult it is. No one sells books (or makes much money on them) about how to boil water, mow the lawn, or wash dishes. We don't need help. But foregoing our own interests? Putting other people first? Those are things we just can't figure out, much less master.

> *Not only does intimacy in marriage take mountains of work after the Fall, but singleness is back, and this time it can be permanent instead of process.*

By now you'd think we'd have discovered the fool-proof formula for unity. Perhaps we have, but we haven't made it work yet. Why? Because the heart, as Jeremiah the prophet says emphatically, is desperately wicked (Jer. 17:9). We are shockingly selfish, and shockingly deceived about our righteousness. It takes one lane closure, two lanes of stalled traffic, and one maverick racing down the merging lane to remind me I'm selfish. How dare he make *my* wait any longer?! Our "hot buttons" are as varied as we are—but we don't have to think too long to identify minor inconveniences that irritate us. And we don't have to dig too deeply to realize that we are usually irritated because of pride or selfishness.

Nowhere is selfishness more evident to us than in the marriage relationship, because nowhere are we closer to another human being. Ever since the initial breakup, reestablishing the intended oneness of *imago Dei* has been the greatest challenge men and women face. Now we have to learn the very hard way what once came as naturally as breathing—loving. Oh, I don't mean the physical aspects of love. There is still a very natural and strong desire for physical oneness, although it too has been corrupted by the Fall. But God's design for oneness was not merely physical. To think that sex is the primary component of oneness is actually to diminish the significance of oneness and, in fact, miss the whole idea of total intimacy. Sex was designed as a picture, a demonstration of what was true about the relationship between perfect man and perfect woman—nothing hidden, no barriers, and no shame.

Not only does intimacy in marriage take mountains of work after the Fall, but singleness is back, and this time it can be permanent instead of process. It's no longer just a step to "very good" for some of us. It's the way life is and very well could stay, whereas if creation had continued in its perfect condition, there would have been one man for one woman for everyone for life.

While permanent singleness is a result of the Fall, we must make the distinction between something being "bad" and being "not good," as God declared singleness during creation. There *is* a difference. Because singleness existed before the Fall within the period of creation, albeit for a short time, it cannot be *morally* bad, or wrong. Blossoming trees in the Garden without fully developed fruit were not bad. A deer whose buds had not grown him into a ten-point buck was not bad. Fields of wildflowers that had not yet bloomed were not bad. They were in process. On a much more significant scale, aloneness was a step in the human process of becoming "very good." Without his relationship with Eve, Adam *was* less and *had* less than what God intended. Singleness, then, is not morally wrong, but neither is it "good." It was never God's intention that His image bearers would be without the intimacy of a marriage relationship that mirrored the intimacy of God Himself.

The Fall changed everything about relationships, between God and people and between man and woman. Humanity is separated from God. Marriage is no longer the *perfect* delight it was created to be; instead it is laden with struggles to relate. Singleness is no longer the temporary step it was in creation; instead, it has become a long-term and even permanent state for many. The path to God's intended relationships has been blocked by the effects of sin.

In the moment Adam and Eve sinned, they received what they thought they wanted—knowledge of good and evil. Obviously, though, they lost much more than they received. As the inheritors of their decision, we find ourselves driven by an insatiable craving to regain what we lost in that fateful Edenic event—identity, acceptance, value, and intimacy.

Who Am I? The Search for Lost Identity

God was the source of Adam and Eve's existence. Without His continuing sustenance, the two would have died on the spot when they ate the fruit. It was only the Creator's grace in the face of their sin that kept them alive. It is only the Creator's sustaining grace that keeps *us* alive—a remarkable contemplation for those who deny and mock God, speaking against the very One who enables them to speak!

> We don't know whose *we are* anymore, and therefore, we don't know who *we are*.

However, God is more than the source of human life; He is also the source of human identity, an identity He partially defined for Adam and Eve when He brought them together. Adam and Eve were designed to be one with each other, and they were designed to be in relationship with God—forming another sort of tri-unity. God, man, and woman in perfect fellowship together. When Adam was still alone and it was "not good" and God provided the solution, the solution was only "very good" because *He* was part of it. Their identity as man and wife was dependent on their identity in God.

When Adam and Eve sinned, they sacrificed their source of identity. To think that the two image bearers could have significance and complete identity apart from the One they imaged is as ridiculous as thinking an invisible man can see his face in a mirror. While Adam and Eve certainly found degrees of enjoyment in each other after the Fall, without God they could no longer be "complete." Apart from Him, they had no significant purpose. This loss of relationship with God created a monumental crisis of identity for Adam and Eve that has shaped the lives of all their descendants. We don't know *whose* we are anymore, and therefore, we don't know *who* we are.

Will Anyone Want Me? The Search for Lost Acceptance

Adam and Eve also lost their acceptableness in the sight of God, a consequence with far greater impact than they could have foreseen. God was the absolute center of their lives and the hub of their relationship wheel. When that hub was ripped out, their "spokes" of human relationships no longer had a center. They were disjointed and separated. By sinning and trading God's approval for some juicy fruit, Adam and Eve also forfeited each other.

Interestingly, when their "eyes were opened" they didn't like what they saw and immediately started to hide. First they hid from each other by covering the most intimate parts of their bodies, a poignant act that visualized the loss of unhindered intimacy. Then they pointed fingers at each other in self-defense. Adam and Eve became instant strangers who were ashamed of themselves and afraid of each other. Finally, they hid from God, knowing they had violated His requirement. They were afraid because they were naked. Exposed. Shamed. Unacceptable.

The loss of God's acceptance has sent all of rebellious humanity on a crazed search for acceptance from the people around us. We shape our identities by others' opinions of us and do almost anything to be accepted so our lives can be complete—or so we think. A romantic relationship, and ultimately marriage, is believed to offer the unconditional love and acceptance we desperately need, so we pursue it with fervor.*

Yet for all our sophistication and life experience, we are no different than Adam and Eve simultaneously needing the acceptance of the other and covering themselves to hide from each other. We self-consciously shield ourselves, presenting falsified fronts to others because we are afraid of what might happen if others really see us. We are shamed by what we are, and we are sure acceptance would never be possible if others really knew us.

Will You Love Me? The Search for Lost Value

When we believe marriage provides the answer to our need for identity and acceptance, singleness becomes a condition of lesser value, a problem to be fixed at any cost. We generally have enough tact not to actually state matters this way, but frankly, we don't have to—it is clear from repeated innuendos and actions. A church I visited promoted

---

* It is sadly ironic that marriage, the "solution" to our problem, is wrought with its own problems of acceptance and unconditional love. The divorce rate, as high in the church as outside of it, serves as a sober reminder that even our best human attempts at "completion" apart from God are insufficient.

in-home dinners for members to get to know each other better; the flyer noted that singles should sign up in pairs. At a wedding I attended, the officiating pastor told us that marriage is a "little bit of heaven on earth"—which left my single friends and me wondering what that makes singleness . . . ? We are loners in a couples' culture and a couples' church.

The destructive nature of the Fall means that value is determined by other people rather than God. The first effect of this is a loss of self-esteem. Singles now listen to a nagging voice inside that wonders if there's something wrong with us. We listen to the shouts of society that say successful people have someone. Secondly, with such high stakes, we are willing to settle for far less in a spouse than perhaps we should. We sacrifice high standards and self-respect just to feel valued in a relationship with anyone who's warm and breathing. I have watched single friends move from person to person to person, trading one pitiful relationship for another (not much different than the way we wear out, throw out, and replace toothbrushes—except toothbrushes usually last longer.) To a shortsighted single, the false sense of worth provided by such expendable relationships can be more important than the price of promiscuity.

How Do I Know You Love Me? The Search for Lost Intimacy

Fifth grade is the year for learning states and capitals. My coworkers and I drilled the spellings of Montpelier and Connecticut into our students' heads, and we made sure they connected Bismarck to North Dakota. When we finally reached Honolulu, Hawaii, in April, the entire fifth grade celebrated by traveling to Hawaii (on an airplane we set up on the school stage) and attending a luau (in the school cafeteria). Concocting a meal of poi and pineapple for one hundred kids, transforming a curtained stage into an airplane, and recreating a Hawaiian scene in the cafeteria required excessive hours of planning and preparation.

In the midst of luau day, while my tireless colleague Barb worked feverishly to get the airplane ride off the ground (so to speak), a visiting parent said to her, "These special days must be just like vacations for you teachers!" Depending on the nature of your family vacations, she could have been closer to the truth than she realized, but certainly the luau didn't *feel* like a vacation for us. It was a lot of work. So why did we bother? You know the answer. Because experience is the best teacher. The more senses involved in the learning experience, the better. It's the difference between looking at a friend's pictures of another country and traveling there yourself. When our whole bodies become involved in an experience, we remember it.

> *God's precious gift has been devalued into a social activity that we trample on afternoon talk shows and laugh about during evening sitcoms. We are obsessed with sex.*

God purposefully gave Adam and Eve an intensely physical experience to help them fully understand the otherwise abstract idea of intimacy. Sex is a multisensory expression of a nonphysical reality— oneness. It is God's gift to husbands and wives, a vivid manifestation and reminder of the unity of their whole persons.

Our culture has snatched this precious package, ripped it open, and tossed it to the crowd like candy at a parade. There's plenty to go around and it's easily within everyone's reach. God's precious gift has been devalued into a social activity that we trample on afternoon talk shows and laugh about during evening sitcoms. We are obsessed with sex.

And while we bemoan this sad state of affairs, no alternative exists for humans who both crave intimacy and rebel against God. God created man and woman to have an intimate relationship, but remember—He is the lifeblood of all relationships. Without Him, the best we can do is achieve pseudointimacy. In human terms, this is spelled s-e-x. We settle for the expression of intimacy and miss the real thing.

Sadly, the situation only gets worse. When intimacy is perceived as primarily physical, the devastating effects of its misuse abound. Instead of expressing unconditional love and acceptance, sex feeds lust and multiplies rejection.

Society assumes (and practically mandates) that sex is a natural part of life for anybody who knows what it is and how it works, regardless of age or marital status. We distribute condoms to teens, expect dating singles to share the rent, and wink at unfaithful spouses. Sex is a symbol of freedom and a banner of independence. No one has the right to tell us what we can or can't do with our bodies. Sexual activity is a sign of normalcy. Anyone who managed to make it to adulthood with virginity intact isn't normal. A single who chooses celibacy over unmarried sex is just plain weird. Gay, perhaps. Virginity and celibacy are as out of place in our culture as an Amish buggy on the autobahn.

Unfortunately, hints of this attitude have filtered into the church where marriage is often presented as the solution to the unconquerable problem of sexual temptation. While marriage does provide an antidote for sexual temptation, it does not eliminate the heart issues behind lust, and focusing on this aspect of marriage only serves to cheapen its higher purpose and turn it into a mere vehicle for lust.

The Bottom Line

God never intended us to live independently—in any way. As His creation, we were made dependent on Him (Col. 1:15–18). As His image bearers, we were also designed for the dependency of interpersonal relationships, especially that which accompanies the intimacy of oneness in marriage. When sin entered the human heart, the design of humanity didn't change—we are still dependent on God and we still need intimacy. However, our perspective of these realities changed radically. In our independent human natures, we now refuse to recognize our dependence on God and think we are self-sufficient. And God's original remedy to the "not good" of aloneness isn't enough to satisfy the nagging emptiness we now have in our hearts. Beneath our best efforts lies an immense dissatisfaction, and when as fallen creatures we lie awake in the middle of the night, we realize how alone we really are—whether or not there's anyone in the bed beside us.

Just as God provided a solution to the original problem of aloneness, so He provides an even grander solution to the isolation brought upon us by the Fall. The Story isn't over yet.

chapter four

The Church

As I prepared to move out of state, I began my hunt for a church like any true citizen of the new millennium—on the Internet. I surfed Web sites of churches in my new town, trying to get a feel for far away places. I perused doctrinal statements, compared various ministries, read about the pastors, and noted incorrect spelling and punctuation on the Web sites (misused apostrophes really drive me crazy). One of the most frustrating things I encountered during my search (besides incorrect usage of its and it's) was the absence of a good map. A Wisconsinite moving into Michigan territory recognizes city names like Detroit, Lansing, and Grand Rapids. We might know roadways like I-94 and I-96, but much beyond these cities and roads, a true foreigner is in trouble. Without a zoomed out map of the entire area, I couldn't figure out if a church in Bad Axe was across the street or the state (incidentally, it's across the state).

At times the universal church suffers from the same kind of problem these cyber sites have. Its members—and sometimes its leaders—are uncertain where it fits in the big picture. We've got the "streets" and "landmarks" down—worship services, children's programs, Bible studies, community involvement—but we aren't as sure about the Church's place in the great plan of God. Where *does* the Church fit? In this chapter we'll zoom out and see the magnificent scope of God's design and the Church's role in it.

We've already discovered that in the Garden of Eden, God provided the solution for man's original problem of aloneness. He created woman, the exquisitely designed counterpart to man. When humanity rebelled against God, they created for themselves a problem far greater than the original aloneness of creation. They brought sin's lonely separation upon themselves, isolating them from God and from each other. Now we'll see how in His grace, God provided the solution for this problem, too. We call the solution "redemption," and its scope goes far beyond what marriage did for the solitary Adam's problem. The solution of redemption is cosmic in nature, and the heartbeat of this plan throbs in the Church.

Seeds of Redemption

Since that fateful day in the Garden of Eden, every part of God's once flawless creation has groaned in agony under the curse of sin. Slinking into every space and creeping into every crevice, sin's deadly poison has left nothing untouched. This is the bad news—the very bad news. The plotline that develops after the events of Genesis 3 is much more familiar to us than the far-away days of Eden. We understand hatred, selfishness, and human suffering, although we seldom understand why such things are allowed to dirty the pages of God's Story.

> *Another Man, a different tree, and an act of obedience*—this *was God's greatest work, His plan to buy back the world for Himself and remake it into a new creation.*

The good news, however, is that in spite of the colossal collapse of God's original design, the Story is not over in Genesis 3. It's really just beginning. Although creation was a spectacular piece of divine handiwork, it wasn't God's *greatest* work. The seedling of His supreme act was sown in the shadow of the Fall's forbidden tree and it took root in the unfolding events of God's continuing Story.* It sprouted and grew

---

* After Adam and Eve's sin, God's curse on the serpent is twofold. He curses the physical serpent, causing him to slither on his belly, and He curses the "spiritual serpent," Satan, in Genesis 3:15: "And I will put enmity between you and the woman, and between your seed and her Seed; He shall bruise your head, and you shall bruise His heel." The Seed of the woman was Jesus Christ who would deal the death blow to Satan and his strategy when He was crucified and rose from the grave.

in the tumultuous life cycle of a tiny nation of farmers and shepherds, and it stood firm through the storms of hard-hearted human rebellion and gruesome idolatry. Its branches wove their tenacious way into every page of the Old Testament, swelling with buds of promise waiting to burst into bloom.

In a backwoods village called Nazareth during an age of Roman oppression, the buds began to open in the womb of an obscure teenage girl, and on a starry night months later, the sky lit up with an angelic declaration that God's greatest work was underway. For the next thirty-three years, God in the flesh walked among men, experiencing firsthand what a man, a tree, and an act of disobedience had done to His world. Jesus came to undo it all with His perfect life and eventual death. Another Man, a different tree, and an act of obedience—*this* was God's greatest work, His plan to buy back the world for Himself and remake it into a new creation.

In many evangelical traditions, we've often missed the significance of the *whole* Story. We have dissected and trisected biblical narratives. We've dog-eared the pages of our Bible dictionaries and concordances, and yet sometimes we've missed the message for the words. We act as if the four Gospels contain the bulk of the message and the rest of the New Testament merely expounds on the Gospels, but we skip past the huge part of the Story written before Jesus formally appears. Oh, we know there are analogical pictures and prophetic snapshots in the Old Testament that allude to His coming, but on the whole, many of us are perfectly happy with our New Testaments or with morals gleaned from Old Testament stories.

Yet the whole Story matters because everything Jesus did happened within the entire framework of God's written revelation, so without the beginning of the Story, Jesus' life and death are meaningless. Just reading the Gospel accounts of the crucifixion and resurrection and then thinking I understand the Story and scope of redemption is like claiming to write a comprehensive biography of somebody I've interviewed for thirty minutes.

Without God's authoritative words in the Old Testament, our concept of the Fall's devastation would be skewed and the need for redemption would be minimal. We would convince ourselves that things aren't as bad as we think. We would keep the hope alive that, given enough time, we can save ourselves. But with vivid imagery and graphic details, the Old Testament destroys any thread of hope for humanity's self-rescue. God needed to enter the Story again in an extraordinary way, like He did at creation. Apart from His intervention, the effects of sin and the reign of Satan would eventually drive the cosmos into an abyss of self-destruction.

I rightly rejoice in God's redemptive plan and the hope that it brings me, but God's plan to redeem the world is much bigger than my personal salvation. Although humanity is incredibly important to God, Jesus didn't live and die just for me—or just for you. Redemption is not only personal. It's cosmic. Jesus came to undo *all* the effects of Adam's sin. He came to restore creation, to remake it in a new and better way.

The Tale of Two Men

The Bible talks about two Adams—the first Adam who was also the first man, and the last Adam who is Jesus Christ. Let's take a closer look at how the stories of the first and the last Adam form the structure for the entire Story of redemption.*

All for One and One for All

George Washington is called the father of our country for good reasons. He was the first President and prior to that, he played a key role in the Revolutionary War. Without his leadership, it is possible we'd call our mums on Mother's Day, enjoy crumpets with our afternoon tea, and retire to our bedchambers when the sun goes down. But Washington did not single-handedly win the war or draft our cornerstone documents or rally all thirteen colonies to fight. We use the word "father" metaphorically, but if we wanted to be technical, we'd

---

* For background reading on the two Adams concept in Scripture, read Romans 5 and 1 Corinthians 15.

have to say that America has many fathers. If we wanted to be literal, of course, we couldn't use this title at all.

> *We live in the land of pioneers and possibilities— we blaze our own trails and control our own destinies. How can someone we've never met, who lived thousands of years before us, control our destinies?*

Adam is called the father of the human race for better reasons. He was *the* first man, and everyone—including Eve—must trace his or her physical beginning back to Adam. In spite of what you suspected about your alien-like brother while growing up, none of us got here any other way. Every human being on the planet—dead and alive— shares the same human genes. We are bonded together as a race in an inseparable relationship.

Adam was given a mandate from God at creation. Care for the earth—develop, use, and enjoy its resources. Fill the earth—create more image bearers who can help with the task of caring for the planet. In the physical absence of God, Adam and the people that would come from him were to rule over the earth, overseeing its operation and being God's "hands" in the world to see His purposes accomplished.

> *We are born into sin, based on the long-ago decision of Adam, and nothing we say about it can change this reality. Because of sin, we are born hating God . . . and apart from a work of grace, we live it out every day of our lives.*

As the father of the human race, Adam stood as our representative, even though we didn't exist yet. What he did, or didn't do, would affect the entire race to follow. He was one man with one job—obey God. Adam sinned. We all sinned in him. He fell. We all fell in him.

Perhaps you're squirming over the "injustice" of this very un-American way of doing things, this one man for all of us. Whatever happened to independence? After all, we live in the land of pioneers and possibilities—we blaze our own trails and control our own destinies. How can someone we've never met, who lived thousands of years before us, control our destinies? This is such an impossibility in our national psyche (and sometimes, sadly, our church psyche) that, quite frankly, sometimes we choose not to believe it.*

Impossible or not, it's true. The Bible is clear about that: "Therefore, just as through one man sin entered the world, and death through sin, and thus death spread to all men, because all sinned" (Rom. 5:12). Our lives are filled with realities that are based on others' decisions and over which we have absolutely no control. No one consulted me, for example, about whether or not I wanted Richard and Nancy Widder as my parents. That choice was made for me. (It was a good one.) Likewise, I didn't choose to be born in suburban America instead of rural Asia. I had absolutely nothing to do with these life-shaping realities, but more than anyone else, I have to live with the unalterable consequences of others' decisions. And while I could disown my parents and try to find someone else to adopt me, and I could move to Finland and change my citizenship, I can never *undo* what has already happened. It is the same for us as an entire race. We are born into sin, based on the long-ago decision of Adam, and nothing we say about it can change this reality. Because of sin, we are born hating God—whether we recognize it or not—and apart from a work of grace, we live it out every day of our lives.

The Last Adam—Jesus Christ

Into this race of God-hating people came the "last Adam," a second representative for an entire race of people (1 Cor. 15:45). While Adam's actions affected those who would be *physically* born, Jesus' actions

---

* This problem is not uniquely American, although it's perhaps amplified for Americans because of our culture. Because of our fallen human natures, we *all* think we are autonomous—able to do what we want, when we want, with no one to interfere. We like to think of ourselves as independent and accountable to no one. "No one has the right to tell me what to do" is a deeply ingrained cultural, but definitely not biblical, motto.

affected all those who would be *spiritually* born. Adam represented all
who would come from the original creation; Jesus represented all those
who would also become *new* creations.

> *The truth is never diminished by our inability to
> grasp it.*

Only Jesus qualified to do this because, just as the first Adam had
been created sinless, Jesus was born without sin. He was the second
Person of the Triune God and He was also a man with a perfect human
nature like Adam had before the Fall. He was one person with two complete natures: divine and human. All the nuances of this truth, like the
Trinity, are impossible for us to fully understand, but again, the truth is
never diminished by our inability to grasp it. Jesus came to give creation
a fresh start by undoing what Adam had done. He accomplished this
mission through both His life *and* His death and resurrection.

In His life, He faced temptations and tests like Adam never had.
Adam had it easy. He faced temptation in a pristine garden on a full
stomach—or at least with a full menu. No societal garbage existed to
tug his heart away from God. He delighted in God's presence in the
misty cool of each day. Adam was wonderfully naive, in the purest
sense; he had absolutely no knowledge of evil and no awareness of
any other kind of life. And in the midst of all this, unimaginable as it
already is, Adam had only one—ONE!—official restriction that we
know about: don't eat from the Tree of Knowledge of Good and Evil.
Does life get any better?!

Jesus, gaunt with hunger and surrounded by the harsh terrain of the
Judean wilderness, squared off against the tempter who had every motivation to bring Him down—like he did the first Adam. But there was
no naïveté in Jesus; He knew better than anyone the destructive forces
of sin, and He understood them even more fully by the time His mission on earth was finished. Jesus was never caught unawares by Satan,
and He likely lived every moment with full anticipation of the devil's
assault. This was, after all, the reason He came. To succeed where Adam
failed. To obey where Adam disobeyed (Matt. 4; Mark 1; Luke 4).

Jesus lived in perfect obedience to every divine command—all those recorded in Scripture and all those that came directly to Him from the Father. More was demanded of Jesus than has ever been, or will ever be, demanded of a human being. He accomplished what no one else could have.

The culmination of Jesus' mission was His death on the cross. Unjustly accused and maliciously condemned, the Son of God stumbled under a criminal's cross that rightly belonged to every other person in the crowd that day—and to every other person throughout all of time. It wasn't just the weight of the cross and the searing pain it brought to His pulverized back that made Jesus stumble, however. He didn't stumble simply because of the agony awaiting Him on the rocky hill at the end of the *Via Dolorosa*. He stumbled under the impending weight of sin and guilt that He knew would fall upon His broken body before the excruciating ordeal was over.

I have quite enough trouble dealing with my own sin and guilt, distributed incrementally through life as the occasions unfortunately arise. I cannot fathom the mental anguish I would experience at having to bear the knowledge and shame of *all* my sin at once. The torturous flood of guilt would be overwhelming, and it's a certainty that I wouldn't be able to stand it. Never mind my trying to bear any or all of your sin too.

It is no wonder that between twelve and three o'clock on that Friday darkness blanketed the earth as all the sin of the world from the past and the future funneled onto the Person of the Incarnate God, Jesus Christ. The Creator Himself bore the sin of His own fist-shaking creation. What *is* a wonder is that the darkness, so often used symbolically of sin, didn't simply crush the entire planet, leaving a mere cloud of dust in the Milky Way. Instead, for three unspeakable hours of horror, our sin converged on the only Person who justifiably didn't deserve any of it—and He bore it, to save us and the rest of creation.

As Jesus hung there—naked, bleeding, and virtually abandoned by those who loved Him—even the intensity of the physical pain was minimal in comparison to the pain of alienation from God. His cry, "My God, My God, why have You forsaken Me?" echoed from the depths of hell's despair. We will never know the magnitude of Jesus' anguish during those moments because alienation from God is a second and very familiar nature to us. We are born with it and even after coming to know Him, we still slip so easily from close fellowship with Him. Not Jesus. Having *always* lived in perfect communion and ecstatic fellowship with God the Father, Jesus had known none of this miserable kind of existence.

The end finally came—the Father's righteous wrath against humanity satisfied by the sinless sacrifice of His Son. At that moment, Jesus mustered enough physical strength to cry out, "It is finished" (John 19:30). What was finished? The darkness? The pain? His life? If you've spent much time in church at all, you're probably answering that Jesus meant the price for our sin had been completely paid. You'd be partially right. In God's Bank of Righteousness, our accounts were so deep in the red there was no hope of ever seeing black. Christ's death paid the debt, erasing both the massive guilt we inherited and the guilt we've accrued with mind-boggling speed since birth. He brought our accounts to zero.

I don't mean to shake the foundations of your faith, but if that's all He did, it wasn't enough. While zero righteousness is better than megasinfulness, God's standard is *absolute* righteousness. A big fat goose egg of righteousness just doesn't measure up. And since Isaiah compares human righteousness to filthy rags, it appears that although no longer indebted, we are still in pretty dismal shape (Isa. 64:6; 1 Cor. 1:30–31; 2 Cor. 5:21).

> *Making the decision to acknowledge our sin to God, seek His forgiveness, and trust fully in the saving work of Jesus may not have changed a single thing about the way we felt.*

When Jesus said, "It is finished," He meant the entirety of His mission to earth. The Last Adam didn't just come to die a horrible death—He came to live a sinless life. That sinless life is credited to the account of Jesus' new race, just as Adam's sin was attributed to his race. From Christ's death we receive forgiveness from our sins and from His life we receive His righteousness, the two essentials for a restored relationship with God. Not only has our debt been cleared, but our accounts are now off the charts with righteousness—we have the absolute righteousness of Christ.

What We Are: It's a . . . Baby!

So, what does a restored relationship with God mean? It certainly didn't time warp us back to the Garden of Eden. Neither did it erase every ugly effect of the Fall in our lives or in the world around us. It didn't send us instantly to a perfect new world either. Lightning bolts probably didn't come through your window, and I didn't even feel a warm fuzzy sense of peace. Making the decision to acknowledge our sin to God, seek His forgiveness, and trust fully in the saving work of Jesus may not have changed a single thing about the way we felt. And our lives may very well have looked exactly the same as when we closed our eyes to cry out for His mercy.*[1]

But we would be mistaken if we thought nothing happened. Everything happened. In that moment, heaven exploded with praise because we were brought to life. God made us new creatures, giving us spiritual life where before was only physical life. This restored spiritual relationship is the cornerstone of God's redemption—He breathes life into a new race of His image bearers.

Just as a healthy baby—small as it is—enters the world fully equipped for a long full life, so we are reborn spiritually with everything we need for a long full life of godliness. We have a relationship with the One who establishes our identities; we are acceptable in His sight because of Christ; we are highly valued . . . just the way we are; and we can enjoy genuine intimacy. But just as a newborn doesn't walk home from the hospital and converse at the dinner table, neither will we instantly "walk and talk" spiritually. Our new lives in Christ develop slowly, one skill at a time as we grow and mature. One of the most defeating things in the Christian life is trying to dance when we haven't even discovered we have feet.

---

* For more information about how to have a restored relationship with God, see note 1 in the endnotes for this chapter.

When God planned how human beings would develop, He made us absolutely dependent on other people. Leave a baby to care for itself and you get arrested. "But," you protest, "you said a baby is born with everything it needs to live a long full life. Why am I responsible?" Ridiculous? Physically speaking, of course. But it's just as ridiculous in the realm of spiritual life. When God planned how *spiritual* babies would develop, He made them dependent on the care of other people—more spiritually mature people. He birthed them into a Family—He is the Father, and Christ is the Brother. Babies grow up in this Family, and eventually they learn to care for younger siblings, while continuing to learn from older ones.

What We Are: A New Kind of Bodybuilder

> *Jesus didn't come to create a loose band of lone rangers who heroically save their parts of the world and then get together around the fire to swap stories.*

The spiritual family we are born into is the Church, the community of people who are spiritually alive (although, sadly, we've fooled many a visitor). The sin that once separated us from God also separated us from one another. When our relationship with God is restored, we are joined to a community of redeemed people inextricably bound together by a common relationship to God in Christ (Gal. 3:26–29).

One of God's most poignant analogies for the Church is the body of Christ—a single entity comprised of many individual members, but expressed locally in thousands of churches around the world (1 Cor. 12). While we remain uniquely individual, our identity is best defined and our roles best fulfilled in our relationship to the body of Christ. A dismembered arm or toe or earlobe is useless and ineffective without the rest of the body, and so are Christians who are not actively involved in the ministry of the local church.

Redemption leaves no room for human authority and independence. Jesus didn't come to create a loose band of lone rangers who heroically save their parts of the world and then get together around the fire to swap stories. He came to create a new race of people bound together in a new kind of oneness. In His heartfelt prayer on the night of His betrayal, He prayed that His followers would be one just as He is one with the Father (John 17:20–26). Sound familiar? In the original creation, God intended man and woman to be one just as He is one. In the new creation, Jesus broadens the scope of oneness to include *all* His followers. Oneness is no longer an exclusive feature of marriage (although, as the New Testament makes clear, the physical expression of oneness remains exclusive to marriage). Jesus also adds a new dimension to this oneness when He prays that His followers would be one with Him and the Father.

A Possible Impossibility?

How does *that* happen? We have enough trouble figuring out how to be "one" with the people in the pews around us—and we can see them! (Perhaps that's why we have so much trouble.) Jesus isn't here. The Father is not a physical being. Did Jesus ask for something impossible?

It isn't any more impossible for us to *be* what He asked us to be than it is for us to *do* what He told us to do: care for and develop the new creation. Jesus' mission was to start the new creation, to make restoration for the Fall's destruction. He finished all that was needed to set the new creation in motion, but the new creation is not complete. It's an "already—not yet" creation. It's already here in the lives of His followers, but it's not yet complete. The total rule and reign of Jesus over all the earth is an event still to come. We are living in the chapters between the first coming of Christ when He conquered death and His cataclysmic second coming when He will clean up all the pieces of that decisive battle and assume His throne forever.

But Jesus is not here. As Adam's descendents, we were left with the responsibility to care for and cultivate the initial creation; as Jesus' followers, we have the added responsibility to care for and cultivate the new creation. We are Jesus' representatives on the earth—His body, in fact—commissioned to be fruitful and multiply in a different sort of way over all the earth: "Go therefore and make disciples of all the nations, baptizing them in the name of the Father and of the Son and of the Holy Spirit, teaching them to observe all things that I have commanded you" (Matt. 28:19–20a). We are agents of God's redemption on the earth, actively extending the new creation until Jesus comes back.

Given the extent of the Fall's damage, the enormity of this task is overwhelming—impossible, even. Thankfully when Jesus left, He did not leave us stranded. Before He left, He made provisions for the care of the infant new creation during His absence by sending His Spirit to indwell the lives of a motley crew of followers, giving them a continual connection to Him—we *can* be one with Him!—and empowering them to carry out His work on the earth—we *can* do what He told us to do! All of us who are descendents of this Last Adam receive the same Spirit when we are born into this new race (Eph. 1:13–14).

Redemption Wearing Shoes

And so, we the Church, the body of Jesus Christ, stand as God's redemptive agents in the world. Through the power and presence of the Spirit, we can put shoes on what Christ started. The responsibility is huge. It includes the reclaiming of *everything* God created.

> *We miss a great part of the redemptive picture if we are only concerned about signing up new people for our Christian club.*

Everything matters because everything is a means by which God can receive the glory He deserves. Humanity is obviously the most important part of God's creation—but when humanity changes, the world ought to be changing too. We miss a great part of the redemptive picture if we are only concerned about signing up new people for our Christian club. Jesus came to reconcile *all things* to Himself.

It's frightening that God let us be the ones who bear His image— and the image of His Son. We are the body of Christ, and as such we are the primary representation of God in the world. When someone wonders what God is like, our answer should be "Look at the Church!" If that makes you cringe, I hope it also gives you goose bumps to realize that God ascribes such value to the Church that He entrusted His reputation, His name in the world, to us. When He told us to be one with each other and with Him, He had a good reason. His name is on the line. When He told us to extend His kingdom by redeeming the world around us, He meant it. His kingdom depends on it. With such a responsibility, we must be diligent in our efforts to best represent His name and accomplish His work as the Church.

Conclusion: Connecting the Dots

God created all things—even singleness. In Adam we all sinned, ruining everything—including singleness by changing it from a process into a possibly permanent life situation. God provided for the redemption of everything—a provision that must therefore include even singleness—through the life and death of Jesus. Jesus then assigned the Church as His agents in the world, and until He returns, we have the task of proclaiming and practicing the good news of His redemption. We *tell* the world that He has made all things new, and we *do* everything we can to reclaim all of His territory—even singleness— from the powers of darkness.

> As a church of married and single members, we have to give up our quest for an Edenic world—a world where everyone gets married.

We must see both marriage and singleness as comparable, even complementary, ways to accomplish the task Jesus left us. We don't have a hard time understanding how marriage fits into this assignment: it mirrors the love of Christ and the Church, demonstrates the Tri-unity of God, and provides for procreation of image bearers. It is singleness that we often struggle to understand as clearly. But if we are to function as a fully operative body of Christ, we must redeem singleness from the clutches of culture and set free those people who may never know the pleasures and pain, joys and sorrows, of lifetime marriage on this earth. As a church of married and single members, we have to give up our quest for an Edenic world—a world where everyone gets married. Redemption doesn't take us back to the goodness of Eden. It takes us beyond to something better—both now and forever.

Better? What could be better than a perfect marriage? What could be better than spending *forever* in a perfect intimate relationship with someone you love more than life itself? What could be better than an eternity of genuine wedded bliss? Jesus made it quite clear that there is no marriage in heaven, and by extension, on the new earth (Matt. 22:30). If marriage as we know it (or wish we knew it) disappears, how can things possibly be better? And if marriage, in its purest form, is such a genius invention of God, why would He do away with it?

Good questions. Let's hang out together a little longer. Maybe we'll come to understand what seems so perplexing right now. Maybe we'll be able to nod in earnest agreement, instead of confused resignation, that God's plan—minus marriage—really is better.

HANGING OUT TOGETHER

Alex called it his secret place, and one Sunday night late in the fall he decided I could be trusted. Cohorts in the conspiracy that was our budding relationship, we skirted past the growing group of singles trying to decide where to eat after the evening service—a weekly ritual that always seemed to take longer than the actual going, ordering, and eating. Safely in Alex's hand-me-down family station wagon, we congratulated ourselves on a successful escape and stole out of the parking lot under the cover of darkness.

The streets we traveled were familiar to me, but when Alex finally stopped the car and turned off the ignition, I was perplexed. The deserted parking lot of one of the city's largest furniture stores didn't seem like such an impressive "secret." When I expressed my skepticism, however, the twinkle in his bright brown eyes assured me we weren't there yet. We locked up the car and took off walking—across the empty lot, under a spooky bridge, through a damp field, between a gap in the fence, and up a steep hill. At the top of the hill, Alex proudly presented his secret place: a bridge of railroad tracks that ran over the interstate.

For the next several hours we walked the tracks, watched the headlights zoom under us, and sat in the chilly October air wishing upon faraway stars. And we talked. Of all the things we had discovered since returning from Atlanta months earlier, the most frustrating was that there was never enough time to talk. Someone else always needed the phone. Classes and work ended our e-mails before they were finished. Responsibilities beckoned when we still had so much to say.

And there was a lot to say—much had happened during that summer and fall, and most of it had taken us by surprise. During the countless hours we'd spent serving side-by-side in ministry, we'd discovered windows into each other's hearts and had been taken aback by the obvious similarities and the complementary differences we found there. We had stumbled upon the delectable sweetness of someone who understands what few people do, someone who wants to hear all the silly things, someone who is willing to risk saying what nobody else will say. We had found out just how much fun doing absolutely nothing could be—as long as we did it together.

The seedlings of what seemed to be an unlikely friendship had quickly sprouted and grown into a flourishing relationship that sparkled with the promise of more. The accompanying emotions we had begun to experience rushed at us like the traffic racing below the safety of our railroad bridge— except, unlike the cars, we hadn't seen them coming. We were delighted and baffled all in the same breath.

So we talked. We talked of dreams and disappointments, families and futures, successes and failures. As the moon moved across the sky, our conversation danced through the years, a slow dance that let us share and savor the memories that shaped who we were and the dreams that defined who we'd become. We were just beginning to discover the wealth of each other and the rich diversity we brought to each other.

The hours slipped away easily—like so many before had and like so many after would.

Reluctant to let the evening slip away, we asked one more question, told one more funny story, shared one more brazen dream. I fought hard to control my chattering teeth, hoping Alex wouldn't notice I was shivering in the cool night air and decide we needed to go. I didn't want to go—the rare warmth of such companionship and the growing thrill of discovery more than made up for the cold that penetrated my light-weight denim jacket.

Somehow we knew that such a moment wouldn't come again soon. Long before we wanted to, we would have to inch back down the steep hill, squeeze through the gap in the fence, amble across the dew-covered field, hurry under the spooky bridge, and cross the empty lot. Monday morning would come quickly, and the pace of life would resume. But for a few magical moments on a crisp Sunday night, time stood still. While the world raced by, a special secret place had lifted us above the rush of experiences and let us take it all in.

chapter five

A Picture of Perfect Singleness

"Don't mock him! As if it's not bad enough that he has to spend his life riding an ostrich!"

Jeanine has a made-for-the-mall Christmas tree. Every square inch sparkles with colorful glass balls, glittery gold curly-cues, and hundreds of white lights. Atop her holiday masterpiece perches a slightly unconventional tree-topper. It's not a shimmering star or a dazzling angel. It's not a glitzy spire or a flashy ornament. No, my single friend rejects all those traditional tree-toppers and awards the most prestigious spot on her Christmas tree to a stuffed cowboy riding a stuffed red ostrich—a relic from the Island of Misfit Toys in the classic Christmas tale of Rudolph the Red-Nosed Reindeer.

The story begins, in case your Rudolph memories are dusty, when Donner and Mrs. Donner discover their new fawn has a glowing and bleeping red nose. They are horrified, and Donner voices dismay that Rudolph will never be one of Santa's reindeer unless they can hide his obnoxious nose. A visit from Santa confirms their fears when the jolly man himself sounds more naughty than nice—"Great bouncing icebergs!" he exclaims, just before telling Donner that he certainly hopes Rudolph outgrows his offensive nose. You'd think if *anyone* in this story would have been understanding and accepting it would have been Santa! But being different is apparently so terrible that even Santa can't handle it.

It doesn't take long for Rudolph to realize he's different, and therefore not wanted. He runs away and meets another runaway, a misfit elf named Hermey, who wants to be a dentist. The two misfits decide they don't need anybody; they are independent!—but as long as they're being independent in the vicinity of the Abominable Snow Monster, they may as well be independent together. Rudolph and Hermey acquire another misfit friend in Yukon Cornelius, and after barely escaping the Abominable Snow Monster the three friends find themselves ashore on a remote island where they meet a spotted elephant, Jeanine's tree-topping cowboy, and a Charlie in a Box. It's the Island of Misfit Toys, a place for toys that no little boy or girl wants. The runaways finally feel at home.

> *My single friends and I often feel like we've washed ashore on our own intangible island, far from the real world where marriage is the norm. We are misfits, isolated in a little-understood place where the most earnest attempts at rescue come in the form of blind date offers.*

Eventually Rudolph decides he can't run away from his problems, so he returns to Christmas Town and the taunts of "Fire Snoot" and "Neon Nose." He discovers that his parents are searching for him, so Rudolph braves the weather to save Christmas by bringing home Donner, Santa's lead reindeer. The town welcomes the misfit as a hero and admits that perhaps they'd been a little hard on him: "Maybe misfits have a place, too." A wave of politically correct generosity sweeps through Christmas Town and all three misfits are accepted. Rudolph's hero status only grows when a horrible snowstorm threatens to cancel Christmas, and he goes down in history for single-nosedly saving Christmas by guiding Santa's sleigh through the blizzard. Happy endings abound for the three misfits who proved themselves useful.

The story of Rudolph and his friends is nice—rejects turned heroes. But most of us can't relate, at least to the hero part. I much prefer the tale of the misfit toys, stuck on an island to rot and rust because they couldn't do anything extraordinarily special. Stuck there because someone decided they had the curse of being different, of not being "normal." The only thing they could do was stay together and dream of being rescued, waiting to be valued just because they existed.

The *real* happy ending occurs when the misfit toys find better days because Rudolph and a reformed Santa come to their rescue. Someone understood what it was like to be rejected just because of being different. Someone recognized their inherent value, plucked them from alienation, and gave them a place to be loved.

I'm not the first person to draw the analogy between the Island of Misfit Toys and singles in the church. Through no particular fault of our own, my single friends and I often feel like we've washed ashore on our own intangible island, far from the real world where marriage is the norm. We are misfits, isolated in a little-understood place where the most earnest attempts at rescue come in the form of blind date offers.

Nothing New Under the Sun

It's really nothing new for singles to be misfits. Ever since God gave Eve to Adam, marriage has generally been the expected and preferred way of life. While history is full of notable exceptions who chose the single life when they very well could have married, for most singles, singleness is what happens to us when we don't get married. It's definitely Plan B, and the majority of us scramble to figure out how to do it—or how to get out of it. We don't particularly like being abnormal . . . and alone.

If ever a culture revolved around marriage and the family, the Jewish culture of Bible times did. With a fuzzy concept of the afterlife, the Jews viewed marriage and family as a very tangible kind of "eternal life": the family name would live forever through descendents. Such a perspective made it unthinkable for a Jew to remain unmarried, and once married, it was nothing less than God's curse if a couple remained childless. Understandably then, barrenness brought horrible shame, and it also signaled the end of the family name. Consider Sarah and Abraham and the extreme action they took to have a child. Hear the words of Rachel to Jacob, "Give me children, or else I die!" This may sound a bit melodramatic, but it makes clear that marriage and family formed the overriding purpose of life in Jewish culture (Gen. 16; 30:1). The prominence of the family in Jewish culture is also rooted in God's promise to bless Abraham by making him into a great nation. Obviously procreation was an essential part of fulfilling this promise—the nation of Israel was built one family at a time. Marriage and family were understandably the "marrow of Israel's identity and purpose."[1]

This perspective did not wane over time, but instead was etched into formal Jewish teaching. According to the Mishnah, the rabbinic commentary on the Torah (the first five books of the Old Testament), Jewish men were *required* to get married and have families. One rabbi said that a man who didn't fulfill these requirements was not a "proper man."[2] Other rabbis taught that God watches and if a man reaches twenty and is still single, He exclaims, "Blasted be his bones!"[3] Quite simply, Jewish society didn't have a place for singles and found it unthinkable that anyone, and especially a religious leader, would be unmarried.

Throughout the Old Testament, the misfit nature of singleness is sustained:

> Only rarely did unmarried people play a role in Old Testament history. These exceptions include some of the prophets, such as Elijah and Elisha. Daniel may have been a eunuch in Babylon. Jeremiah was commanded by God, "You must not marry and have sons or daughters in this place" (Jer. 16:2), as part of his prophetic testimony. Though used mightily by God, these singles did not enjoy the affirmation of Jewish society. Rather, they were viewed as eccentric, ascetic anomalies.[4]

> *Jesus actually talked very little about marriage and family, giving us scant material to use as a how-to manual for single living. Perhaps He bypassed these issues because they are really only symptoms of deeper issues.*

Into this culture came the Incarnate Son of God, who lived the misfit single life well past the expected age of marriage and died without a solitary descendent to carry on the family name of Joseph and Mary. I wonder sometimes what the people of the day thought and said about this situation. It seems likely that, somewhere along the way, well-meaning friends hinted that there were plenty of nice girls in Galilee and certainly one of them would make Jesus a fine wife. It's not hard to imagine that at some point, His family asked if it wasn't time He stopped traipsing all over the countryside with His little club of boys and settled down to start His own family.

Given the cultural priority of marriage and family, I have little trouble believing that such things occurred during the life of Jesus, and I dearly wish the gospel writers would have included just one of these incidents so my single friends and I could finally have the perfect answer to give during such awkward encounters. It would have been nice if they had clearly spelled out how Jesus handled the day-to-day challenges of the single life. It would have been helpful if Jesus had given direct answers to the seemingly all-consuming questions of singleness, like "What if I never get married?" and "How do I make it through lonely holidays year after year?"

But God didn't answer these questions when He recorded the life of Jesus for us. Jesus actually talked very little about marriage and family, giving us scant material to use as a how-to manual for single living. Perhaps He bypassed these issues because they are really only symptoms of deeper issues. They are like a rumbling stomach during Sunday morning church—the growl is not the real problem; hunger is. Address the hunger, and silence the rumble. A deep hunger gnaws at our souls, a craving for significance and purpose. Why are we here? What should we do with the wisp of time we have? What really matters in life? Address these intense issues, and the rumble of circumstances will be silenced. For the majority of people in Jesus' day (and a majority of people in the twenty-first century American church) the answer seems simple: "Get married and have a family. That's what ultimately matters in life." Interestingly, God never answers our gnawing questions this way (perhaps we should stop answering them this way then, as well.) because the true hunger goes beyond the rumbling desire for marriage and family.

A Man with a Mission

God's message in the four Gospels redirects us to the answers that Jesus' life gives for much bigger questions. You cannot read the Gospels and come away without the impression that Jesus lived a life of purpose and focus. His decisions were defined by clear intentions. He lived with absolute focus. He knew exactly why He was here. If I asked *you* why He was here, you might say He came to die, to pay the penalty for the sin of the world and make a way for us to stand righteous before God. Everything He did drove Him toward that goal.

> *We take out the trash, wash behind our ears, change the sheets, and pick broccoli out of our teeth. None of these activities seem very important when we think about mission and purpose.*

You'd be right, but have you ever wondered exactly how He did this every day? What did it mean for His entire life to be defined by His mission? Did He wake up in the morning and say, "When I grow up, I'm going to be brutally beaten and nailed to a cross"? Did He play, or not, with His neighborhood friends on a given day because of His mission? Did He choose His disciples' lesson for the day with this purpose in mind? Did He stay a day longer here or there because of the impending cross? Perhaps, but Jesus was human and sometimes human existence is pretty mundane. We take out the trash, wash behind our ears, change the sheets, and pick broccoli out of our teeth. None of these activities seem very important when we think about mission and purpose. They're just, well, they're just life. How did such a big mission, such as dying on the cross for the sins of the world, define the commonplace routines of Jesus' daily life?

> *What if Jesus had decided, as so many Christian*
> *singles do, that satisfying one's sexual drive is not*
> *only expected but totally acceptable?*

Jesus had a mission that superceded His eventual death on the cross. It was a mission that ultimately led Him to the cross, but it was also a mission that He could pursue when He was five, fifteen, and twenty-five. The defining purpose of Jesus' life was to obey God all the time. We first hear Him voice this mission at the fresh-faced age of twelve when His distraught parents finally found their "lost" son expounding on the intricacies of Jewish Law with the silver-haired religious experts in the temple (Luke 2:41–50). Jesus called it being about His Father's business or doing the will of His Father, and it was an intention He would repeat often to His followers for the remainder of His life. He lived every day to do whatever God wanted Him to do, to be obedient every step of His thirty-three years, all the way to the cross.

Our mission as children of God is essentially the same—whether we are single or married. We are called to live every day to do whatever God wants us to do, to be obedient every step of our unknown number of years, all the way to wherever God plans.

If you're thinking that because Jesus is God, it was easier for Him to be obedient and to be single than it is for you or me, you'd be wrong. It was *harder* for Him, as all of life was. As the only man who could feasibly carry out redemption, He bore the responsibility of doing right what we do wrong. He lived under perpetual satanic attack of a magnitude we can't imagine. Think about it. What does Satan gain when you are discontented with your singleness? What happens when you fall into sexual sin? To be sure, Satan gains. He gains territory in your life, he gains another foothold in the world, and he makes it easier for you to lose sight of your mission. But think about what Satan would have gained if Jesus had been discontent with His singleness? What if Jesus had decided, as so many Christian singles do, that satisfying one's sexual drive is not only expected but totally acceptable? The next time you want to think that Jesus had it easier, think again. He *does* understand what it's like to be human—and to be single in a culture of families.

Do not misunderstand—I am not putting our lives and our obedience on the same level as Jesus'. Obviously, His accomplished mission produced results that ours never can. Only He could provide redemption. However, I, and hopefully you, have been made children of God and therefore agents of His redemption. By our daily obedience, we carry God's redemption to places it might not have reached before. I don't know where your obedience takes you. I'm not always sure where my obedience takes me, but I'm pretty sure that during this chapter of my life, obedience takes me to singles and churches, doing what I can to redeem singleness. God has put within our individual orbits people that only we can reach and places that only we can go. Accomplishing our mission demands that we obey Him faithfully, taking His message to those people and those places.

The Unexpected and the Unacceptable

Misfits, with all their foibles and peculiarities, have always fit into God's plan, and often in more significant ways than "normal" people. God has long delighted to shower His special, undeserved favor on those who are blanketed with shame and rejected by others, and He's done it not for their own sakes, but for His. Working through the weak manifests His strength.

In fact, the entire Story of redemption is woven with strands of shame—God uses the broken, scorned things of the world to carry out His plan. When He promised Abraham that he would be the father of many nations, it seemed like a joke. Sarah, the de facto mother in the story, was barren. A shamed misfit in a culture of marriage and family. But this was God's Story, and Sarah miraculously had a son. The promise stayed alive. That is, until Isaac, Abraham and Sarah's child of promise, married and discovered that his wife was barren. Another shamed misfit without the ability to rescue herself. Once again it appeared that God's grand plan had run amuck. But barren Rebekah gave birth to the next son of promise. In spite of horrible human odds, God's promise lived. God chose the unlikeliest people to carry out the early stages of His redemptive plan (Gen. 17–21; 25).

Reading through the Old Testament, we come to expect the unexpected from God: imprisoned and forgotten Joseph rises to second in Egyptian command; Moses the murderer is snatched from obscurity in the desert and appointed leader of the Hebrews; widowed Ruth leaves behind her chances for remarriage when she sticks by her bitter mother-in-law—and then ends up living out a time-honored love story; a lowly shepherd boy named David is anointed to replace the stately King Saul. The stories are often so familiar to us that we rarely notice how surprising the events really were. God's plan often spins on the axis of the unexpected (Gen. 37–41; Exod. 1–5; Ruth; 1 Sam. 16).

> *Jesus' life was full of the "unacceptable," from the way He entered the world to the way He left it.*

But God's plan also spins on the axis of what we would call unacceptable. At the climax of the redemption Story, God turned a "normal" person into a misfit, subject to the rejection of those around her. Mary wasn't barren and shamed like her matriarchal predecessors—she was an innocent God-fearing teenager whose life stretched before her with all the promise and anticipation of youth. She eagerly awaited and prepared for life with Joseph, a godly man who loved her deeply. But God broke into what looked to be a scripted life, and Mary found herself doubly scandalized—she was pregnant and Joseph wasn't the father. In the culture of her day, she could have been stoned and no one would have protested the injustice. But in God's plan, misfit Mary lived to tell a story that most people found hard (okay, impossible) to believe, and she did it with all the grace and beauty of a century-old saint.

From the moment we meet an embryonic Jesus in the womb of Mary, the theme of God's Story returns again and again to the "unacceptable." What's acceptable about a king, *the* King, sucking His thumb in a feeding trough? What's acceptable about the Bread of Life nearly starving to death in the desert? What's acceptable about the Owner of everything not having a place to lay His weary head? What's acceptable about the Righteous One being found guilty? What's acceptable about the Rose of Sharon wearing a crown of thorns? What's acceptable about the Living Water gagging on a vinegar-drenched sponge? What's acceptable about the Giver of life dying?

Nothing, that's what. Nothing is acceptable by any definition about God doing what He did through the life of Jesus, the misfit. Jesus' life was full of the "unacceptable," from the way He entered the world to the way He left it. Again, we've heard it so often that we barely flinch at the scandalous nature of Jesus' presence here. My unchurched niece, after hearing the Story for the first time, was right in her assessment: "It's so unbelievable it has to be true. We would never have thought to ask God to do *that*." It just doesn't fit our concept of what's right, what's sensible, what's appropriate.

Misfits Redeemed

In all these irreconcilable realities, it does seem appropriate that the kinds of people God has delighted to use are also the ones that Jesus came to save. The rich and the popular and the prestigious didn't want what Jesus offered—what could He have added to their bank accounts or popularity polls? Jesus came for the destitute, the untouchables, and the oppressed—the ones who had nowhere to look but up. He lived among them, understood them, and loved them. He ascribed great value to them when everyone else saw utter poverty in their existence.

> Being a misfit isn't the problem. Misfits form the very apple of God's all-seeing eye.

On a larger scale, Jesus came to rescue another kind of misfit. He came to redeem *us*—a group of people displaced from the kind of world we were designed to occupy. We were never meant to live a life alienated from God and any kind of meaningful existence, but, unlike the misfit toys stuck on their island, we have done everything to deserve banishment. We have wholly earned God's rejection and repeatedly shown ourselves to be misfits in His once sinless creation. We desperately needed Someone to recognize our inherent value as God's creation, pluck us from alienation, and give us a place to be loved.

That's exactly what Jesus did. Into this misfit environment came God-in-the-flesh to rescue us and give us a place where we are loved and valued for no reason other than that He wanted to. Ultimately, that place is in His presence on the new earth forever, but He's also provided a place on this earth, in this life, where we can be unconditionally loved and accepted. That place is the Church, where we are all redeemed misfits, people loved by God and given to each other.

Interestingly, though, once we are rescued from our alienation, we don't stop being misfits. In fact, we become a *new* kind of misfit. We may now "fit" in a relationship with God, but we should no longer fit within the values system of this world. Jesus came to obliterate the misplaced values of humanity, and He replaced them with His own. He chose for Himself a remnant of people who would *choose* to become temporary misfits to follow Him—swimming upstream against the raging waters of cultural acceptability. Someday when Jesus comes back, all this will change, but until then, being a follower of Christ is *not* a culturally acceptable thing.

So, you see, being a misfit isn't the problem. Misfits form the very apple of God's all-seeing eye. He's demonstrated His power through them, sent His Son to become one, and will one day re-create the world for them. The more important matter is where we're misfits. If we don't fit in the culture, that's understandable. If we don't fit in the church, that's inexcusable. We stand before our Redeemer on equal ground—there is nothing that distinguishes one's value over another. Marital status, economic situations, and educational backgrounds don't determine value and shouldn't form class distinctions. The only actual misfit in the Church is the person who is not really part of the Church at all.

chapter six

The Rest of the Story

Daniel doesn't eat, breathe, or move. But for all his shortcomings—mainly that he's just a stuffed animal—he managed to accomplish what my sister and brother-in-law couldn't. He opened the world of words to my five-year-old nephew, Philip. Suzy and Peter had worked hard for months to teach Philip the alphabet and how the letters form words and how the words form meaning. They bought him the delightful BOB Books, engaging stories that build phonics skills through the life and times of Mat, Sam, Cat, and Dot. Philip knew *how* reading worked—he just didn't want to do it. Decoding words and deciphering meaning was a lot of hard work. It was much easier to just look at the pictures or wait for an available adult to read the stories.

Daniel changed all that. When Philip made the eleven-inch stuffed Bengal tiger at Build-a-Bear Workshop—the store where you select the furry fixins of a toy animal, position a fabric heart in it, stuff it, and name it—he could have been the poster child for their company slogan: "where best friends are made." Philip didn't just make another stuffed animal for his collection; he made a first-rate friend. Philip and Daniel, in the tradition of Calvin and Hobbes, are an inseparable pair in search of adventure.

In a stroke of brilliance (or parental desperation), my brother-in-law mentioned to his reluctant little reader that Daniel had told him how much he would enjoy it if Philip would read to him. The power of suggestion began its work, and reading slowly took on new meaning for Philip. It wasn't just something Mommy and Daddy wanted him to do; it was something Daniel needed him to do. What had previously been a chore became a chance to make his friend happy, and, in the process of pleasing his stuffed buddy, Philip discovered the wonder of words and story. He didn't just learn to read—he learned to love it. Philip's life will never be the same.

On one level, Philip enjoyed books immensely, even when he couldn't read the words. He could follow the stories or make up his own just by looking at the pictures, and he was content with what he knew. Fortunately for Philip, his parents are smarter than he is, and they know that the initial invested pain of decoding words pays dividends for a lifetime. Between the covers of books lie inexhaustible treasures waiting to be discovered and experienced.

Moving Beyond the Picture

Pictures are helpful ways for us to learn—and the Bible provides a lot of word pictures to make things clear for us. But if we are content to just look at these pictures and never get to the rest of the Story, we will miss much—just as Philip did before he learned to read the words that accompany the pictures.

> *Jesus was the perfect single adult—but in somewhat ironic reality, His entire purpose for coming to earth was all about marriage.*

One such picture that Scripture gives us is that of Jesus' life as an unmarried person. Certainly one of the beautiful themes in the grand Story of redemption, as we looked at in the previous chapter, is that God provided salvation for the human race and the entire cosmos through the life and death of a single adult. A human being who lived with all the emotions, desires, and temptations we do. A human being who understood what it meant to be lonely, deserted, and rejected. A human being who loved more deeply, purely, and passionately than we can because His love was unhindered by selfishness. A human being who fully understood yet lived without the intensity, significance, and ecstasy of sex. (He was, after all, the One who designed it.) The way Jesus lived His life as a single adult offers defining answers to how we can actually live—fully and purposefully—without a spouse.

But if we only see Jesus' life as a picture perfect model for Christian singles, we have missed the totality of the Story that shapes the picture. We have missed the full significance of the words—and the Word. Jesus was the perfect single adult—but in somewhat ironic reality, His entire purpose for coming to earth was all about marriage. Really. He lived and died so we could all get married and live happily ever after—eventually.

Redemption is all about marriage, but it isn't about finding an earthly spouse; it's about looking forward to a heavenly one. Because of redemption, we can look ahead to a day when the bride of Christ will be united with her Bridegroom and live in perfect union with Him forever.

Jesus came to take a bride in the true fashion of a Palestinian Jew, a tradition that follows a slightly different process than Western dating, engagement, and marriage. In both cultures, marriage takes place in two stages: betrothal or engagement and then full-fledged marriage. The betrothal and engagement periods begin when the woman accepts a gift from her prospective husband. For those of us in the West, that gift typically entails a trip to the jeweler, a diamond that costs what my parents paid for their first house, and a carefully planned romantic evening of "surprise." (At least, this is what girls hope for.) In Middle Eastern culture, however, instead of the prospective groom giving an expensive gift to his beloved, he offers a dowry—a payment of some kind—to her father since the man will lose what his daughter contributes to the household economy. (Things haven't changed much in the Middle East as my friend Tammy and I, both glow-in-the-dark Americans, discovered when we visited there. We often heard dowry offers barked in our direction: "Five camels? How 'bout six?" Lacking knowledge about the going rate for camels in the Middle East, we didn't know if we should be flattered or insulted.)

This gift-giving is where the similarities between Jewish betrothal and Western engagement end. The betrothal period, called *kiddushin*, comes from a word meaning sanctified or set apart. The woman is set aside to be the wife of a particular man and no other. We'd say this is true in our engagements as well, but in reality, engagements are broken all the time. While this usually causes a lot of pain and varying degrees of inconvenience, it's not the same as breaking *kiddushin*. Even though the couple does not live together, the legal relationship created by *kiddushin* can only be dissolved by death or divorce.

In Bible times, *kiddushin* was a busy phase for both the man and the woman. He maintained his regular work responsibilities, but also worked diligently to prepare a place for them to live after the wedding. Unlike our modern families, biblical families functioned like multigenerational communities, living in houses that featured several rooms surrounding courtyard areas. Various family members lived in the rooms, and when a son prepared for marriage, he added another room to the family residence—a place for him and his new bride. While the groom-to-be made living preparations, the bride-to-be was busy preparing for the wedding and learning everything she could from her mother and grandmother about how to care for her own household. At the end of *kiddushin*—a time determined and known only by the groom's father—the groom came for his bride, taking her and an assembly of friends and family on a grand procession through the city to their new home where they would officially start their lives together with a full week of wedding festivities.

> We will marry the Lamb and live forever in the presence of God as the ultimate spouse, the bride of Christ.

Jesus' first coming initiated the *kiddushin* stage of His marriage. He came to pay the bride-price determined by His Father. The cost was extraordinarily high; He paid it with His own life. Then He returned to His Father's house where He has been ever since, preparing a place for His bride to live with Him forever. On a future day known only to His Father, this divine *kiddushin* will end and Jesus will come to claim His bride. He will take her to the place He's been preparing since He left two thousand years ago. We, the Church of Jesus Christ, are that bride, and until the much-anticipated day when He comes, we are set apart for Him alone (John 14).

Jesus' return to claim His bride, the Church, will begin what we can rightly call the consummation. All of God's Story since the beginning—creation, Fall, redemption—has been leading to this day when everything will be completed, filled up to perfection. We will marry the Lamb and live forever in the presence of God as the ultimate spouse, the bride of Christ.

It Only Gets Better

So, you see, there *is* marriage—or at least *a* marriage—on the new earth, but not the kind of marriage that's been around since the creation of the world. That kind of marriage is no longer needed. Remember its original intent (besides procreation)? God wanted Adam and Eve to mirror the oneness and intimacy of the Godhead. Marriage gave them a human expression for what God is like. On the new earth, we will be in the very presence of the One who marriage has always imaged, and the human expression will pale in comparison.

But that's not all! In the presence of God, we will enjoy a new kind of oneness—an intimacy and fellowship between Creator and creature, a relationship with Jesus Himself in the flesh. All that accompanies any human experience of oneness is just the prelude to this unfathomable experience of truly *knowing* God.

But that's still not all! Not only will we live in this kind of incredible relationship with God, but also with each other as a community of His children. It will be marriage perfected, intensified, and enlarged—the intimate, untainted oneness of marriage will be expanded to include the entire community of believers.

Think of the person you most love to be with. Subtract all your combined weaknesses, and then add all the time in the world. Forget about busy schedules, ulterior motives, limited resources, and competing friendships. Imagine your relationship if all the things that make both of you unique could be fully enjoyed instead of often being a source of annoyance or misunderstanding. Imagine having forever to fully enjoy and be enjoyed by your friend. Now multiple this delight by every other believer through all of history, and you begin to get a foretaste of glory divine! We will have forever to enjoy God and the perfect company of *all* His image bearers in a world without sin.

> *Thinking about what God has planned for the future can stir your appetite for something truly better than anything we've known. It's so indescribably good that our minds can't handle it.*

I don't pretend to know how this really works. In fact, I find the whole idea mind-boggling. But it's an exhilarating kind of mind-boggling, not the kind that threatens to make your head explode. You understand the difference. I liked to force the latter kind on my fifth-graders when we studied the solar system. Armed with an array of spherical items, including a yellow recess ball, a pea, a Ping-Pong ball, and a marble, we ventured outside to the nearest corner. There we left a student with the yellow recess ball—a severely undersized sun—while we took off walking, counting steps in our close-to-scale reconstruction of the solar system. Thirty-five steps later we left a student with a poppy seed for Mercury; after thirty more steps we left a student with a BB for Venus. Twenty-eight more steps and we had reached the cosmic position of planet earth—the pea. About this time, we called in the stranded students so they wouldn't miss traveling into deep space (and since it violated school policy and common sense to leave students standing alone on city sidewalks). Seven hundred fifty-seven steps and a pinhead, Ping-Pong ball, and big marble later, we had to call it off. Walking nearly two more miles to get all the way to Pluto would have been a bit much. By this time, they'd had enough. Their minds were numb from pondering the expanse of infinity and the magnitude of the God who could create it all.

Thinking too hard about space can threaten the sanity of an average person, but thinking about what God has planned for the future can stir your appetite for something truly better than anything we've known. It's so indescribably good that our minds can't handle it. It's so incredible that God quite possibly withheld the details lest we'd flip out with excitement (like kids waiting for Christmas) and perhaps be rendered useless now while there's so much to do. And yet what He has told us and what He has provided in the present are just enough to bring comfort and hope in the midst of a relationship-challenged world.

When we get to the new earth, marriage will both pass away and be present at the same time. The shadow—what we know now—will be gone, eclipsed by the brilliance of the real thing. Redemption really does lead to something better.

Living in the In-Between: Kingdom Life

Yeah? So what. That's *then* and this is *now*. I'm still single with no viable prospects on the horizon. So not only am I stuck waiting for an earthly spouse, but now I also get to wait for a heavenly Spouse. And this is supposed to make me feel better?

Well, yes and no. The "better" of redemption wasn't meant to only be a distant reality—like the planet Pluto. We obviously won't know the reality of the consummation until Jesus comes back, but He has already laid the groundwork for a new way of living. The fact that it often seems a distant reality isn't His fault. It's ours. As fallen people in a fallen world, we've failed to understand the nature of what Jesus came to do, what He taught, and how it affects life now. We've missed the beauty of oneness in Christ and instead live in increasingly fragmented ways.

The very first message we have recorded that Jesus delivered was about the kingdom of God. He made it clear that this kingdom, whatever it was, was happening—"The kingdom of God is at hand"—and later in His ministry He made it just as clear that the kingdom was still coming—"I will no longer drink of the fruit of the vine until that day when I drink it new in the kingdom of God" (Mark 1:15; 14:25). What are we to make of this? How could the kingdom be "at hand" and still be a future event? The simplest answer is that it just is. Jesus started it when He came, and He will complete it when He returns. We are living in the in-between.

I don't know what goes through your mind when you hear "the kingdom of God" or its interchangeable expression, "the kingdom of heaven." You might think of pearly gates and golden streets. Or maybe you think of some state of spiritual existence where everyone gets along all the time. Perhaps you think warm fuzzy thoughts about all the Christians in the world. If you're not really sure what it is, don't feel bad—it's one of the bigger entries in my Bible encyclopedia and after reading it, I can tell you this: theologians aren't really sure what it is either.

I can tell you what first-century Jews, Jesus' original audience, expected it to be. They looked for a very physical kingdom, a place where wars only appeared in the history books, crops overflowed the barns every year, and government truly existed for the benefit of all citizens. They expected the kingdom of God to sweep Roman rule aside and inaugurate God's rule at every level of life.

> *Jesus came to establish a new kingdom that would not physically overthrow existing kingdoms, but it would change them one person at a time from the inside out.*

That's not quite what happened. In fact, Jesus' kingdom was "a total reversal of what had been expected. His kingdom had not come to replace the kingdoms of this world, but was intended to exist among them and in doing so transform . . . every sphere of human experience."[1] He taught His followers principles that made them scratch their heads. The least shall be greatest. The poor are rich. You must die to live. Serve instead of being served. I guarantee this didn't fit their ideas of leadership and power anymore than it fits ours. Although the term hadn't been coined yet, they lived according to the pervasive human rule of the survival of the fittest.

To establish this radical kingdom, Jesus chose the most ordinary of people. They were an unimpressive collection of men with hands that smelled like fish, feet that raced to be first in line, and ears that usually missed the point. These men with varying skills (and non-skills), rough personalities, and minimal education were the intentional choice of

Jesus—in quality and, as David Ashton suggests, in quantity: "[Jesus] chose twelve—apostles who would be the counterpart of the twelve leaders of the twelve tribes of Israel. Later in His ministry He chose a larger group . . . He chose seventy—seventy was significant. There were seventy leaders in the Sanhedrin who ruled Jewish life. These were the successors to the seventy elders with whom Moses shared leadership. What was Jesus up to? He was building a church that would be a shadow cabinet to the current systems that operated. He was creating 'His Majesty's Loyal Opposition' that would out-think, out-live and out-die the governments in power."[2]

Jesus came to establish a new kingdom that would not physically overthrow existing kingdoms, but it would change them one person at a time from the inside out. And it would do its work by means of a *new* kind of family. Jesus introduced this new Family to His followers early in His Galilean ministry.

A New Family: The Means to Build the Kingdom

On this particular day when Jesus' mother and brothers came looking for Him, they weren't bringing Him home-baked chocolate chip cookies or an extra change of clothes—although both of these would have been nice given the circumstances Jesus faced in Galilee. They came because they thought He had snapped. Gone crazy. Sold the farm. They came to take Him home where He belonged—or at least where they could keep an eye on Him. As they approached the house where He was, though, the crowd was so thick that they ended up standing outside while the announcement of their arrival rippled through the mob (Matt. 12:46–50; Mark 3:31–35; Luke 8:14–21).

Crowds were all in a day's work for Jesus. People swarmed around Him, forcing Him to retreat into wilderness areas where traffic wasn't a problem. And even there, Mark records that the people still came from every direction.

His miraculous acts in Galilee gained Him many friends (or at least fans), but Jesus had earned some enemies, too. He was a renegade by Pharisaical standards, blacklisted for Sabbath-breaking and cavorting with societal scum. (Wouldn't some motherly love packaged in choco-late chip cookies have been nice?) Just a few chapters into the Gospel record, the conspiracy to get rid of Jesus was already brewing.

> *While Mary and her boys said, "He is out of His mind," Peter and his buddies were getting ready to say, "You are the Christ!" While His family tried to stop what He was doing, His followers thirsted for more.*

The word of His family's arrival finally made it to the front: "Look, Your mother and Your brothers are outside seeking You" (Mark 3:32). Instead of calling intermission and pushing through the crowd to greet them as *any* Middle Easterner would have done, Jesus turned to the one who delivered the message. "Who is My mother and who are My brothers?" (Matt. 12:48). The crowd fell silent. If a bystander had dropped a shekel on the stone floor at that moment, its clink would have echoed in the room. With a sweep of His hand around the inner circle of His disciples, Jesus said, "Here are My mother and My broth-ers! For whoever does the will of My Father in heaven is My brother and sister and mother" (vv. 49–50).

Gasp! Many of us are so familiar with these words that we aren't shocked anymore, but I guarantee His audience was. What would possess Jesus to practically disown His family, or at the very least to displace them? What happened to shift His primary allegiance from His own flesh and blood to a ragtag band of men who quarreled among themselves and vied for position in whatever kingdom He was establishing?

What happened is that the ragtag group of men believed in Him. His own mother and brothers did not. While Mary and her boys said, "He is out of His mind," Peter and his buddies were getting ready to say, "You are the Christ!" While His family tried to stop what He was doing, His followers thirsted for more. His family's intentions may have been good—they only wanted what they thought was best for Jesus, but undeniably, as Rodney Clapp says, "if Mary and her other children [could not] accept Jesus' vocation, He [could not] recognize their kindredness. Mary [came] as mother; her Son [called] her to something even more fundamental—He [called] her to discipleship."[3]

With His actions and words, Jesus established a new Family built not on biological connections but on allegiance to His mission and obedience to His commands. In a sense this idea was new, but not really. Like so many things in the life of Jesus, it was hinted at in the Old Testament. The community of Israel was not made of only biological Jews. It was a hodge-podge of people who identified themselves with the God of Israel through obedience to His commands and association with His wondrous acts on their behalf.

The Torah also highlights the relationship between family and obedience. When children disobeyed and rebelled against their parents, they could be killed or disowned. (I'm not suggesting that we reinstate this practice, but it makes me laugh that our society considers spanking a condemnable offense!) As severe as this seems to us, it is clear that something is more important to God than warm, fuzzy family connections. God also told His sons and daughters that if they failed to keep their covenant with Him, He could sell them into slavery and even declare them no longer to be His people (Deut. 32:19–20; Hos. 1:9). Again, God makes it clear that there is something more important than biological "rights." Jesus affirms this truth in the parable of the prodigal son who insisted that he was no longer worthy to be called his father's son because of his despicable behavior (Luke 15:11–32). Family is not a matter of mere biology. It's really about obedience and honor.

Do not think that by prioritizing this new Family Jesus intended to undermine the biological family. He actually affirmed its importance during His ministry. When He spoke strongly against divorce, raising the bar higher than the spiritual leaders of the day had, His disciples responded with amazement in Matthew 19:10, "If such is the case . . . it is better not to marry." (When was the last time we heard this perspective propagated in church?) The sanctity of marriage, Jesus reminded them, was established by God at creation and was not to be treated lightly. As for children, Jesus gently welcomed and loved them when His followers would have brushed them off like pesky mosquitoes.

Jesus gave a final affirmation of the biological family in His last excruciating moments on the cross—but He did it within the framework of the new Family. As He hung dying, He gazed on His mother (who believed by then) and did for her what His position as oldest son demanded—He took care of her by making arrangements for her continued care in His absence. But even while fulfilling His sonly duty, He didn't do what was expected in terms of the biological family. The logical person to care for Mary would have been one of His brothers, but they didn't believe in Him yet. Instead of entrusting her to them, Jesus gave her to His beloved disciple John—a devoted member of the Family of believers (John 19:25–27).

Focusing on the Family

Jesus came to institute a new kingdom and a new Family. The advantage of hindsight makes it fairly easy for us to cull these truths from Jesus' words. But the ideas that Jesus was inaugurating were revolutionary and the people grappled with their meaning. The Jews had long anticipated a new kingdom established by the Messiah who would overthrow Rome, but they had trouble understanding a kingdom that wasn't comprised of political rulers and physical territory. Family was obviously nothing new to them; it was the essence of their existence and had been the bedrock of their society since the time of the patriarchs, but they wrestled with the notion that another Family, or community, could be more important than the biological family.

> *If we think that building strong families will produce strong churches, we've got it backward.*

Twenty-one centuries later, we may nod our heads in agreement at Jesus' teaching of a new kingdom and a new Family, but truthfully, we struggle with it perhaps as much as Jesus' first listeners did. For decades, strong nuclear families have been heralded as the way to save America. Definitely there is validity in these efforts—encouraging the godly leadership of dads, deepening the spiritual walks of moms, and nurturing the hearts of children can't hurt in the efforts to affect America with the gospel. But if we think it's the answer, we've missed the point. If we think that building strong families will produce strong churches, we've got it backward. Building strong churches will produce strong families. Jesus redefined our order of priorities.

> If the American church doesn't survive, there's not much hope for the American family. And there's not much hope for American singles either.

We have to rethink things. The nuclear family is not the marrow of identity and purpose. Instead, our significance is rooted in a relationship with Jesus and membership in His Family—the institution officially assigned to reach the world. No longer are we primarily identified by our individual family name, but rather by His name. No longer is our personhood and character most significantly determined by the blood of the biological family, but by the blood of the Lamb.[4]

This Family supercedes the biological family in importance because it is a permanent Family. Rodney Clapp calls it the First Family because it should receive first allegiance and function as "the primary vehicle of God's grace and salvation for a waiting, desperate world."[5] This will only happen as the Church forms "a community . . . among the world's fractured and divided communities [that] will live in unity and truth, worshiping the God of Israel, who is the Lord of all creation."[6] It is our commitment to one another as believers and our devotion to the truth of God's Word that will reach the world, not the success or failure of our individual families.

I am not trying to destroy the nuclear family any more than Jesus was, but is it possible that we've so focused on reclaiming families that we've sacrificed the Family Jesus created to accomplish His mission? Churches are dying every week across this country, while others limp along on life-support. Christianity has an ever-increasing number of nominal followers, unaware of or unconcerned about the cost of true discipleship. If we can't figure out how to fix these issues, we may as well forget our families. If the American church doesn't survive, there's not much hope for the American family.

And there's not much hope for American singles either. Jesus redeemed singleness. He made it absolutely okay for people to be single—and not just because He was. His life may give us a beautiful picture of single living, but the Story itself tells us what we wouldn't have known if we'd just looked at the pictures. Jesus opened up a whole new world to His followers by joining us together in inseparable relationships and forming a new Family where each member matters equally. He gave significance where there hadn't been any, dignity where it was missing, and belonging for those cast aside. He made the standard for acceptability contingent on *Him*, not us. In Him we are given the most precious of relational names—individually we are the sons of God and corporately we are the bride of Christ. Knowing the Story that lies behind the picture means our lives should never be the same.

chapter seven

Making Sense of Church

"I can check it out on the Internet, and I don't miss a thing," says sixteen-year-old Mike, who can't make it to his church every week because he doesn't always have a ride. He logs on to the church's Web site, catches the sermon, and considers himself present. "It's really cool to be able to go online to hear my pastor speak right to me," he says of being able to pose a "live question" to the pastor while he's preaching—and then wait to see if he answers. "When you're at church, it's cool too, because the pastor might talk about a lot of things that will relate to you. But when you're on the Internet by yourself, it's directed at you almost."

This exuberant teen is not alone in his so-called church experience. The Barna Research Group estimates that 12 percent of teenagers use the Internet for religious or spiritual experiences, turning "to the web for personal support and encouragement they don't find in a bricks-and-mortar church."[1]

Mouse-and-modem or bricks-and-mortar? What *is* the Church? How *does* it really work? In a previous chapter, we introduced the Church by zooming out and seeing its role in the grand Story of redemption. In this chapter, we will zoom in, taking a closer look at what it means to be the Church and how its individual members fit into God's purposes.

The identity and purpose of the Church is so rich and colorful that the New Testament uses over one hundred different metaphors to describe it. Some we have alluded to in other chapters—the Family of God, the body of Christ, the bride of Christ—so we won't repeat them here. Instead we'll focus on another prominent theme that runs the breadth of Scripture, appearing over and over again from Genesis to Revelation: the Church is the dwelling place of God, a living temple.

Delight Multiplied

Every spring, my mom "creates" her flower gardens. While the winter snow is still melting and icy Wisconsin air is still whipping through naked trees (brr!), she's busy at the kitchen table sketching out designs, mapping flowerbeds, and figuring out what to change from the previous year. As soon as is humanly possible, she's out in the yard planting, pruning, and transplanting. For the next several months, she spends day after day outside, delighting in what her green thumb and the ground have brought forth.

> *He didn't need us or anything in all creation to complete His delight, but because pure delight bubbles over, we shouldn't be surprised that God created beings who could also enjoy Him.*

A few years ago, she put my dad to work turning over sod to make a new flowerbed—her "friendship garden." In this section of the yard, she now annually cares for a broad sampling of her favorite flowers—and then she invites friends over one by one. They tour the yard, "oooh" and "ahhh" in every quadrant, and then go home with a boxful of snippets, clumps, and sprigs of various living things to plant and pray over in their own yards.

If my mom never gave away a single flower, she would still delight in gardening. But pure delight bubbles over, waiting to be shared, and when my mom gives others the opportunity to enjoy flowers and gardening, she somehow increases her own delight. She doesn't need to share her plants to enjoy them—but neighborhoods all over southeastern Wisconsin are richer because she does. When she shares her flowers, she shares pieces of herself—her creativity, her tenderness, her expertise. By creating, cultivating, and passing on her flowers, she opens new worlds of enjoyment to others.

It's hard to draw comparisons with God because He is absolutely "otherly," but consider this idea. My mom shares what she's created with others so they also can enjoy it, but God shares *Himself* with His creation so we can enjoy Him. God has delighted in Himself from eternity past. Medieval theologian Anselm of Canterbury called Him "that than which no greater can be thought." God is the greatest possible good. He is the very essence of delight. He didn't need us or anything in all creation to complete His delight, but because pure delight bubbles over, we shouldn't be surprised that God created beings who could also enjoy Him. And almost inexplicably, His already complete delight only multiplies. He takes great pleasure in us as we enjoy Him.

Creation was God's first act of sharing Himself with us. When I gaze into a night sky thick with stars, I understand a little bit of God's vastness. Standing in the spray of thundering Niagara Falls, I feel mere droplets of God's power. As I cradle a newborn and caress the perfect, tiny fingers, I marvel at the tenderness of God. Immersing my face in a bouquet of flowers (which I don't get often), I breathe in a little of God's beauty. In thousands of ways, God has shared Himself in creation.

And yet, amazingly, all of creation is just a glimpse of what God is like. It is not God Himself, just a limited reflection of Him. So, while we find great delight and enjoyment in creation, it's just a teaser for the real thing. Since the beginning of the world, God Himself has desired to *dwell among us*—ponder that idea for a minute—sharing the bubbling over delight of His very person with us.

Adam and Eve tasted this unfathomable, delicious reality until they traded it for a piece of fruit and a promise of freedom. Ever since God banished them from the Garden, He has been seeking a place to live among His image bearers. However, image bearers were no longer interested in God dwelling among them—when Adam and Eve forfeited the delight of His presence, they also lost perspective on what that presence means. Because of them, we now *think* we are happier without God. The effort, therefore, to make a way for men and women to be back in His presence had to be all God's.

A Holy Quest

God states His clear desire in Exodus 25:8, just after delivering the Israelites from bondage in Egypt: "And let them make Me a sanctuary, that I may dwell among them." Here was God's purpose, the entire reason He had saved the people from bondage. He wanted to bring them back into His presence. Throughout the Pentateuch, we see the details of how this plan could be carried out. Half of the book of Exodus gives the nitty-gritty building plans for the tabernacle, God's tent dwelling, and its furnishings. Then the book culminates with the glory cloud of the Lord—the Shekinah—filling the tent. In Leviticus we see the way things had to work for sinful people to enjoy the presence of a holy God. It describes a sad contrast from the way God met with Adam and Eve—He walked with them in the serenity of the Garden, but in the tabernacle God met with His people in an environment of violent death and spattered animal blood. In Numbers we witness Israel's stumbling first steps as the newborn children of God, and by the time we reach Deuteronomy, the nation needed a refresher course in how to enjoy God's presence.

The tabernacle continued to serve as God's mobile home while the Israelites settled a bit too comfortably in their new homeland. Admiring the gods of nations they hadn't quite conquered, the Israelites cycled a dozen or more times through sin, judgment, and deliverance. (For this head-spinning read, check out the book of Judges.) About this time, the people grumbled about being different from their pagan neighbors; they wanted a king. God obliged them, and after a dismal tenure under King Saul, one of the brighter chapters in Jewish history played out as David, a man after God's own heart, took the throne. While he basked in the comforts of his palace home, he wondered why God was still dwelling in a tattered, road-weary tent. King David drew up the blueprints and gathered the materials for a magnificent temple that his son Solomon would build. Spectacular by any standard, the temple was made even more resplendent by the reappearing presence of the Shekinah. It looked like God had finally arrived among

His people. Surely He would gain the kind of devotion that could only lead to utter delight.

It *should* have led to utter delight, but sin's grip on the human heart is strong, and the people soon forgot God. The nation split and hurled headlong into apostasy, despite the flaming condemnations of their eccentric prophets. Finally brought to their knees, the people of God were dragged to captivity in far away Babylon while the temple, their national pride and joy, was stripped of its beauty and left to crumble. Generations later, the humbled captives returned home, cleaned up the rubble of the once glorious temple, and set about the business of rebuilding. With a new sense of devotion—captivity had been good for them—the Jews resumed their temple sacrifices and religious rituals, with one notable difference: the Shekinah, the glory-cloud of God's presence, never graced their temple again—neither the one repaired by the returning exiles nor the breathlessly beautiful structure built by Herod the Great in the earliest days of the New Testament.

> *God Himself got up every morning and dealt with the effects of bed-head and morning mouth. He was, in short, an approachable, likeable, ordinary sort of guy.*

The Shekinah glory of the Lord *did* eventually appear again, just not in or over the temple. It shone in an unlikely place (there were no blood-stained altars) to some unlikely people (these were not priests). The Shekinah, accompanied by the exuberant song of a host of angels, exploded in the starry sky above the heads of third-shift shepherds on the outskirts of Bethlehem. Centuries of absence and anticipation burst out in the spine-tingling pronouncement, "Glory to God in the highest! And on earth peace, goodwill toward men!" God's presence was among His people again, but in a most unexpected way. The leader of the angelic array directed the shepherds to the express image of God's person, the fullness of the Godhead in bodily form . . . lying in a manger (Col. 2:9; Heb. 1:3). Who would have thought God would stoop so low just to be with us?

God, in the Person of Jesus Christ, found His dwelling place among humans as a human. God Himself got up every morning and dealt with the effects of bed-head and morning mouth. He was, in short, an approachable, likeable, ordinary sort of guy that seemingly bore no resemblance to the fearsome, distant, "otherly" God the Jews had come to know during their two thousand year existence. And yet, for those who saw the Shekinah on that first Christmas night, and for those who witnessed it thirty-some years later at the Transfiguration, there was no doubt—God was dwelling among men. As gospel writer John says, in Jesus, God became flesh and tabernacled "among us, and we [John and other eyewitnesses] beheld His glory, the glory as of the only begotten of the Father, full of grace and truth" (John 1:14).

> *The entrance and sojourn of Jesus on the earth was the key that opened the door to God's expansion plan—a dwelling place that ultimately fills the earth.*

Yet for most of Jesus' lifetime, His glory was veiled. Even when people did get a tiny glimpse of it, He urged them to keep the truth to themselves. Jesus was God undercover, working to carry out a bigger plan than just letting everyone see God's glory in the first-century person of Jesus Christ. God's desire since the beginning of time has been to dwell among *all* people *everywhere* for *all* time, not just a few thousand Jews in a dusty corner of the Roman Empire. The entrance and sojourn of Jesus on the earth was the key that opened the door to God's expansion plan—a dwelling place that ultimately fills the earth.

The Expansion Plan

On the night of His betrayal, Jesus assured His followers that He needed to leave and that it was, in fact, *better* for them if He did. I imagine the disciples were a bit skeptical about this—how is anything better when someone you love tragically dies? Yet Jesus knew that only in His physical absence would the Holy Spirit, the Spirit *of Christ,* come to dwell in each of them. God would no longer be among His people—He would be in them. As Jesus breathed His last on the cross, God tore in two the temple curtain that had always blocked access to the Most Holy Place, the place of His presence. On the day of Pentecost fifty-odd days later, the Spirit came down and created a new temple—the living, moving, breathing temple of God that would spread into every culture and include every generation to come.

The followers of the resurrected Christ finally understood that He had come to replace the Jerusalem temple with those who worship Him "in spirit and truth" (John 4:21–24). Paul marveled at the truth that the church replaces the presence of Christ, the fullness of God, in the world: "And [God] put all things under [Christ's] feet, and gave Him to be head over all things to the church, which is His body, *the fullness of Him* who fills all in all" (Eph. 1:22–23). Unbelievable as it sounds, considering the magnificence of the Shekinah, we are able as the temple of God to be "filled with all the fullness of God" (Eph. 3:19). Because of what Jesus did, we can enjoy a new kind of relationship with God—as individuals, local churches, and the universal Church, we are the temple of God (1 Cor. 3:16; 6:19).

The Stone and Its Stones

Peter, one of the followers who witnessed the unveiled glory of Jesus at the Transfiguration, adds some ideas to the image of the living temple. In the following passage, he identifies Jesus as both the Living Stone and the Chief Cornerstone. These two metaphors help us understand His and, therefore, our roles in this new temple.

Coming to Him as to a living stone, rejected indeed by men, but chosen by God and precious, you also, as living stones, are being built up a spiritual house, a holy priesthood, to offer up spiritual sacrifices acceptable to God through Jesus Christ. Therefore it is also contained in the Scripture,

"Behold, I lay in Zion
A chief cornerstone, elect, precious,
And he who believes on Him will by no
means be put to shame."

Therefore, to you who believe, He is precious; but to those who are disobedient,

"The stone which the builders rejected
has become the chief cornerstone,"

and

"A stone of stumbling
and a rock of offense."

They stumble, being disobedient to the word, to which they also were appointed.

But you are a chosen generation, a royal priesthood, a holy nation, His own special people, that you may proclaim the praises of Him who called you out of darkness into His marvelous light; who once were not a people but are now the people of God, who had not obtained mercy but now have obtained mercy. (1 Peter 2:4–10)

The idea of a living stone is a bit peculiar—I doubt you've ever seen one (and if you have, you probably ought to get your eyes—and the gray matter behind them—checked). A stone is so *not* alive that we use it to describe death—a corpse is "stone cold." Ironically perhaps, Christ the Living Stone *was* stone cold and yet now is astonishingly full of life—resurrected life. This is life He has in Himself; He is not dependent on any other source for life.

As *the* Living Stone, then, Christ gives life to those of us who trust in Him, and we, in turn, become living stones as well. Left to ourselves, we are "stone cold" spiritually, but from Him we derive new life. This derived life is not like the sprigs of greenery my mom gives to her friends. Once part of a larger plant, the shoots can be separated and, if properly nurtured, grow into their own plants. Our "living stone life" is not *from* Christ; it is *in* Christ. Like fish in water, we are dependent on the surrounding and filling presence of Christ in order to live this new life.

> There is no such thing as a pile of loose stones around this new temple. Only as each stone is rightly aligned with the Cornerstone and closely connected to the surrounding stones, is it truly part of the building at all.

Jesus is also the Chief Cornerstone of this new temple. The cornerstone of a building is the first stone laid, placed at a corner to establish the level and angle of every other stone that is joined to the building. Without the absolute standard of the cornerstone to determine each stone's placement, the walls will wander like a sleepy driver on the road. The building will never take shape—or at least, it'll never take a shape that any building inspector would approve. Jesus is the foundational stone of the new dwelling place of God. His finished work and His spoken words established the level and angle for every stone that is joined to the building—we don't get to decide how things work in this building. It's already been decided.

The stones of this living temple are placed according to intended tasks and according to lines established by the Cornerstone. Stones have different colors, shapes, sizes, and strengths, and each fits in a unique place in the building, and only together do the stones comprise the temple. Coming to Christ means taking on a corporate identity—much like getting married means acquiring a host of relatives you never had before. You can't escape the collective nature of the living temple of God. There is no such thing as a pile of loose stones around this new temple. Only as each stone is rightly aligned with the Cornerstone *and* closely connected to the surrounding stones, is it truly part of the building at all.

From these two metaphors of Jesus as the Living Stone and the Cornerstone, we discover our roles in the Church, God's new dwelling place. As living stones, we are immersed in the life of Christ, aligned to the purposes of Christ, and joined to the body of Christ. Apart from the Living Stone, we have no life, and apart from the Cornerstone, we have no purpose.

Keeping House

Because this new temple is comprised of living stones it must be a living temple. It is not a cold granite edifice, but is, instead, an "amorphous 'building' that continually takes on the changing dimensions of God's assembled people."[2] We are continually being shaped and built into a spiritual house, a temple in which God can dwell more and more fully. The beauty of this temple is not seen in the gold, marble, and ornate decorations that characterized previous temples, but instead it is evident in the lives of its living stones—individually and collectively.

But just as the tabernacle and subsequent temples did not exist merely for looks, neither does the living temple. It exists for much the same reason as God's previous dwelling places did—to provide the means for the people of God to present sacrifices to Him. We no longer need priests to offer our sacrifices for us—*we* are the priests with rights and privileges to approach God because Jesus, the great High Priest, sacrificed Himself as the ultimate sin atonement. We also offer different kinds of sacrifices. Obviously, we don't slaughter animals or bake cakes to present to God, but instead we offer "living sacrifices"—in our daily living we give, or withhold, continual offerings to God. The New Testament writers describe a litany of such sacrifices: praise and thankfulness (the "fruit of our lips"), good done to others, resources shared with those in need, those we've won to Christ, imitation of Christ through loving sacrifice, and prayers (Rom. 12:1–2; 15:16; Eph. 5:2; Heb. 3:15–16; Rev. 8:3). Even a quick reading of the list informs me that it would be much easier to offer God an animal (although I'd rather someone else kill it for me) or a freshly baked cake. With good reason, then, Peter calls these *spiritual* sacrifices—only through the power of the Holy Spirit can we hope to offer such sweet, aromatic gifts of gratitude to God.

Being living stones is not only an immense privilege, but it is also an awesome responsibility. We comprise the new temple, the priesthood, and the sacrifices!

Corruption in Today's Temple

We have not always done a good job of maintaining this living temple, but its corruption is often subtle, as I was reminded on a recent trip to the office supply store. While there I observed that if, perchance, I wanted to buy a phone, I had no fewer than sixty-four choices. I could choose a display in English, Spanish, or French. I could have my phone hang on the wall, rest on the table, or convert for either. My new phone could remember sixty-eight different numbers (do I call that many people?), accommodate four-party conferencing, time my calls, speed dial twenty different numbers, and tell me the time and date. Did I want a single line, double lines, or multiple lines? Cordless? Caller ID? Built-in answering machine? Call waiting? Ivory, black, white, cream, or chartreuse? The only thing that didn't appear to be available was a rotary phone—you know, the kind you actually have to *dial?*

> *Every outing to the store, commercial on television, and ad in the paper screams our cultural slogan—"It's all about me!"*

Thankfully, I didn't need a phone. I have one that works just fine, and, in fact, already has two buttons that I neither use nor know how to use. When you think about it, the purpose of a phone is relatively simple. I need a way to talk to you when we are not in shouting distance. As I surveyed my options that day, however, I was reminded that it really wasn't about phones at all . . . it was really all about me. Why should I settle for a plain old phone? I can have whatever shape, style, color, and kind I want . . . except, apparently, the rotary phone. But I bet the office store down the street could get even that for me.

Every outing to the store, commercial on television, and ad in the paper screams our cultural slogan—"It's all about me!" Consider the

American way of life imbedded in popular advertising slogans: Have it your way. You deserve a break today. Just do it. Be all that you can be. Whether the advertisers are selling hamburgers, cross trainers, or army stints, they are really capitalizing on our beliefs. Says Bob Garfield of *Advertising Age,* "The greatest advertising isn't great for moving merchandise any more than the greatest literature is great for compelling plots. Somehow . . . these [ads] have discovered our humanity. They have touched us, understood us, reflected our lives . . ."[3]

We really do believe we deserve to have it our way, and not just when it comes to flame-broiled burgers. We really do believe it's our calling, and even responsibility, to be all that we can be, in whatever career or pursuit we choose. Can you hear the echoes of Eden in our drive for self-gratification and self-actualization? Satan baited Eve with the very same things—you deserve to eat the fruit because God is keeping something from you; you can't be all you were meant to be without it. She (and he) bit, and we've believed it ever since. "Self" is probably the single most powerful force that drives our culture. And sadly, often the church.

For scores of nominal attendees and even committed members, church and Christianity are means to make life better. We have often "marketed" God and the church as the answer to every problem and the way to true fulfillment. Jesus wants to be your Friend. God wants to see you reach your full potential as a person, and He is just waiting to bless you in every area of your life. The church is the place where you can have your needs met.

Am I saying Jesus isn't the answer to all your problems? No. Am I suggesting He doesn't want to be your Friend? No. Am I implying that God doesn't want to bless you or see your gifts and abilities maximized? No.

> *When, as a member of the Lord's army, I am consumed by the need to "be all I can be" (for Christ, of course), I slowly pull away from the inherently corporate nature of the living temple of God.*

What I am saying is that we've often presented truth out of context. It's a bit like an experience I had with a fifth grader during my first year of teaching. I caught Josh lying and in an attempt to discipline him in a productive way, I assigned him to use a Bible concordance to find verses related to his sin, write them out, and then choose one to memorize. It all sounded very beneficial until I checked in on Josh's progress to see what verse he had chosen. He was working on a text from Leviticus: You shall not lie with your neighbor's wife.

True? Definitely. In context? Definitely not. Josh had an incomplete picture of what the Leviticus verse meant (thankfully) and he didn't take the time to check the rest of the passage (I didn't even suggest it).

Much of our modern perspective of who Jesus is and what the Church is about is incomplete and out of context. Notice the emphasis when I say "I'm not getting anything out of this," or "My gifts aren't really being used here." When I pursue the dangerously strong duty I feel to discover and develop who I am, I risk making the Church just another means to my personal fulfillment and self-actualization. When, as a member of the Lord's army, I am consumed by the need to "be all I can be" (for Christ, of course), I slowly pull away from the inherently corporate nature of the living temple of God and instead allow *my* relationship with God to be the primary concern of my life. My Christianity is, in truth, "all about me."

> We don't understand what true fellowship is and how genuine unity works because there are very few places, if any, that we experience it.

The difficulty is that *both* things are true. I matter *and* the church matters. The greater difficulty is holding both of these truths in appropriate balance—and even tension. On one hand, the individual does matter, but on the other hand, the goal of Christianity isn't self-fulfillment.

Both the individual and the church are important in the plan of God. As ruggedly individualistic American Christians, we have done a superb job of teaching personal regeneration, but we haven't done as well at teaching how such regenerated individuals fit into the community that is the living temple. Instead our church "communities" are much like modern neighborhoods—filled with people living separate and private lives in increasingly bigger houses, running to-and-fro caring for family interests, and barely knowing the names of those who live mere steps away. We are content with superficial "over the fence" relationships, and don't really need each other. When we bring this kind of mindset to church, it becomes another item on the list of responsibilities that we fulfill—we show up for services, do our ministries, and hurry home to be about the business of whatever it is we really do. We don't understand what true fellowship is and how genuine unity works because there are very few places, if any, that we experience it.

And yet we instinctively crave it. "Community" has become a national buzzword—both inside the church and out of it. While I haven't tried, I'm almost certain I could find a club, league, or organization for former fifth grade teachers, Packer fans living in western Michigan, and left-handed dog lovers—if not in "real life," then certainly on the Internet. As much as we love our independence, we don't want to do things alone—and as much as we hate to admit it, we can't make it on our own.

That's because we were never meant to. Augustine, the premier theologian of the early church, perceptively observed that "there is nothing so social by nature, so antisocial by sin, as man."[4] Originally created from one man to be one large community, humanity severed their connection with God and therefore with each other by sin. Sin breeds individuality and independence that can only be cured through the recreation of humanity through redemption—and the construction of the living temple. "The very purpose of [Christ's] self-giving on the cross was not just to save isolated individuals, and so perpetuate their loneliness, but to create a new community whose members would belong to Him, love one another, and eagerly serve the world."[5]

While it is true that only in Christ can we find meaning in our personal lives, such meaning can only be fully understood as we also discover the joy of belonging to each other in a dynamic, transforming way. We are living stones because of the Living Stone, and we are joined to the rest of the building. The Christian life is about interdependence, not independence. We must be in this together—growing, sharpening, helping, challenging—or we're not really in it at all.

Biblical community doesn't come without a cost. It's hard work being part of the living temple. It's frustrating to watch people hear the truth, nod their heads, and change nothing. It's discouraging to recognize the magnitude of the need and the weakness of the workforce. It's time-consuming to get close enough to ask each other hard questions. It's heart-wrenching to pour your life into another person and then watch him walk away. My teacher friends and I used to say jokingly (sometimes) that teaching would be a great job if it weren't for the kids. Church can be the same—it would be a great place if it weren't for the people. Church is chock-full of sinful people with selfish goals and rough edges. I'm one of them.

Being part of the living temple may bring great responsibility, accountability, and sometimes pain. But the temple is who we are and how we grow. Church is neither mouse and modem *nor* bricks and mortar. Church is us, together, growing "up in all things into Him who is the head—Christ—from whom the *whole* body, joined and knit together by what *every* joint supplies, according to the effective working by which *every* part does its share, causes growth of the body for the edifying of itself in love" (Eph. 4:15–16).

When we settle for a Christianity of "personal fulfillment," we not only sell ourselves short, but perhaps we've missed Christianity altogether.

chapter eight

Making Sense of Singleness

Not so terribly long ago in this country, the dictionary would have declared me a spinster—a single woman over the age of thirty. (If your dictionary still says this, please get rid of it.) I'd have been an oddity in society and the church. However, society has changed and now I'm a member of one of the fastest growing demographic groups in America (unfortunately, this growth rate is not mirrored in the church). Nearly half of all adult females in this country are single.

No one dares to call them spinsters anymore . . . single women own their own homes, buy their own cars, and take their own vacations. Some raise their own children, start their own companies, and run for public office. Perhaps most surprisingly, a whopping 66 percent of them admit they aren't desperate to get married.[1] They've rejected the philosophy of Yenta, the hobbling matchmaker in *Fiddler on the Roof*, who declares that "even the worst husband, God forbid, is better than no husband, God forbid!" They'd rather be single than stifled in a relationship that denies the opportunity to develop abilities and attain goals. A thirty-nine-year-old single woman summarizes the conclusion reached by this new breed of unmarried women: "You don't just want a man in your life. You only want a great man in your life."[2]

> *After so many years of societal shame and sympathetic whispers, redemption has finally arrived!*

It doesn't appear that this trend will reverse itself anytime soon since these numbers are fed by a generation of unmarried women in their twenties who are educated, independent, and making money to burn. Labeled the "Me Years" by *Mademoiselle* magazine, the twenties have become a decade of "discovery and self-indulgence, of fledgling autonomy and social sampling" for its single female members who unashamedly "indulge their every whim [and] answer to no one but themselves."[3] The twenty-somethings who live with such flagrance may find the burden of raising a family less and less appealing. And those who eventually do marry may find the personal sacrifices that marriage demands more than they want to handle—the odds are high that they'll end up single again.

It is obvious that in recent years singleness has undergone a sort of cultural redemption. Singles are no longer the outcasts. Unmarried women, especially, now stand at the center of our social and cultural life, essentially free to pursue whatever kind of happiness they want. Chic, savvy, and competent, they comprise a growing market of consumers who have money to spend . . . on themselves. And after the sexual revolution, they are free to do what they want with their bodies. Who needs the restraints of marriage when sex can be free? After so many years of societal shame and sympathetic whispers, redemption has finally arrived!

It may be a sort of redemption, but it's redemption without God. This new face of singleness is one of self-fulfillment, personal satisfaction, and independence—not exactly what God has in mind for those who don't marry. Rather than racing to catch up with culture or holding tenaciously to tradition, those of us in the church need to make sense of singleness according to God's purposes. We must rediscover—and celebrate—God's redemption and its incredible impact on the single life. How does singleness make sense in the plan of God, and specifically in His plan for the church?

What Kind of Gift Is This?

One of the many absolutely adorable things about dogs is the way they welcome you home. No one is as glad to see you walk through the front door as Buddy, Max, or in my family's case, Lady Roxanne the Fourth, our chestnut boxer who was as distinguished as her name sounds. We just called her Rox, a name not quite as prestigious but slightly more endearing and definitely easier to say. When she heard the car doors slam, her entire stocky self shook with pure delight, from the stubby sausage tail that wagged her whole back end to the splitting of gums that revealed the dog smile she reserved for the most exciting of occasions. (I'm not kidding—she really smiled.) Absolutely no one says, "Hey! It's about time you got here!" like a dog.

On those rare occasions when Rox didn't meet us at the door, we immediately knew something was wrong—and our noses usually confirmed it. With a little exploration, the verdict almost always returned the same, with slight variation in location: "She left a gift in the corner of the living room." These are not the kind of gifts dog owners like to receive.

> *The majority of unmarried Christians don't feel any kind of unique ability or desire to deny sexual urges and be forever content as singles.*

Christian singles hear a lot of talk about the "gift" of singleness. I need to pause here and clarify what I mean by singleness. Perhaps it is obvious, but given the nature of culture, the cultural influence in the church, and our own sinful selves, I don't want to assume that everyone understands singleness in the way I'm using it. Singleness implies celibacy—the choice to refrain from sex. Sex is explicitly reserved for marriage, with no exceptions. Singles, by biblical definition, are to be celibate for as long as they are single.

It's beginning to change, but for a long time, the predominant teaching in the church community has been that singleness is a *spiritual* gift, a supernatural ability given to believers by the Spirit of God at salvation. The lucky chosen few are given some kind of special capacity to live their entire lives in blissful contentment as unmarried people, happily and easily existing without sex and intimate companionship. While I suppose these things are true for some singles, the majority of unmarried Christians don't feel any kind of unique ability or desire to deny sexual urges and be forever content as singles. And a lot of those who supposedly have this gift think of it with the same excitement they'd have for a pile of dog poop in the corner of the living room—a gift they need to discard as soon as possible before it stinks up their lives.

Is singleness really a gift? The short answer, according to Paul in 1 Corinthians 7:7, is yes, sometimes: "For I wish that all men were even as myself. But each one has his own *gift* from God, one in this manner and another in that." The better questions to ask, it seems, are what kind of gift is it and who has it? Is it a spiritual gift, and if so, why don't we feel unwedded bliss? Is it a stinky gift, and if so, how did we get stuck with it? If I'm single, does that mean I have "the gift"? If singleness is not, as the world says, the gift of self-indulgent freedom, what could possibly be good about it?

Albert Hsu, in his must-read book *Singles at the Crossroads,* argues convincingly that while singleness is certainly a gift, it is not a *spiritual* gift, and claiming that it is raises significant problems.[4] For example, if single people want to be married and don't *feel* particularly content with their singleness, can we assume they don't have the gift of singleness? If they don't have the gift, are they allowed to be discontent? Is it permissible for them to have sex since God hasn't especially equipped them to deny their urges? Obviously, the answer to all these questions is no—contentment and purity are required of all believers.*

> Singleness may be a gift, but it is not one that is contingent on a special work of the Spirit.

Our error and misunderstanding about singleness as a spiritual gift, Hsu says, has resulted from an inappropriate combination of Paul's teaching about marriage and singleness in 1 Corinthians 7 with that

---

* Contentment does not mean ignoring the painful feelings that accompany life's disappointments—which we all have, regardless of marital status. Contentment is agonizingly learned by acknowledging that God is both sovereign and sufficient. Unfortunately, the issue of contentment is bigger than can be addressed in this context. For additional thoughts in this area, I refer you to my book, *Living Whole Without a Better Half* (Grand Rapids: Kregel, 2000), and some other excellent titles mentioned in the additional resources at the end of this book.

of spiritual gifts in 1 Corinthians 12. The Corinthians were confused by cultural clutter related to lots of things, and in 1 Corinthians 7, Paul especially addresses their misaligned views of marriage, sexuality, and something he understood from personal experience—singleness. In chapter twelve, Paul shifts topics and begins by saying, "Now about spiritual gifts." Paul has shifted from whatever issue he was addressing and moved on to a new topic—spiritual gifts. He uses the word "gift" in both texts, but only in chapter twelve does he talk about spiritual gifts.

The word "spiritual" has nearly endless meanings and connotations in modern vocabulary—ranging from having personal devotions to conversing with dead relatives. Our understanding, however, is a corruption of what Scripture means when it uses "spiritual." When the Bible refers to that which is "spiritual," it means those things that are specifically of the Holy Spirit. We are "spiritual" because we've received new life through the Spirit, not because we act religiously. "Spiritual" blessings are those things directly related to the work of the Holy Spirit, not just good things that happen. In the case of gifts, some are called "spiritual" because the Holy Spirit is active in accomplishing particular tasks through the lives of Christians. This is the focus of 1 Corinthians 12—gifts bestowed on the believer by the Spirit for the benefit of the body of Christ.

This "Spirit language" is absent in Paul's discussion of singleness in chapter seven. Singleness may be a gift, but it is not one that is contingent on a special work of the Spirit.[5] For the most part we are not *supernaturally* equipped to be single or to be married. We can choose to be married if the opportunity presents itself or we can choose to stay single. Often circumstances more than choice dictate singleness— we never meet someone to marry, a husband walks out, a wife dies— but regardless, the point is that we have *no* control over genuine *spiritual* gifts.

So, if singleness is not a spiritual gift, what kind of gift is it? Frankly, Paul himself is a little vague on the answer to this question—probably because he wasn't trying to answer it. He was writing to a community with the exact opposite viewpoint that our Christian culture has: they elevated singleness (more precisely, celibacy—even within marriage) above marriage, while we elevate marriage above singleness.

In 1 Corinthians 7, he addresses several groups of people: married people who were depriving each other of sex, widows and widowers, those contemplating separation or divorce, those married to unbelieving spouses, and engaged couples. He voices his preference for singleness on two separate occasions—first, when talking to widows and widowers, and second when talking to engaged couples.*

His reference to the "gift" occurs in his remarks to widows and widowers, which casts a vastly different light on the way we understand his comments. Apparently Paul himself was a widower, but was at a place in his life where he could live contentedly without a spouse and sex. This is not the case for many who have lost a spouse—after having experienced the physical and emotional intimacy of marriage, they are painfully aware of what they have lost and find it overwhelmingly difficult to live by themselves. Paul tells them to go ahead and remarry rather than be involved in immorality—a situation the Greek verb implies was already happening in Corinth—because they are burning with passion.

Unfortunately, this passage has often been snatched out of its context and universally applied to never-married singles: we're told if we burn with passion then we don't have the "gift" and we should get married. To a certain extent this may be true, but the never-married single with virginity intact can't compare his or her "burning with passion," intense as it may be, with that of a widow or widower.

So, what was Paul's gift? Maybe it was a lack of sexual desire. Maybe it was greater self-control—although none of us, "gifted" or not, are exempt from the requirements of self-control. Maybe it was a greater focus on his ministry that enabled him to live contentedly without a spouse, although he'd previously had one. Maybe it was a combination of all of these things.

---

* First Corinthians 7 poses many interpretative challenges and few definitive answers. Based on my own work with the text and my reading of others' works, I offer my current understanding—not a solution to the issues. For the exegetical basis of my interpretation of this difficult passage, please see the appendix titled "Paul's View of Singleness in 1 Corinthians 7."

> *The Corinthians were focused on the wrong things. They were most concerned about changing their circumstances, and overlooked the fact that Christ was much more concerned about changing them.*

Whatever it was, Paul doesn't bring it up later when he addresses the engaged couples who were unsure whether they should go through with their marriage or not. The "no sex" standard of spirituality in Corinth had prompted them to reconsider their plans. Paul affirms the goodness of marriage (and therefore sex within marriage; vv. 1–6) and their freedom to choose, but he also says it's good to stay single. His reasons, however, do not include some kind of special gifting. He first encourages them not to marry because of distressful circumstances happening in Corinth—perhaps a famine or some sort of persecution. The burden of caring for a family in such times is heavy. His second reason for encouraging singleness was the soon return of the Lord. The present order of things—including marriage—is on its way out and Christ is coming to usher in a new order.

We have trouble following Paul's thinking here because we can't relate to either of these reasons. Our lives are fairly comfortable—no "great distress" in sight—and if we are honest, we are pretty nonchalant about the second coming of Christ. Instead, we are preoccupied with the "passing order" of things, unable to see their relative insignificance in light of eternity.

The resounding theme of Paul's arguments in 1 Corinthians 7 is that the Corinthians were focused on the wrong things. They were most concerned about changing their circumstances, and overlooked the fact that Christ was much more concerned about changing them.

Like the Corinthians, we have often failed to understand that contentment, spirituality, and abundant life have nothing to do with our circumstances. They can be acquired no matter what life is like. Guy Greenfield sums it up well when he says, "The abiding truth of [1 Cor 7:17–31] is that believers should find satisfaction, fulfillment, and meaning for life from *within* and not in outward circumstances.

Christian faith brings a new reality *within* a person, but not necessarily *around* him or her."[6]

So, again, what kind of gift is singleness? Sometimes, it's what Paul had—whatever it was that enabled him to live as he did. Do most singles have this gift? I doubt it. Does that mean all singles who don't have it should get married? Not if we believe the rest of what Paul said.

I'd like to suggest that singleness is a gift even if we don't have what Paul had, and we'd rather be married. It may not be a gift like we're accustomed to defining gifts—but, like everything else we receive from the gracious hand of a loving heavenly Father, it *is* a gift. If you are single, your life circumstances are a gift, and despite what you want to think about it, it's not a stinky gift.

> None of God's gifts are ours to do with as we please. They are His resources entrusted to us for something far beyond ourselves.

Maybe it helps if we think about this type of gift in terms of tools, things in our lives that we can put to use for God's glory. They are God-ordained conditions of our existence. I happen to be a Caucasian female. I am five feet six inches tall. I am single. These are not disasters or punishments. They describe the God-ordained "gifts" of my existence. My brother happens to be a Caucasian male. He's six feet six inches tall. He's married. None of these facts are disasters (unless he hits his head on a low door frame) or signs of God's supernatural gifting.

Neither marriage nor singleness, Paul affirms, is bad—God does not give stinky gifts. In fact neither is merely neutral—rather, both are good. And both come with certain privileges and responsibilities. Just as my brother has the responsibility (or is it a privilege?) to reach something on a back shelf that I can't, and just as I once had the privilege of helping him match his clothes, so marriage and singleness each offer unique opportunities to serve God and others. Paul's concern is not whether someone should or shouldn't marry—he leaves that open to individual choice. Singleness is a gift that can be exchanged, guilt-free, for the gift of marriage. Paul's primary purpose is to say, "Look, what-ever you are—married or single—you need to serve God in your situation. Get busy." Instead of singles worrying so much about how to get rid of what we—and lots of well-meaning people in the Christian community—wrongly assume is a stinky gift, we would find life more fulfilling if we worked harder at living obedient, focused lives as singles.

Opening the Gift

None of God's gifts are ours to do with as we please. They are *His* resources entrusted to us for something far beyond ourselves. With His gifts, we are called to carry out His purposes in the world, that is, the expansion of His kingdom. Against every instinct of the human heart, we are not our own, but rather everything about us belongs to Him. We are merely the managers of His resources. This is the essence of stewardship.

> *Lots of singles have been conditioned to believe that their most valuable gift to the church is being the on-call workforce for the nursery.*

Singleness, then, is not a resource to be used for self-advancement and fulfillment (the same is true for marriage). It is not an enviable ticket to absolute independence and carefree living. Instead it is a means by which the kingdom of God can benefit. If we see it any other way, we've missed its primary purpose. Since today's primary manifestation of the kingdom of God is the Church, we must ask how singleness benefits the Church. What unique gifts does the Church possess because of its single members?

Lots of singles have been conditioned to believe that their most valuable gift to the church is being the on-call workforce for the nursery. Most of the singles I know don't mind taking their turn caring for children in the church, but does this really represent the fullness of what single members offer to the body of Christ?

I'd like to suggest that singleness offers the church much more than just a steady supply of childcare workers. We are full-fledged members of the body, and as such, all that we are is very much needed in the church. Consider the familiar words of Paul:

> For in fact the body is not one member but many.
> If the foot should say, "Because I am not a hand, I am not of the body," is it therefore not of the body? And if the ear should say, "Because I am not an eye, I am not of the body," is it therefore not of the body? If the whole body were an eye, where would be the hearing? If the whole were hearing, where would be the smelling? But now God has set the members, each one of them, in the body *just as He pleased.* And if they were all one member, where would be the body be?
> But now indeed there are many members, yet one body. And the eye cannot say to the hand, "I have no need of you"; nor again the head to the feet, "I have no need of you." (1 Corinthians 12:14–21)

By our lives and status, singles provide valuable truth that the church might not be able to receive any other way. In the fourth section of this book, "Saying I Love You," we will look more closely at how singles can meet some concrete needs of the church, as well as how the church can meet some specific needs of singles. In the remainder of this chapter, however, we will consider the meaning of singleness in the body of Christ, especially related to the love of God and to human relationships.

Singleness and the Love of God

What can a life devoid of lasting romance contribute to an understanding of holy love?

One of the pervasive themes of Scripture is God's love for His chosen people, the Israelites. He selected them from among all the nations of the world to be His own, established a covenant with them, and vowed His faithfulness to them. Throughout the writings of the

Old Testament prophets, this relationship between God and His people is expressed in the metaphor of marriage. Israel, the bride, spurned God and prostituted herself with other gods, and yet because of His covenant, God's love for her endured. In the New Testament, marriage images the relationship between Christ and the Church.

Marriage provides a beautiful reflection of some of our most treasured spiritual truths. It pictures genuine commitment and unconditional love in a world of no-fault divorce, and it provides the framework for our concepts of spiritual birth and the Family of God.

What could singleness possibly add, if anything, to this array of rich images? What can a life devoid of lasting romance contribute to an understanding of holy love? Perhaps it merely serves to amplify the beauty of marital love, much like a dark sky enhances the splendor of a rainbow or a Hollywood villain magnifies the goodness of the hero. Or maybe it's a grand test that, if we pass, we get to move on to the higher ground of wedded life.

> While marriage is designed to illustrate the restrictive nature of God's covenant love for His people, singleness can beautifully display the treasured truth that God's love is open to all.

Or maybe it's none of these. When understood properly, the picture of singleness can help round out our concept of the love of God. While marriage illustrates what we can call the *exclusive* nature of God's love, singleness allows us to better understand the *inclusive* nature of God's love.[7]

Generally speaking, singles have a freedom in relationships that married people don't have. They are free to befriend and love many people without being unfaithful to any of them. I can be friends with men and women alike and not worry about being disloyal to my spouse—although I must always be careful not to give someone else's spouse the opportunity to be disloyal. I am able to invest in a wide variety of relationships without cheating a husband out of the time that is rightfully his. It is this freedom that portrays the inclusive dynamic of God's love—the fact that the gospel message is open to all who will receive it. While marriage is designed to illustrate the restrictive nature of God's covenant love for His people, singleness can beautifully display the treasured truth that God's love is open to all. His relationship quotient is never filled—there's always room for one more.* Because the friendships that singles form are not restricted in the same way that those of married people are, singles "reflect the openness of God's love that seeks to include within the circle of fellowship those yet outside its boundaries"[8]

We must never forget that the message of love in the gospel has two sides. God jealously guards and provides for His own. He chastens us as children. He reserves space for us in His everlasting kingdom. We are precious in His sight. However, if we overemphasize His exclusive love we start to think like elitists in a special Christian club. God is also always seeking the outsiders so that they, too, can be enveloped by the fellowship of the Christian community. If, however, we overemphasize God's inclusive love, we start to think that God is just a nice guy who will accept everyone, whether or not they believe in Him. Both sides of this mysterious love must be kept in balance, even tension. The complementary natures of marriage and singleness can help the church picture this difficult task.

Singleness and Human Relationships

One of the great luxuries of singleness, according to Lucy in the movie *While You Were Sleeping,* is sole possession of the remote control. One lazy afternoon I was enjoying this luxury to its fullest, and predictably, nothing worth watching was on. However, something about being positioned in front of a screen with a bowlful of popcorn makes me feel like I *must* watch something, so I continued to flick through the stations with the half-hearted expectation that something

---

* The pictures of love presented by both marriage and singleness are flawed. Exclusive love in marriage is flawed—but God's love is not. Inclusive love in singles' relationships is flawed—even singles have a limit on how many relationships they can adequately nurture while God does not.

would magically appear (a habit akin to opening the refrigerator door and staring into it every ten minutes. Do I think food grows in there? And if it does, do I want to eat it?) Well, something did magically appear (or the commercials finally ended) and the remote screeched to a halt at a talk show whose topic shocked me into stopping. (I think my hand froze in the popcorn bowl, too.) "I'm a virgin. SURPRISE! Wanna be my first?"

I watched in astonishment as teenaged girls confided to the hostess (and the national viewing audience) that they were virgins, but, whew, had picked the guy friends they wanted to be "their first." These unsuspecting friends were stashed backstage, awaiting their moments in the "hot seat" when each girl would confess her unfortunate predicament and ask her male friend if he'd be willing to fix this regrettable situation.

I listened to this sordid script long enough to see two girls turned down, and even though the reasons were "good" and the girls told their friends it was okay, it was obvious that it really wasn't. In desperation they had humiliated themselves, embarrassed their friends, and experienced rejection in the most intimate of matters. Why? Because according to cultural standards, sexual activity has a lot to do with value and identity. The shock of their friends and the pity of the audience said that it was unthinkable and nearly tragic for these teen girls to be virgins. Sex happens for "normal people." If you're not having sex, you're not quite normal.

Sex is certainly a good thing—Paul affirms this against the backdrop of immoral Corinth when he told the church that marriage is good and sex is part of marriage. Withholding sex from a spouse was not a commendable thing, as many in the Corinthian church had determined (1 Cor. 7:1–9). Sex, as we discussed in an earlier chapter, is God's incredible design for oneness. He didn't have to make us male and female. He could have come up with another way to populate the earth. In fact, by the time He created man, He had already invented some pretty ingenious forms of reproduction; He could've designed us to be fruitful and multiply like budding fungus or like the broken-off body parts of starfish. Really, He could have. Instead, He made us male and female for the very reason that He intended us to need each other. It is biologically obvious that men and women were meant to go together.

> *The gift of godly singleness is a continual reminder to believers, and we are prone to forget, that sexuality is not defined by sexual activity.*

But maleness and femaleness encompass more than the physical relationship between a man and woman. Whether or not one's sexuality is expressed in the physical act of sex, it is expressed in thousands of other ways because sexuality defines who we are. In every cell of my body, every thought in my head, every emotion in my being, and every nuance of my personality, I am female.

Because God made male and female—and designed them to need each other—the sexuality that defines us also reminds us that we are not all we can be by ourselves. "Sexuality," say theologians Stanley Grenz and Roy Bell, "lies behind the human quest for completeness, expressed through the drive toward bonding."[9] Most obviously, this drive of sexuality is what attracts us to members of the opposite sex for intensely physical bonding. But because sexuality is not limited to a physical act, it is also the drive behind our craving for nonsexual relationships. Although I am a complete person, I do not have everything I need for fully balanced living. Sometimes my thinking is way out in leftfield and I need the logical perspective of another person to bring me back to reality. At other times my emotional scales are tipped beyond apparent retrieval, and I need the balancing response of another person to make my world level again.

Sexuality lies behind our desire, our *need*, for friendship and community. Because God made us social, only in each other are we complete people. God is a triune community; we, His image bearers, reflect Him best in community.

This quest for completion cannot be satisfied by a spouse, by friendships, or by any of the traditional solutions of fame, fortune, and fun.

Page through Ecclesiastes—it's all been tried before, and it all comes down to fearing God and keeping His commandments. Rephrased centuries later by Augustine, another man who had tried it all, our hearts are restless until they come to rest in God.[10] Completeness is only found in God through Christ—a relationship that joins us to a community of people looking forward to the ultimate fulfillment of all human restlessness—or sexuality—the consummation of all things, when we will live forever with God.

The gift of godly singleness is a continual reminder to believers, and we are prone to forget, that sexuality is not defined by sexual activity. Sexuality is a God-given aspect of His image that drives us first to Him and then to one another in nonsexual relationships. We need Him to be satisfied and we need each other to be complete. We need the community of Christ's body.

In Pursuit of Happiness

Americans staunchly stand by their rights to "life, liberty, and the pursuit of happiness"—although truthfully, we really care the most about the last one. After more than two and a quarter centuries of pursuing happiness, we should have found it by now. We ought to be the happiest people in the history of the world. Instead, we're perhaps the richest, most educated, most comfortable, unhappiest people on the planet.

That's because the pursuit of happiness can be like chasing a greased pig, which I've never actually done. I have, however, chased a Crisco-covered watermelon "pig" in the murky lake at Camp Fairwood in central Wisconsin. Catching the slippery impersonator was virtually impossible because as soon as a camper threw his arms around the watermelon, it'd pop out on the other side, bobbing in imagined laughter. Impossible as it was, though, the lure of victory kept us splashing around the lake in wild pursuit of an elusive object.

Of all the childish things I left behind when I became an adult, I have to confess that the game of greased pig hasn't always been one of them. I bet you can relate. Watermelons bob all around us, promising the end of the happiness pursuit. Television, picture of realism that it is, tells us that the right toothpaste, the right toilet paper, and the right spaghetti sauce are the end-all to happiness. Of course we're smarter than that and know that if we can just find the right person, the right job, and the right friends, *then* we'll be happy.

But we won't. The problem with the pursuit of happiness is that the goal keeps moving. The new generation of American singles will discover this—if they haven't begun to suspect it already. They've got the pursuit all wrong. They're chasing happiness, fulfillment, and satisfaction in places they will never be found. The pursuit God ordained for singles looks very different, and it has a fixed goal. Paul puts this goal in plain language in 1 Corinthians 7:32–35:

> He who is unmarried cares for the things that belong to the Lord—how he may please the Lord. But he who is married cares about the things of the world—how he may please his wife. There is a difference between a wife and a virgin. The unmarried woman cares about the things of the Lord, that she may be holy both in body and in spirit. But she who is married cares about the things of the world—how she may please her husband. And this I say for your own profit, not that I may put a leash on you, but for what is proper, and that you may serve the Lord without distraction.

> *If singleness becomes a means to acquire what I want out of life, I have missed the point of the gift.*

Paul is not suggesting, as some have, that singleness is a more spiritual state than marriage. He is, instead, highlighting the obvious—without the responsibilities of a spouse and family, singles are more free to give undistracted attention to the "things of the Lord." I don't think Paul is saying that every single should go to the mission field—although perhaps more of us ought to consider it. Neither is he saying that we should all work for churches or Christian organizations. The "things of the Lord" encompass those areas of the Christian life that specifically build us up in the faith—we often call them spiritual disciplines, and they include a variety of things from Bible study to church involvement to community service.

While the stages of life and the situations of singleness vary dramatically, singles need to take honest inventory of their time, energy, and money commitments to assess the wisdom of their investments. It is irrelevant whether we've "chosen" to be single or not—the reality is that we are: now what are we going to do with it?

If singleness becomes a means to acquire what I want out of life, I have missed the point of the gift. Likewise, if marriage becomes a means to acquire what I want out of life, I have missed the point. The purposes of both are *essentially* the same—we are being formed in the image of Christ. The difference is the means by which it happens.

The pursuit of happiness is a waste of time, not to mention unbiblical. Instead, says Paul in 1 Timothy 6:11, "Pursue righteousness, godliness, faith, love, patience, gentleness." Obedience to God ought to be the pursuit that defines my life. Conforming my actions and attitudes to that which makes Him happy is the only investment worth my energies.

The irony is what ultimately happens when I shift the pursuit from *my* happiness to *His* happiness. Paul continues in 1 Timothy, "Command those who are rich in this present world . . . to put their hope in God, *who richly provides us with everything for our enjoyment*" (v. 17 NIV). Hmmm, it sounds like happiness is possible after all. While it should never be the goal, genuine enjoyment of life—without bondage to that which can never satisfy—will be the result of a life lived in obedience to God.

SAYING "I LOVE YOU"

It had been more than a year since Alex and I had forced our way aboard the overcrowded Marta bus at Stone Mountain, and during that year, we had taken the ride of our lives— through the ups and downs of a growing relationship. There had been moments of exhilaration and excitement, and there had been moments of pain and stretching. We had clung to commitment during the tough times, and we had relished the rewards when the path leveled out. Discovering the intense heartache and the immense delight a relationship brings, we had grown to love each other.

Late that summer, I had an unbearable week at the office, and on the heels of this very long week came an even longer weekend. By the time Friday afternoon arrived and brought with it the annual planning retreat for the singles ministry, I already felt beat up and overwhelmed—an especially bad thing since I knew the twenty-four-hour "retreat" would provide little respite and relief for me. As the primary coordinator of the ministry, I loved serving my church and its singles, but I always came away from leadership retreats buried by twelve months of events to pull off. Digging out from under the avalanche of responsibility usually required several days of sorting through the mess and several friends reminding me that, indeed, I would not have to single-handedly implement the entire calendar of events.

As part of the leadership team, Alex was also at the retreat but needed to leave early. Several hours after he had left, I arrived home, wearily set my bags down in my apartment, and noticed the red message light blinking on the answering machine. It was Alex—he just wanted to talk about the retreat. Knowing me as he did by then, he knew he'd get far more than just a summary of what he'd missed. I didn't disappoint him. A week's worth of frustration and a weekend's worth of stress poured into the mouthpiece of my phone. Added to the already crushing load was my Saturday evening, an evening that loomed before me with an unfinished ministry project for the next morning—the weekly newsletter for the singles.

Alex just listened. He didn't correct me, didn't minimize what probably wasn't that big of a deal, didn't belittle my inability to "get a grip," and didn't change subjects. When I had finally worn myself down with the telling, he responded to the tired, beat-up, and exhausted pieces of a person on the other end of the phone, "Don't worry about the newsletter. I'm gonna do it for you." A hundred other things were on his list to do that evening, but he moved me to the top. Setting everything else aside, he lifted my burden, made it his own, and told me to go take a nap.

Alex had told me he loved me often before this particular night, but I doubt I ever heard it so clearly—and this time he didn't even use the words. It was like he had found me on the side of the road just crumpled in a heap, and he picked me up, carried me the rest of the way, tenderly tucked me into bed, and said he loved me. With characteristic gentleness, he responded to the cry of my heart and did what he could to make it better.

chapter nine

Loves Me, Loves Me Not

I met my knight in shining armor at school one day. He whisked into the building, swept me off my feet, and we rode merrily into the sunset to live happily ever after.

Well, not exactly. What actually happened is that a somewhat eccentric single man who collects and displays replicated medieval armor and weaponry all over his house clanked into the elementary school building, clumped down the stairs, and mesmerized my fifth-graders with his hands-on exhibit of the age of chivalry—all at the request of a damsel in distress (me, trying to interest fifth-graders in learning on a warm Friday afternoon). As he made the long trek from the office to my classroom, students and teachers alike gaped at the fairy tale figure come-to-life right outside their classroom door. He seemed not to notice that he sounded like a combination of the Tin Man and Jacob Marley as he moved down the hall. Wearing a full suit of armor was all in a day's work for my knight. When he finished his unusual presentation, he packed up his weapons, kept most of the armor on, and drove off into the afternoon sun in his Toyota pickup (without me).

Admittedly, he was fascinating (when was the last time you helped a knight put on his gauntlets?), but he wasn't real. Medieval knights don't exist anymore, but their long ago feats earned them a permanent spot in fairy tale lore. They are the representatives of a bygone era, when real men speared each other with lances and prized women hung their golden tresses out of stone towers (the things they did for love).

Medieval knights may not exist anymore, but the ideal for love that grew out of that era lives on. The legendary chivalry of knights on behalf of fair maidens has mushroomed to mythic proportions and given us a working vocabulary for "love," encompassing phrases like knight in shining armor, riding a white horse, damsel in distress, Prince Charming, swept me off my feet, Camelot, and—for those still without a prince—the ladies in waiting.

We all know this idea of love is unrealistic, but somehow we still hope for it. I know this because I watch blockbuster movies where perfect strangers meet, fall in love, and live happily ever after—all in the span of two hours. I watch "must see TV" sitcoms where the commercials take longer than the tidy resolutions of major relationship crises. We know this kind of love isn't *true* love, but we can't quite get it out of our minds. For most of us, "falling in love" means finding a relationship based on mutual attraction, satisfaction, and delight. When one of the people in such a partnership stops being attractive, satisfying, or delightful, we often fall out of love, walk away from the relationship, and look for another one.

Our understanding of romantic "love" is badly diseased and has, unfortunately, infected our understanding and practice of non-romantic love, too. Nearly all parents say they love their children, and yet thousands of children know they will never measure up to their parents' hopes; love apparently includes expectations—and resulting disappointment. Friends who said they'd be friends forever drift apart over the years and miles; love obviously has limits. Love as we've experienced it in romance, family, and friendship can be superficial, conditional, and temporary.

Into this lovesick culture comes a Church that, according to its Founder, will be known by its members' love for one another (John 13:35). And into this Church come an enculturated people who are a little fuzzy about what *true* love is—primarily because they've rarely, if ever, experienced it. Thankfully, such fuzziness doesn't have to persist, because into this confusion comes the purest definition—and example—of love: God Himself. God *is* love. He, in His Person and activity, defines what love is and how it works. He provides the motivation, the model, and the manner in which we truly love each other.

The Motivation

Sandy's backyard met mine at the fence, and most of the time I left my turf to go play on hers because she had cool toys. She had everything a seventies child could possibly want—Lite-Brite, the Inchworm, the Fisher Price castle, a Crissy doll, Creepy Crawlers, a sandbox, an inflatable swimming pool, and a basement playroom that looked like the toy aisle of a local department store. I think she even had the Snoopy Sno-Cone machine. And as if that weren't enough, Sandy's mom bought all the snacks that rarely made my mom's grocery list, like Doritos, Twinkies, and Ho-Ho's. Furthermore, Sandy didn't have to contort her face into pathetic expressions to get these snacks (not that that kind of stuff really worked on my mom, but it was always worth trying)—snacks were there to eat whenever the spirit moved (and it moved often).

I could tell you that I loved Sandy, but mostly I loved her stuff. It was a selfish "love" motivated by what she could give me. I was nine when my family moved out of the neighborhood, and Sandy's friendship didn't move with us. I don't remember ever seeing her—or her stuff—again. I always felt kind of bad about that friendship—like I should have learned to love Sandy for who she was instead of for her enviable toys and desirable snacks.

> My shining displays of "love," the whole of Christian character, were sometimes motivated by the desire for public praise and recognition.

A few years later, Ty and Rachel entered my life. My mom watched them after school every day while their mom worked hard to make a living for the three of them. Rachel was fine, although a year or so younger than I (and, therefore, not quite as cool), but Ty was absolutely unbearable. He was in my sixth grade class, and he was annoying—like most boys that age are to their female classmates. Having him in my house every afternoon was almost more than I could stand, not to mention the teasing I took from my best friend because I had to spend so much time with him.

Begrudgingly, I offered Ty patience, kindness, and limited access to my stuff, but I gritted my teeth the whole time and rejoiced when vacations came. I could tell you that I "loved" Ty, but mostly I was nice to him (sort of) because I knew I should be—and I would have gotten into big trouble if I weren't. Any love I demonstrated was motivated by the guilt I knew I'd feel if I was unkind.

Later when I entered eighth grade, I did so with a clearly defined goal for the year. Every year at eighth grade graduation several awards were presented. The highest honor was given in recognition of Christian character—the Citizenship Award. I wanted that award more than any other graduation accolade. It was, in my warped estimation, the ultimate acknowledgement of achievement. I know there were times during that year that I paid attention to someone I might have otherwise ignored, simply because a teacher was nearby. I know there were instances when I sacrificed and served primarily because someone else would see it. My shining displays of "love," the whole of Christian character, were sometimes motivated by the desire for public praise and recognition at the end of the year.

If I am honest, I will tell you that my life has adult versions of Sandy, Ty, and the eighth grade Citizenship Award. I demonstrate what looks like love because of what I will gain in return, because I know I should, and because I crave the praise. My motivations for "love" are rooted in selfishness more often than I'd like to admit. I sometimes "love" my brothers and sisters in the church because there's a payoff if I do and a penalty if I don't. Obviously these less-than-praiseworthy motives are not the ones Jesus intended to characterize love within His Church.

> *Loving people who fend off friends like a good insect repellent requires a stronger motivation than the sheer enjoyment of friendship.*

Fortunately, not all my relationships are driven by such negative motives. I love lots of people who give me nothing but the sheer pleasure of their company and the stimulation of their friendship. We have oodles in common and find it easy to love each other. And if either person ever needed it, we'd go to the moon on the other's behalf. The love of friends is like that.

The love demonstrated in such reciprocal relationships is positive, but it's not particularly impressive, as Jesus pointedly reminded His listeners in Luke 6:32–34: "But if you love those who love you, what credit is that to you? For even sinners love those who love them. And if you do good to those who do good to you, what credit is that to you? For even sinners do the same. And if you lend to those from whom you hope to receive back, what credit is that to you? For even sinners lend to sinners to receive as much back."

The love I have for my friends may be a good thing, but it's not enough when it comes to love in the church. The church is not just a happy gathering of close friends. If your church is anything like mine, it has people who seem almost intentional about making themselves hard to love. Loving people who fend off friends like a good insect repellent requires a stronger motivation than the sheer enjoyment of friendship.

We have one. John, the beloved disciple, says it plainly:

> Beloved, let us love one another, for love is of God; and every-one who loves is born of God and knows God. He who does not love does not know God, for God is love. In this the love of God was manifested toward us, that God has sent His only begotten Son into the world, that we might live through Him. In this is love, not that we loved God, but that He loved us and sent His Son to be the propitiation for our sins. *Beloved, if God so loved us, we also ought to love one another.* (1 John 4:7–11)

We love because we've been loved. We love because God has loved us, knowing what we are and what we've done against Him and to His beautiful creation. When describing this kind of love, John Ortberg compares us to a battered and tattered rag doll named Pandy that his little sister loved with indestructible love. "We are all of us rag dolls. Flawed and wounded, broken and bent."[1] And yet God loves us because we are His rag dolls. He not only made us, but He redeemed us with the life of His Son. His love gives us all the reason we need to offer love.

This love, however, does not simply reach up to the One who first reached down. Because of the love we've received from God, we now reach *out* to share the same kind of love with others. The New Testament puts our response to God's love in the form of two commands and, says Ortberg, "They cannot be separated. The whole of God's will comes down to this, Jesus said, 'Love the Lord your God with all your heart, soul, and mind and strength; and Love your neighbor as yourself.' The primary form that loving God takes in the Bible is loving the people who mean so much to him. . . . 'Love me, love my rag dolls,' God says. It's a package deal."[2] God's love toward us creates an irresistible compulsion for us to love those He loves.

The Model

> God's love was more than some intense emotion for humanity; it was a choice to act sacrificially on our behalf.

When I started taking seminary classes, I quickly discovered that professors are involved in a conspiracy. They are committed to shattering the deeply entrenched theological ideas of unsuspecting students. They do this by dropping bombshells of knowledge on us. Not only are they intentional about this kind of thing, but they actually seem to delight in it. With apparent nonchalance, they launch statements guaranteed to wake up dozing seminarians and send our worlds into a tailspin of questions, uncertainties, and perplexities. Then they grin slyly and move to the next point in their material until someone stops spinning long enough to formulate a question. It is not my goal to rock your world too hard (you have to pay lots of tuition money for that sort of thing), so I'll share an illustration that shouldn't do more than mildly rearrange some of your ideas while demonstrating the model of love God sets for us.

Indisputably John 3:16 is the verse that has been memorized by the most people, sung in the most churches, and displayed at the most professional sports activities. More than any other verse, its twenty-five words seem to encapsulate the entire message of the Bible. (Relax, I'm not going to shatter this idea.) The way we often recite the verse shows the way we understand it: "For God *soooo* loved the world that He gave His only begotten Son, that whoever believes in Him should not perish but have everlasting life." Then we usually go on to say something like, "God loved you *so* much that He sent His Son to die for you." We read the "so" to mean the extent of God's love, the intensity with which He loved us.

It's true that God loves us immensely—so much so that He sent His Son to redeem us (and the rest of creation). It's true that God has lavished a kind of love on us that is unlike anything we can completely understand. But this is probably not what John had in mind when he wrote these familiar words. The first part of John 3:16 is better read, "For God loved the world *in this way*—He gave His only begotten Son." "So" describes *the way* God loved the world; He loved it by giving His Son to redeem it. He demonstrated His love by giving His Son. God's love was more than some intense emotion for humanity; it was a choice to act sacrificially on our behalf.

John emphasizes the sacrificial nature of love again in 1 John 3:16: "By this we know love, because He laid down His life for us." We don't know what genuine love is apart from the unfathomable sacrifice Jesus made. But John doesn't stop there with his description of love. He continues and says this sacrificial love provides the model for us to imitate. We, like Christ, are to "lay down our lives" for our brothers and sisters in Christ. Whoa. That sounds pretty serious. Laying down our lives sounds like more than an exchanged greeting in the hall on Sunday morning or a quick rehearsal of the items on the weekly prayer sheet.

While Jesus physically gave up His life at Calvary for those He loved, He laid it down a thousand times before that dark Friday. The Gospels abound with examples of Jesus sacrificing His "rights" in response to the needs of those around Him. As He encountered the demands and inconveniences of ministry to selfish, short-sighted, and spiritually slow people, not once did He say what I probably would have in the most exhausting of moments—"I am stinkin' tired of this. People, people everywhere—and not a moment to think. They are always taking and never giving me anything in return but a bad headache and a lousy night's sleep." Instead we know that He swallowed a lump in His throat when He saw the beaten-down masses consumed by a hunger they couldn't even describe. They were befuddled sheep, and when the Shepherd stood in their midst, His heart turned inside out with compassion. Loving them meant He put His own interests aside and made their interests His.

In Philippians 2 Paul tells us to do the same: "If there is any consolation in Christ, if any comfort of love, if any fellowship of the Spirit, if any affection and mercy [and the clear implication is that there is], fulfill my joy by being likeminded, having the same love, being of one accord, of one mind. Let nothing be done through selfish ambition or conceit, but in lowliness of mind let each esteem others better than himself. Let each of you look out not only for his own interests, but also for the interests of others" (vv. 1–4). Love within the body of Christ means your needs are as important, and sometimes more important, than mine. It means that I am willing to lay aside my interests to minister to you. And it means that you are willing to lay aside your interests to serve me. Robert Webber says it well: we, as "a fellowship in faith . . . [are in] mutual slavery to each other."[3]

I was on the receiving end of this kind of service from the "fellowship in faith" when I moved to Grand Rapids. My family's entourage of three vehicles made it successfully through Chicago, stopped for a leisurely picnic lunch just inside the Michigan border, and marveled at how painless the trip had been. We still had an hour and a half to go, but with Chicago's maze and craze behind us, our travel concerns primarily consisted of hoping our two travelers under the age of five could hang on until we reached the hotel and its promised swimming pool.

Three hours later, the car I was driving had been to the hotel, my apartment, the hotel, and back to my apartment again. To this day, I can't tell you where the other two vehicles were during that time because their drivers are unsure and any kind of probing for landmark information is like picking off a scab—it's better left untouched. When all three vehicles were finally at my apartment, the last thing we wanted to do was what we had come for—unpack the van and move me in. We were tired and crabby, and the thought of the hotel swimming pool was infinitely more appealing than the thought of unloading my life's belongings, meager as they were, in ninety-degree heat. And then the "fellowship in faith" appeared—three guys recruited from an area church to help me move in. They did it with ease and disappeared before we could gather our frazzled thoughts enough to thank them. I can't even tell you their names, but the sacrifice of their summer Saturday afternoon was an act of love, small as it may seem, toward another member in the body of Christ.

> *Love is mostly about relinquishing my rights on behalf of another person.*

Dying to self can be as simple as giving up a Saturday afternoon or it can be as costly as the sacrificial gift Larry and Annie Mercer received when Annie faced her first cancer surgery. Larry relates the story of a friend from church who gave up her trip to Israel so she could be there if they needed her. "Instead of taking a once-in-a-lifetime trip to Israel, she was standing by, caring for our children and running errands. Her words were simple, but her actions were profound."[4]

Laying down our lives for each other requires that we make ourselves available to meet needs in whatever ways we can. I know what you're thinking because I'm thinking it too. If we are willing to do this, what's to keep someone from walking all over us and effectively deflating our enthusiasm for ministry? Maybe this is more than a "what if" thought for you—maybe you've experienced it. The simplest answer to this very real issue is that if *everyone* in the body of Christ sacrificed for each other, we wouldn't get stuck carrying the heavy load alone. Idealistic? Perhaps, but Scripture still teaches it. Realistically, though, *any* progress we make in this area lightens the load for everyone else.

The model of love God gives us to imitate demands a lot of us. It has virtually nothing to do with feelings of fondness or common characteristics, but nearly everything to do with the choice to sacrifice. Love is mostly about relinquishing my rights on behalf of another person. However, it's not just *what* we do—it also includes *how* we do it.

The Manner, Part 1

> *What we hold up as an ideal for marital love was really part of an admonition to a church that is never held up as an ideal for anything—except maybe the way a church shouldn't be.*

The New Testament is packed with admonitions for how we should love one another. The most dog-eared chapter about love is 1 Corinthians 13 where Paul paints a poetic picture of genuine love, setting a high standard for relationships among believers.

While this chapter's famous words appear on wedding cards, gift plaques, throw blankets, and dozens of other wedding-related items, Paul didn't write these beautiful words about love because he was officiating at a Corinthian wedding and needed something memorable to say to the happy couple. In fact, marriage was nowhere in his thoughts. What we hold up as an ideal for marital love was really part of an admonition to a church that is never held up as an ideal for anything—except maybe the way a church *shouldn't* be.

Paul wrote to the Corinthians because they divided over leadership, squabbled about spiritual gifts, perverted the gift of sex, and drank themselves silly at the Lord's Table. They were a splintered body, about as far removed as possible from what Jesus had prayed for His followers—"that they all may be one, as You, Father, are in Me, and I in You; that they also may be one in Us, that the world may believe that You sent Me" (John 17:21). Unity in Corinth was virtually nonexistent, and Paul gave them the solution. It wasn't more spiritual gifts, better teaching, or greater knowledge. They had plenty of those things—God had seen to that through the ministry of the Holy Spirit. The antidote for their fractured fellowship was love. Only love could mend the breaks and strengthen the body.

Lest the Corinthians be confused about love, Paul explained it to them—and us. He begins by calling attention to the value-altering presence of love. Its presence is what assigns genuine value to seemingly commendable activities.

"Though I speak with the tongues [languages] of men and of angels, but have not love, I have become as sounding brass or a clanging cymbal" (1 Cor. 13:1). I don't think Paul is making a statement about the spiritual gift of tongues here—I think he's talking about people who are skilled communicators, those enviable people who are always comfortable in conversation regardless of who's involved. I am impressed by those in the church who are like this since I look for ways around the awkwardness of making steady conversation with strangers—like passing out bulletins or washing coffee pots in the kitchen. Yet in God's view, their eloquence is actually obnoxious if they don't love their listeners.

"And though I have the gift of prophecy, and understand all mysteries and all knowledge, and though I have all faith, so that I could remove mountains, but have not love, I am nothing" (v. 2). Often the people in the church who garner the most respect are those who know the most. We stand in awe of people with solid insight and workable answers, and we turn to them again and again when help is needed. Yet according to God, their knowledge is of little value if they don't love those who seek their counsel.

"And though I bestow all my goods to feed the poor, and though I give my body to be burned, but have not love, it profits me nothing" (v. 3). If I become homeless in order that some residents of the local rescue mission can take a step forward, but I don't love the men and women who receive my gifts, God assigns no value to my sacrifice.

This all sounds very spiritual, but I have to confess that it's hard to agree with Paul that all these things count for nothing. Go back and think through each of these scenarios. Aren't people affirmed and valued when someone communicates clearly to them? Don't the recipients of wise counsel benefit? What's not to call good about needy people receiving a gold mine of provisions? I can see value in all these activities—and if you're daring enough to disagree with Paul, I bet you can too.

Taking his words at face value, I think we'd have a case, but since Paul is writing in the context of an entire book, I think he's right after all. (Whew . . . I'd hate to have a standing disagreement with the apostle Paul!) Remember that the "it's all about me" virus had infected the Corinthian church, and Paul wrote to remind them that the "success" of the Church is the unity that results from loving relationships.

I have attended plenty of baby showers, and for most of them, I can't tell you what I gave as a gift. Chances are good I stopped at the nearest store, picked up something snuggly and cute, and had it wrapped "to go" at the gift counter. Or, chances are greater that I wrote a check to my sister or mom who let me share the cost of a gift they'd already bought. Did I do a good thing by taking a gift? Sure, it's nice to help new moms welcome their little ones—and you can't show up at a shower without a gift. Was I motivated by love? Sometimes, but truthfully, more often by duty. Does anybody benefit? Sure, the mom-to-be feels honored and the baby gets a cute new outfit.

> *Growth is impossible apart from unity; unity is impossible apart from love; and love is impossible apart from relationships.*

It all sounds pretty good until I compare it to a story that includes love. When my thirty-something friend Barb was expecting her first baby, I enthusiastically assumed responsibility for her baby shower. I spent my winter evenings and an impressive amount of my discretionary income pulling off what came to be called the "mother of all baby showers." I did everything I could to guarantee a perfect day for her—and almost inconceivably, it all worked even better than planned. After the grand event, Barb took home a carload of baby stuff, but even fuller than her backseat was her heart. She took home the gift of overwhelming love—the gift I gave that would outlast the diaper bag, stuffed lion, and baby books. I also went home with a full heart from having given the best of myself to delight another person. The real "achievement" in the whole event wasn't found in the wrapped presents or tasty treats—the real benefit was the deepened bond in our friendship.

We came out "ahead" because of love—decisions I made on Barb's behalf without any thought for my duty (really a selfish motivator since *I* look bad if I fail to perform) or any concern for the time, energy, and money it cost me.

By God's original design we are incomplete without the giving and receiving of love, and by God's redemption design, we are to find this outlet in the church. It's true that busy lives demand that we often act more out of duty than love, but love—not obligation—is really what we live for. Duty calls long and loud, but we somehow make time and find money for the activities and people we love. And in those loving relationships, the greatest gift we give isn't stuff—it's ourselves.

Ultimately, the purpose of love in the Church is the growth of the body of Christ, a body that grows proportionally and together. Imagine the absurdity (and impossibility) of your elbow taking off on a growth spurt by itself. Instead, it grows as your arm grows, as your torso grows, as your body grows. Each part supports and strengthens the other parts. When the body doesn't grow in this way, it's either unhealthy or pubescent—and nobody wants to stay in either condition very long.

Growth is impossible apart from unity; unity is impossible apart from love; and love is impossible apart from relationships. Without love, I am disconnected from the body, and my good deeds don't contribute to its total growth any more than a cut flower in a vase adds to the beauty of the faraway plant that gave it life. Individuals may benefit for a while, but the greater good—growth of the body—is not accomplished.

The Manner, Part 2

Love, continues Paul, is patient; love is kind. When Paul said this in Greek, it carried a little more oomph than our English versions can.

"Patient" and "kind" are actually action verbs for the subject—love. Love "patients." Love "kinds."

> *Love doesn't just wait; love "patients." Love doesn't just do the right thing; love "kinds." Love is the beautiful combination of action and attitude.*

I have sacrificed my rights on behalf of other people, but I have not always "patiented" or "kinded" them. During my seminary years, I've had a delightful roommate with vastly different shopping habits than I have. When it comes to groceries, I'm a blitzkrieg shopper. I have the list, if not on paper then definitely in my head, and from the moment I park the car, I'm on a mission: I buy the brand on sale, aim for the fastest line, and try not to run anybody over on the way back to the car. In. Out. Home. That's the way to shop.

Norma, however, sees the grocery experience differently. She peruses her options on the shelves. She reads labels. She compares prices, calculates the cost in Canadian dollars (she's Canadian . . . this isn't just a weird habit), contemplates the benefits of one item over another, and finally selects what she wants.

While Norma weighs the advantages of Yoplait yogurt over Dannon, I fetch two half-gallons of milk, a bottle of salad dressing, a box of croutons, three cans of tuna on sale, a jar of spaghetti sauce, a jumbo package of napkins, and a bag of coffee filters from six different aisles in the store. By the time she has her yogurt in the cart, our shopping is nearly done—except for any personal items we might need (although I have probably already grabbed my toothpaste en route to the paper goods).

Norma heads off to get her things and I take everything else through the checkout line . . . and then wait. And wait. And wait. In the early days of our roommateship, I didn't wait very patiently or very kindly. I checked the clock, grumbled to the bagged groceries, and wondered what could possibly take so long. I may have sacrificed my time while she selected the perfect shampoo and conditioner (I didn't really have a choice), but I don't get any credit for loving her in the process. Love doesn't just wait; love "patients." Love doesn't just do the right thing; love "kinds."

Love is the beautiful combination of action *and* attitude. I act on your behalf *because* I value you as a person and fellow-member in the body of Christ—not just because I know I should. I act on your behalf because I have been loved. I love you because you are really part of me—we belong to each other in Christ. *This* is love.

The Manner, Part 3

In further explanation of what it means for love to "patient" and to "kind," Paul gives a bullet list of actions and attitudes that are absent when love is present:

- *Love does not envy.* Love means I'm okay with my aging car, my seemingly endless career preparation, and my chronic difficulty making small talk. It means I don't compare myself to you, but because I love you, I am glad with you that God has blessed you in the ways He has. Love "patients" with my life and "kinds" you for yours.

- *Love does not parade itself.* Love means I don't need to call attention to the fact that I stayed late after the Sunday school picnic to clean up because everyone else left early. It means I don't find a way to work into a group conversation that I postponed my vacation because I gave a little extra money to the building program. Jesus' warning in Matthew 6 adds another element to Paul's words about love: "Take heed that you do not do your charitable deeds before men, to be seen by them. Otherwise you have no reward from your Father in heaven" (v. 6:1). Love "patients" for God's reward, and "kinds" others without needing credit.

> *Love means that every time I walk through the doors, I ask the questions, "How can I serve here today? Who can I help?"*

- *Love is not puffed up.* Love means that when I see a children's church leader frantically pulling things together at the last minute, I don't shake my head and say, "Why do people always wait until the last minute? I don't know why they can't get it done ahead of time—it's not that difficult, and their ministry would run a lot more smoothly." Instead love "kinds" the worker, noticing how the kids love the fun things she does with them.
- *Love does not behave rudely.* Love means I don't huddle in my comfortable cluster of friends and catch up on Sunday morning instead of noticing a person *without* a cluster of friends. And it means that when a newcomer does make it into the cluster, we find things to talk about besides the movie we saw the night before. Love "kinds" those who are struggling to belong.
- *Love does not seek its own.* Love means I come to church with greater intentions than finding friends, a spouse, or a place to be spiritually fed. Love means that every time I walk through the doors, I ask the questions, "How can I serve here today? Who can I help?" Love "kinds" the church body.
- *Love is not provoked.* Love means I recognize that although not everyone is like me, neither is everyone out to get me. It means I don't take offense when the Ladies' Tea committee decides not to use my recipe, someone else plays the position I wanted on the softball team, or my first grade Sunday school class has to switch rooms again. Love "patients" with diversity, change, and inconvenience in the body.
- *Love thinks no evil.* Love means when a leader is late for club I pray for her safe arrival and ability to minister, rather than tallying her tardies in my head. It means I allow lots of room for explanations instead of jumping to hurtful conclusions. Love "kinds" when it's easier to assume.
- *Love does not rejoice in iniquity.* Love means I hear the scuttle-

butt in the hallway and keep walking. If I'm already in the conversation, it means I stay and tactfully redirect the conversation. It means I don't scout for the juicy details of another member's sin, even under the guise of sympathetic sorrow and shock. Love "kinds" those who have strayed and "patients" for truth and goodness to prevail.*

Paul concludes his description of love with a resounding cheer for love—it *bears* all things, *believes* all things, *hopes* all things, *endures* all things. It bears *all* things, believes *all* things, hopes *all* things, endures *all* things. I didn't just stutter—I meant to repeat this description, emphasizing first the activity and then the extent of love. Love *never* fails. Love is tough stuff. It is relationship Superglue in a Post-it world.

Is it any wonder that Paul urges the Corinthians to "pursue love" (1 Cor. 14:1)? Love is the key to unity, and unity is how we, as a church body, reflect the image of the triune God who birthed us. We are many members, but one body. We are diverse, but called into community—the kind of community that is only possible when we love according to God's definition.

It's All About Us

From inside a plush, air-conditioned tour bus, I took in the tragic scenes of human poverty along the rocky roads of Israel's wilderness. The miles of sandy terrain were speckled with what can only be called tents, although no one from *this* country would consider camping in them. Wooden frames covered with a patchwork of tin and trash, these tents are home to the nomadic people of the Middle East—the Bedouins. Goats, sheep, and a few stray mules wander around the "neighborhoods," while disheveled children scamper behind them. As dusk settles over the village, the Bedouin streetlights come on—campfires scattered about for heat, light, and stovetop cooking.

---

* Paul is not suggesting that love excuses accountability for sin—he makes this clear in other New Testament passages. Love doesn't mean we don't hold each other accountable for sin; it means we don't hold it against each other.

> *The Bedouin people that I pitied for their poverty have a wealth we'll never know in this life because we live in a culture that ties us to possessions and prestige, often using people as the means to achieve both.*

As we raced past these unsightly camps, I marveled that people could live with so little, and I pitied them. I had more in my suitcase than they had in their homes. How, I wondered, do they do it? What, I asked myself, do they do with themselves when there is so obviously nothing *to do?*

The more I traveled, the more I realized what they do. They "do" each other. Life, untarnished by the tyranny of the urgent that drives "civilized" cultures, moves at its intended pace, and together the people ebb and flow with it. When the day's work is done, they sit around the fire and talk. Centuries of oral tradition have survived because nomadic cultures, those people with "nothing," mastered with ease the art of talking and listening, of sharing and discovering, of self-awareness and "other-awareness." Without the multiplicity of distractions we consider necessities, Bedouins have no trouble understanding real necessities— the people they live with. "Part of the Bedouin character," says Father Emil Salyta, a Jordanian Roman Catholic priest, "is a sense of dependency on providence and each other. Whatever happens, they will sit together for long, long hours to share together . . ."[5]

A government movement is afoot in Israel to abolish the Bedouin way of life. One of the commendable motives behind the movement is to provide a better way of life for people with such a meager existence, but the Bedouins, in a fashion sadly reminiscent of Native Americans, would rather be left alone to live as they've always lived. While I agree that a higher level of civilization offers certain benefits, I don't blame the Bedouins for their resistance. The Bedouin people that I pitied for their poverty have a wealth we'll never know in this life because we live in a culture that ties us to possessions and prestige, often using people as the means to achieve both. Breaking those ties requires continuous, counterculture effort—and even then, sometimes it's still impossible.

The Church of Jesus Christ is called to make these continuous, counterculture efforts, becoming more and more a place where people matter to each other. Saying "I love you" in the church demands that we use our time and treasures as tools for building relationships. It means that we meet the needs of another by offering the best gift we have—ourselves.

chapter ten

Loving Singles

I met Julie at a single-girls-only New Year's Eve party, and it's hard to think how it could have been a party without her. She is vibrant, personable, and has an extraordinary sense of humor.

It's a good thing. She needed it recently when she attended a ladies' fellowship at her church. After the large general session, the women broke into smaller groups for discussion and interaction about specific topics. Julie's choices for a small group that afternoon included being a supportive wife, homeschooling children, parenting preschoolers, and dealing with depression. I don't think she was depressed when she went to the ladies' event, but I wouldn't have blamed her if she was by the time she left—which she promptly did when she discovered her small group options. Another single friend heard this sad tale and summed it up well: "The Bible is a big book. Couldn't they have found something that applied to everyone?"

Did the ladies at Julie's church intentionally exclude her? I sincerely doubt it. If they are anything like most of the women I know in churches, they are wonderful people. They are gracious and hospitable, make mean muffins, and run circles around any church planning committee.

> *The primary need of singles, and the one, as God would have it, that the church is best equipped to meet, is that singles need to be part of a family—they need to be part of the Family.*

They didn't intentionally exclude her, but—and herein lies the problem when it comes to singles and the church—neither did they intentionally include her. Since we have been conditioned to believe that marriage and family are the norm, we have to learn how to include those who aren't married. Because the marriage mentality is our default, our thought process needs to undergo some reprogramming.

In the first two sections of this book, we laid the foundation for why singles and the church make a perfect match. In the third section, we hinted at how they fit together, how each is uniquely equipped to meet the needs of the other. In this fourth section, we are trying to answer the questions some of you have been asking since you began reading: "So, what do I *do?* How do I *fix* this?" You want to know how the church can meet the needs of singles and how singles can meet needs in the church. In short, you want to know how we can love each other.

The primary need of singles, and the one, as God would have it, that the church is best equipped to meet, is that singles need to be part of a family—they need to be part of the Family. Going through life alone is what God called "not good" in His original creation. The redeemed community of God provides the ideal network of people to "do life" with the single adult, to provide a Family where the single can find a place to belong, feel valued, and develop lasting relationships.

A Place to Belong

Some of you might be thinking, "My church has solved this problem. Singles have a place to belong because we have a singles ministry." Or you might be thinking the exact opposite, "There's no hope for my church. We can't seem to get our singles ministry off the ground." Or perhaps you are somewhere in the middle: "We have a ministry for singles, but it doesn't seem like they're really part of the church family."

Wherever you fall on this spectrum, keep reading. Singles ministries, for all their positive contributions, are not an automatic solution to the need of singles to belong in the church, and in fact, sometimes they are part of the problem. Singles may belong to a singles group, but not really be part of the Family.

Adult Bible Classes

> When we spend the majority of our time with people just like ourselves, we begin thinking everyone is like us—or should be. We develop myopic views of life and ministry.

Most churches have structured their Sunday Bible classes for adults around an "age-and-stage of life" format. Young marrieds meet with young marrieds. Parents of young children fellowship with other parents of young children. Retirees attend class with retirees. Everyone in the church is assigned to his or her "own kind." This kind of arrangement has its advantages—doing life with people like you can boost morale, provide camaraderie, and offer helpful suggestions. Moms with babies like to be with other moms who are losing sleep, changing diapers, and bracing for potty training. Parents of teens often need to swap their war stories—sharing the victories, defeats, and strategies for dealing with adolescents.

Most churches with a strict age-and-stage format have some sort of singles ministry, otherwise singles really don't have any place to belong. Sometimes, though, these singles groups are treated more like extended youth groups than as adult classes. One single friend commented that his church offers adult electives but expects the singles to stay in their group instead of mixing with the larger church family in elective classes.

Age-and-stage of life grouping can also have costly disadvantages. First, when we segregate into age groups, we struggle to truly learn from those who have done life ahead of us and to teach those who are coming up behind us. At best, we dance around Paul's instructions for the older men and women to instruct and encourage the younger men and women (Titus 2) and at worst, we disobey it. Second, when we spend the majority of our time with people just like ourselves, we begin thinking everyone is like us—or should be. We develop myopic views of life and ministry.

> *"I didn't want to be part of a singles ministry because the majority of my needs don't have anything to do with being single. I need prayer. I need to serve others. I need to be held accountable for my sins. And I figure married people need those things, too. I don't want to be segregated with people who, superficially, are just like me."—Lauren Winner*

You can figure out the logical and disastrous consequences of an entire body of church members who think like this. Diane Langberg says of segregated adult classes, "It is so easy to lose sight of our unity in Christ. In essence, we end up with individual Sunday school classes for feet, for hands, and for eyes."[1]

I understand the desire to be with one's peer group every Sunday. Actually, I envy adult classes that have spent a lifetime together, because a singles class can never do this. The transient nature of single life—especially twenty-something single life—means the community of singles will dissolve before most of the class reaches thirty. Every year members will move to a newlyweds class or to another city, and the "leftovers" will try, with decreasing success, to regroup. We had a joke (and not a very good one) in my singles class that once you entered, the only way out was to get married or move out of town—and most of my friends did.

Single and in her mid-twenties, Lauren Winner fought against joining a singles ministry: "I didn't want to be part of a singles ministry because the majority of my needs don't have anything to do with being single. I need prayer. I need to serve others. I need to be held accountable for my sins. And I figure married people need those things, too. I don't want to be segregated with people who, superficially, are just like me."[2]

What rich blessings we miss by staying in our peer groups, and what precious resources we waste by not interacting with those unlike us! I've discovered that as the scope of my church involvement widens, I have less desire to be with people "just like me." Spending time with newlyweds and newly widowed, childless and child weary, first-time parents and empty nesters opens my eyes to the beauty of the body—and the way we are designed to fit together, with all our quirks and foibles, and minister to each other.

Perhaps your church can't upset the apple cart of segregated adult classes without having a revolt. Then you need to create other regular and meaningful opportunities for desegregated small group relationships. And when you do, be careful how you schedule them. If you plan a ladies' Bible study and only offer it on weekdays, you've alienated most single women who work full time. If you plan a men's retreat that focuses on fathering, you've told the single men they don't belong.

> *Many of us have learned the hard way that going to a church "family event" can mean going to an event that is really a collection of families.*

If your church isn't so established or if you're adding new adult classes because you're growing, consider mixing things up and building cross-generational classes so everyone can have a place to belong no matter who gets married or moves out of town.

Special Events

For show-and-tell one day, three first graders brought items that represented their religions. The little Catholic girl brought a rosary, the little Buddhist boy brought a Buddha, and the little Baptist girl showed off a casserole. Churches (and not just Baptist ones) love to gather outside formal Sunday services, classes, and midweek studies. Food is the preferred catalyst for fellowship.

Church-wide celebrations can be wonderful occasions, but they are often "stay-at-home-events" for singles—especially for those singles who are newer to the church or who don't have any family nearby. In the singles culture, both of these conditions are prevalent—because we are a transient group, we're often "new" to a church, and many of us have left our families in another city or state. We come to church without the rich background I enjoyed for thirty years at one church. We come to church needing a place to be drawn in and embraced. We come to church where families are often established and we have to figure out how to wedge ourselves in. Many of us have learned the hard way that going to a church "family event" can mean going to an event that is really a collection of families. So we stay home because it's too painful to be reminded that we don't belong.

My single friend Kate determined to try such an event at a church where she was a fairly new member. She braved the odds, signed up to bring a dish, and attended an all-church potluck. She'd even made the extra effort to adopt herself into a family, finding one that agreed to save her a seat. When she arrived a few minutes late, she discovered they'd forgotten. Looking around the crowded room, she observed that there was nowhere to sit without intruding on a family. I may have bolted by this point, but she squeezed in and stuck it out. After dinner the entire group moved to another room for a service, and Kate sat in a pew with plenty of room in it—but still ended up sitting alone as family after family made their way into other pews. She left church that night in tears. She had gone to a "church-wide celebration" and learned that it really wasn't.

These situations are familiar to singles who haven't found a niche yet, but they can also happen to singles who are established in their churches. When I traveled home for Christmas one year, I attended the Christmas Eve service at the church where I grew up and still know hundreds of people. I went alone and sat alone, and as the sanctuary filled up, I realized that lots of families wouldn't be able to sit together, so I moved to an obstructed view seat near the sound booth. While I sat there, a longtime member who meant it to be funny asked, "What are you doing here? Don't you have a church in Michigan?" Fortunately, I have a sense of humor and I guessed he had no idea how caustic his statement sounded, so I laughed. Just then an extended family with small children in tow entered and surveyed their seating options. There weren't any, except the row of obstructed view seats where I was. I gave them my seat and told them to squeeze in—and I moved to the lobby where I pulled up a chair and parked myself near the information booth to participate in the service from a distance. Eventually, two single friends joined me, and we watched the family event together. Did I mind giving up my seats? Not really—it was a way to serve the body. Did I feel like I really belonged? Not really—it was one of the biggest events of the year for families, and I didn't have one.

"But Wendy," you ask, "what was the church supposed to do? They can't change that you're single and they can't change that others have families. What would have made a difference?" Simple. If one of the dozens of families I knew in the sanctuary would have said, "Are you alone tonight? Join us—we'd love to have you." That's all it takes sometimes to tell a single they belong. (A hearty "good to see you!" from the longtime member wouldn't have hurt either!)

Simple Things

Within the ongoing functions of the church, simple things can alienate singles. Fortunately, they are also fairly simple to fix. With a little bit of awareness, we can demonstrate sensitivity in the way we involve singles and promote church ministries.

- *Sermons and lessons.* It's easiest for pastors and teachers to use illustrations and applications that come from their own lives. This means if the pastor or teacher is married, the examples he or she uses often refer to family life. This is fine, unless these are the only kinds of examples the singles in the audience ever hear. For four years, I served on a mostly-married church staff, and I took it upon myself to help my colleagues understand single life in the church. Over the course of time, I heard a difference in the way my pastor preached—he had trained himself to be sensitive to the diversity of his audience, and he often made appropriate applications for singles. Once or twice he even ran his ideas past me just to see how they sounded to single ears. He worked hard to understand and include the singles, and we appreciated it. We knew we belonged.

- *Church committees and planning teams.* Look around your ministry and notice what singles are doing in the church. Are they involved in every facet of ministry? I doubt any singles were on the planning team for the ladies' retreat Julie attended. (I suspect, too, that many churches that host annual mother-daughter events don't have singles on the committees in charge.) Are there places in ministry where singles can't serve because of their marital status, and if so, is such a standard biblically sound? Remember, if we don't intentionally include singles, chances are we've excluded them.

- *Potlucks and food-related events.* When I asked a male friend what little things the church does that cause singles to feel like they don't belong, he said "potlucks," but for a different reason than my friend Kate encountered. As a single guy who doesn't cook, he's stuck staying home, showing up with a telltale bag of chips, or looking like a leech. Another church announced its potluck in the bulletin and told members to bring a dish to pass for fifteen. Gulp! In my budget, that's two weeks of meals. How does your church communicate that everyone's welcome at these kinds of events?

- *Discounts for couples.* The saying that two can live cheaper than one often applies to paid events in the church. When I read a brochure that says registration for singles is $10 and couples pay $15, I wonder why we can't all pay $7.50 or even $8. Do I get an extra dessert in my lunch? Do I get a better seat? What is my extra money being used for?

- *Promotional pieces and literature.* As I put my lunch in the refrigerator at work one day, I noticed a magnet on the door promoting an area church's ladies' ministry. It had an adorable close-up picture of a baby's face and the phrase "fearfully and wonderfully made." That ladies' ministry is clearly not a place where singles (or those without children) belong.

Says Diane Langberg of these kinds of things, "Anything we have done in the body to cause another to feel or be less a part of that body because of their status, is sin. When we teach and preach and organize the body in such a way that we communicate to singles, 'We have no need of you,' or 'You are of less importance,' then we have failed to be obedient to the Scripture. . . . If we have done this, we have also, by our exclusive ways, deprived the body of the good that was intended to be brought by those we have left out."[3] Not only does the single lose—the church loses what the single can offer.

A Place to Be Valued

> If singles are to step foot in the church and have any desire to stay, they need to know they are valued exactly as they are.

Not too long ago, I was going about my Sunday morning ministry when a dear grandmotherly friend approached me. We exchanged hugs of greeting, and she asked me about a project I was in the middle of. We talked briefly, and as she turned to go, she offered me her encouragement—"I'm praying for a husband for you." I don't mind it when people tell me this. I have learned to take their words as the sweet wishes of people who have been happily married for a long time and desire the same kind of happiness for someone they care about.

Her next words were intended to be the highest of compliments, and she would be mortified to realize they carried overtones of exactly the opposite. "You're too good to waste," she said as she squeezed my arm and walked away. My sensitized single ears picked up the overtones instantly, and even though I knew her heart was pure gold, the words smarted. I blinked hard, took a few deep breaths, kept my smile on, and reminded myself that she did not really think my life was being wasted without a spouse.

This story plays itself out weekly in churches everywhere, and singles are left feeling like they are less valuable single than married. If singles are to step foot in the church and have any desire to stay, they need to know they are valued exactly as they are.

Things to Avoid: Saying Untamed Things

We have no trouble agreeing with James's words, "No [one] can tame the tongue" (James 3:8). Sometimes we intentionally hurt with our "wild" tongues—we sic 'em on people and tear them to shreds. More often, however, our tongues are like the oafish dog that playfully barrels over a small child because he doesn't know his own strength. We often speak before we think, and sometimes we speak and *never* think, never considering the impact our words might have on the person who had to receive them.

> He doesn't promise to give us what we want just because we follow Him. . . . The road this side of the new heaven and new earth isn't paved gold.

Words can be weapons of mass destruction or tools for "temple construction." We can tell singles that they are valued or we can reaffirm their suspicions that they aren't. Some examples of comments that subtly tell singles they are not valued as they are include:

- You're a nice girl. . . . Why aren't you married?
  What singles hear: Perhaps I'm not really as "nice" as everyone thinks.

- It's time for him to settle down and get married.
  What singles hear: I am not a full-fledged adult if I am not married.

- God has someone really special for you.
  What singles hear: If I *don't* get married, God has let me down.

- I hope you meet someone; I really want you to be happy.
  What singles hear: I can't be happy without a relationship.

The majority of these kinds of statements can be avoided if we will follow three simple rules:

1. *Don't promise what God doesn't.* Telling singles that God has someone wonderful for them doesn't match up with Scripture. God does not promise that we will all get married and "live happily ever after." He doesn't promise to give us what we want just because we follow Him. In fact, Scripture testifies to the opposite—if we follow Him, we are often called to suffer. The road *this* side of the new heaven and new earth isn't paved gold.

2. *Don't assume the single life is miserable.* Sure, life without a spouse can be lonely. Combating sexual pressures can be a chore. But singleness is not misery any more than marriage can be misery. I don't have to get married to be happy (and frankly, if I get married for this reason, it won't work anyway). Singleness affords me many opportunities my married friends will never have. It *is* possible to never get married and *still* have a fulfilled, joy-filled life.

3. *Don't wear your shoes—wear theirs.* Walking (at least mentally) in another person's shoes can provide great insight. When an inquisitive church member puts himself on the other side of his question before he asks it, he may decide to swallow it. For example, if the answer to the question, "Are you seeing anyone?" turns out to be no, then the conversation hits a really uncomfortable place. Other questions simply have no good answers—"So, why aren't you married?"—and shouldn't be asked.

Things to Avoid: Playing Cupid

I know a lot of really nice people who have met and married because a matchmaking friend introduced them. Matchmaking is acceptable when singles have given their friends permission to do it—or when it's so covert that nobody but the matchmaker knows his or her intentions. Otherwise, playing Cupid can have dangerous effects on the single's sense of value.

Persistent matchmakers cause singles to question their wholeness. When someone is preoccupied with getting me married off, it makes me feel like I must not be a complete person since I'm single. It raises the familiar questions of "what's wrong with me?" and "why can't people just accept me as I am?"

Matchmaking can also foster discontentment much like going to the mall does for me. Shopping introduces me to a plethora of potential possessions. When I left home, my wardrobe looked just fine as it bulged out of the closet (except for the wrinkles), but before I finish walking one level of the mall, I realize how outdated my clothes really are. Focusing on what I don't have makes what I do have seem inadequate. Matchmaking can do this to singles—it focuses their attention on what they don't have instead of encouraging them to delight in what they do have. Church members serve singles better when they look for ways to encourage who they are and where they are, rather than unintentionally causing them to struggle with discontentment.

Things to Embrace: Begin to Understand Singles

Camerin Courtney tells the awkward story many singles have lived. Diana, a coworker in the church nursery with Camerin, dead-ended on her first few attempts at conversation ("Do you have kids?" "Are you a college student?") When Camerin answered no to both of these questions and offered the fact that she worked at a nearby office, Diana was stumped, gave up, and shifted conversation to another mom in the nursery. "'Well . . . Susan and I are both stay-at-home moms, and it's the best job in the whole world.' They launched into a conversation about their babies, their husbands, and their labor stories. As I listened, I felt as though they were the insiders and I was the outsider. As usual, I wished the conversation would shift to summer plans, faith, work, or anything else to which I could contribute."[4]

I've already confessed that I'm terrible at small talk, so I have great empathy when people don't know what to say to singles. Once they get past the weather, many of them are as lost as New Yorkers in Nebraska. Rule number 3 from the above list can be applied here as well—try wearing the single's shoes and ask about interests, work, hobbies, and plans. The difficult part is getting started. Some of this kind of information you'll have a hard time gathering in the church halls—you'll have to put yourself in situations where you can get to know singles on a personal level. When you do, you'll make the amazing discovery that they are remarkably like you. Once this relationship has been established, you can take steps to understand what it's like for the singles in your church. You might be surprised by some of their answers, but try asking. Singles will know they are valued when you've taken the time to understand them. Diane Langberg offers several helpful prompts for conversations with a single who's become your friend—and it's important that the single is already your friend before you start probing for answers to these kinds of questions:

1. Teach me what it's like to be single in the Christian community at large, and in our church in particular.
2. What is hard, or what hurts about being single?
3. What are the strengths, or what do you value about being single?
4. How does the church contribute to the hurts?
5. How does the church ignore or misuse the strengths of singleness?
6. What kind of messages, overt or covert, have you received from this church about singleness?
7. What could this church do to ease the difficulties and nurture the strengths of your life as a single adult?[5]

Things to Embrace: Sensitivity to Basic Needs

Living as a single includes all the responsibilities of adult life combined with the unique challenge of doing it alone. Sometimes making singles feel valued in the church is as simple as recognizing and helping provide for some basic needs. Most of these are primarily applicable to the needs of single women, although the possibilities certainly extend beyond those I've listed.

- *Car maintenance and repair.* As a single woman living in an area where I don't have any family close by, I am indebted to the friends who came to my aid when my car was out of commission for more than a week. Grocery shopping still needed to get done, my place of employment still expected me to punch the clock, and church responsibilities still beckoned. I know churches that provide regular car services for their divorced, widowed, and singles who need it. This is a huge weight off the mind of someone going it alone.
- *Home maintenance and repair.* For singles who own homes and lack the Bob Vila touch, a church that comes alongside to assist in some very practical matters does a great service. A team of men and boys from my church recently helped a widowed mom remodel her bedroom—a task she could have never accomplished on her own. Not only did the team help her, but they modeled to a younger generation invaluable lessons about what it means to care for one another.
- *Taxes and money matters.* Depending on one's experience with financial matters, the assistance of church members with expertise can be a lifesaver, especially for those single moms whose tighter budgetary constraints prevent them from hiring professional help. For younger singles, and others who have never had good financial counseling, the opportunity to learn some simple spending and investing principles is a valuable service that the church can often supply. I have several single friends whose financial decisions during their early career days were greatly enhanced because they'd met one-on-one for budget talks with their administrative pastor.
- *Holiday invitations.* For many singles, holidays can be a very difficult time, especially if they are far from home or do not have family. My mom and dad did a great service to a group of senior singles one holiday season when they hosted a Christmas

brunch for them. The ladies who came knew they were valued during a season that's filled with family memories. Another family put extra leaves in their Thanksgiving table and invited numerous singles to join their already large family for the holiday. Even if you think the single person has plans for the holiday, don't let that stop you from issuing your invitation. Even if they can't attend, they'll know you cared enough to include them.

• *Caring for single missionaries on furlough.* When a missionary family comes home on furlough, the sending church often helps supply a home, vehicle, and other necessities during the family's time in the States. However, when a single comes home on furlough, it can be easy for the church to assume that the single will stay with his or her parents. It can be frustrating and hurtful when the church assumes that singles do not have the same basic needs as a family.

Things to Embrace: Celebrate Their Singleness

Most of my friends have had their kitchens, bathrooms, and bedrooms well stocked with brand-new items, compliments of church members who celebrated their marriage. My kitchen, on the other hand, is a hodge-podge of dishes, utensils, and appliances gleaned from various family kitchens. The Crock-Pot, microwave, and hand-mixer are hand-me-downs from my mom, sister, and grandma, respectively. Anything that's new, I bought myself or requested for Christmas. My floor mats came from Grandma's bathroom, and many of my towels are leftovers from my college years when my parents sent me away stocked with supplies. Most of the sheets for my bed are former residents of my mom's linen closet. I don't say this to complain—I'm not starving, so apparently my kitchen is sufficiently stocked with food-preparation equipment, and I'm all for good stewardship. But this kind of reality makes a subtle statement to singles that their lives aren't as worthy of celebration as those of their married friends.

Life is punctuated by rites of passage, marks of maturity that we celebrate—learning to walk, riding a bike, the first day of kindergarten, the end of elementary school, getting a driver's license, graduations, marriage, the birth of children, decade birthdays. In the church, we celebrate several of these rites of passage, and many with great hoopla and outpouring of gifts. The Family of God should celebrate milestone occasions, but significant celebrations after college are generally limited to those who marry and have children. No one *celebrates* singleness. Again, the church is not intentionally excluding singles—but it's not intentionally including them either.

> *If only singles are "celebrating" singleness, it's much like singing "Happy Birthday" to yourself, and the greater message from the church at large remains unchanged.*

The idea of celebrating singleness may seem like an awkward proposition since the majority of singles fully expect to get married—and be "showered upon"—someday. It's not so awkward, however, if we start thinking of celebrating *life*, not marital status. Maybe my apartment is a collection of hand-me-downs, but it's okay because I've been part of a church that communicated my value to me with bells and whistles by intentionally planning other milestone celebrations for me. When I turned a traumatic thirty, about as many friends crammed into my apartment to lavish me with love. When my first book was published, dozens of friends appeared at church one summer Sunday afternoon to nibble snacks and ogle over their autographed copy. When I approached my move-out-of-state day, fifty people sad to see me go pooled their resources to pay for a much needed box spring and mattress.

Singles groups can be good safety nets to make sure everyone gets celebrated, but when it comes to communicating value, it takes more than singles. If only singles are "celebrating" singleness, it's much like singing "Happy Birthday" to yourself, and the greater message from the church at large remains unchanged. My single friends spearheaded some of the celebrations for me, but I was fortunate enough to have a network of friendships that connected me to every age and stage of church life—and many of those dear friends, with lives vastly different from mine, initiated and attended celebrations on my behalf over the years.

If singles are to feel valued in the church, we must find ways to celebrate nontraditional rites of passage with them. Some additional events worth celebrating include missions trips, the purchase of a home or condo, grad school graduation, a new job or career, an international trip, a major remodeling project, or a new vehicle. It's not nearly as important *what* you celebrate, but *that* you celebrate. Be creative— life is full of reasons to celebrate!

Things to Embrace: Start Making Singleness a Choice Instead of Plan B

> From their earliest days, we talk to little girls and boys about the time when they'll grow up, get married, and have children. . . . While this is not inherently bad, it doesn't make singleness a choice—it makes singleness what happens when dreams don't come true.

For better or worse, singleness has ridden a pendulum of popularity through the course of church history. In the early and medieval church, the most devoted, most gifted men and women chose singleness because it led to a level of focused spirituality that married Christians could never reach. Intimacy with God was reward enough—who needed marriage?

The Reformation moved marriage to a place of preference and prominence, while singleness started to swing out of favor. This is generally where we are today. We assume that everyone should and would choose marriage if a viable option presents itself. Singleness happens when all options appear to be exhausted. From their earliest days, we talk to little girls and boys about the time when they'll grow up, get married, and have children. With the best of intentions, we feed the dreams of a spouse and family. While this is not inherently bad, it doesn't make singleness a choice—it makes singleness what happens when dreams don't come true.

> Addressing singleness when people reach adulthood is like forming a support group for alcoholics—it's definitely helpful, but it's really reacting to a problem instead of preventing it.

Why don't we ever tell our children that marriage is a choice, and singleness is just as acceptable a choice? Why don't we help them understand that singleness isn't a travesty to cope with, but instead it can be a purposeful decision. I admit this is probably the most difficult area to "embrace" because it goes against everything most of us have grown up believing. This fact alone affirms how deeply entrenched our perspective is that marriage is better.

Lauren Winner comments on singleness in the church, saying there is "very little space in today's evangelical churches for discerning a call to singleness. Catholics—at least Catholics who believe they are called not just to celibacy but also to religious orders—have something positive to do. They don't fall into a monastery by default. Rather, prayerfully and in community, they discern God's calling for them there. Protestants, on the other hand, don't often begin imagining they might be called to singleness until their thirty-fifth birthday rolls around. Then they woefully begin to think, 'Well, maybe I have the gift of celibacy.'"[6]

Of all places, the church needs to affirm the value of singleness—and not just in singles groups or adult ministries. Addressing singleness when people reach adulthood is like forming a support group for alcoholics—it's definitely helpful, but it's really reacting to a problem instead of preventing it. If the church and its families started shaping positive ideas about singleness and presenting it from childhood for what it is—an equal way to love and serve God—we would avoid many of the problems we create by elevating marriage.

Obviously, many kids grow up expecting marriage and family because it's the kind of life they know. Every child is familiar with some concept of family because they are part of one. They *exist* because two people at least had a married-like relationship. The idea of singleness, and especially never-married singleness, is generally foreign to them.

I realize that parents who teach the truth about singleness to their children take a risk—and many parents aren't willing to take it. If their children choose singleness, grandparenting opportunities diminish. But which risk is greater—potentially giving up grandchildren or perpetuating an unhealthy, unbiblical position for singles in the Family of God? And what if their children "end up" single anyway? I guarantee the children will experience guilt for dashing those grandparenting dreams.*

So how do parents instill the right ideas about singleness in their children? The most profound effects will come through exposure to and interaction with godly singles who enjoy wholehearted, purposeful lives. I have spent many hours in the homes of my married friends, and one of the highest compliments I've ever received came from a friend who wished his adolescent daughter could spend more time with me. He understood that her ideas about singleness could be shaped just by being with me. If a child only knows singles who mournfully move from one sad circumstance to another while they wait for marriage to come, who will blame them for thinking it's an awful way to live—it would be!

A Place for Relationships

We've already made the point that the Church is a community—the new community, bonded together in Christ forever. Much of what we do in church is about developing this community for all members of the Body. According to D. J. Burke, "The local church for every Christian should be God's repository of 'life support' systems. These systems consist of groups of other Christians who are both nourishing and realistic in their relationship to us; they are a family whom we can trust, with whom we can be honest, and to whom we can confess our sins and with whom we can be intimate without resorting to playing games."[7]

---

* Again, the beauty of God's Family design shines through. For those parents who never get to be grandparents—or for those people who never get to be parents—the church is full of children who can never get enough "family lovin'."

Building community requires more than putting a group of people together in a room—it requires intentional and committed effort. Most of the issues in this chapter are about creating an environment where singles can become integral parts of their church communities. This will only happen as we remove barriers that tell singles they don't belong and aren't valued.

For singles who have already developed solid friendships in their church families, many of these issues won't apply because when such relationships exist, singles *do* belong. Relationships make them belong. And when something happens in the church that causes them to feel alienated, they have the freedom to broach the subject because they are part of the Family. But when singles come into a new church where they haven't developed the needed "life-support systems," they won't risk trying to build relationships if the environment isn't safe and welcoming to them. They will either go somewhere else or stay halfheartedly—and the church will lose the unique contribution these single members could make to the body. Once, however, we remove the barriers, the church can help meet singles' need for community.

Building Bridges: From Old to New

Singles, especially never-married singles, are a demographic group on the move. Moving out of town, state, or even country is par for the single course. And while relocating carries the excitement of newness, leaving the old behind isn't necessarily easy. With every move, singles experience the death of relationships, the death of familiarity. Walter Wangerin describes this death:

> We are woven into communities, though we may be unconscious of the webbing that supports us—the shopkeepers, neighbors, church families—until we move to a new town. And then we become terribly conscious, because of the breaking. A thousand tiny *snaps!*
>
> Should anyone wonder, then, why even the happy move that one had planned for can cause such mortal grief? As if

someone had died. . . . Someone did die. You, at displacement. And the period of distress, the overwhelming sense of vulnerability and loneliness and even the heavy lethargy that follows, are natural after all.[8]

Singles suffer these deaths alone, adjusting by themselves to a thousand nuances of a new environment—not the least of which is a new church. Finding a church without a spouse and family to help ease the discomfort and pain of trying to fit in is a daunting task. The church can come alongside singles and walk with them through this difficult process by doing what my singles group called "bridging." When new people walked in our classroom door, we committed ourselves to help them find a place to belong—we wanted to "bridge" them from being painfully new to belonging. If I was the first to spot a new girl walking in, I immediately "adopted" her, assuming full responsibility for her initial experiences at church. Sometimes it meant not sitting by my friends so she wouldn't have to sit alone. Sometimes it meant inviting her to the service, to lunch afterward, or to an activity during the week—an activity I would attend in order to befriend her. For those initial days, weeks, or even months, I became her best friend at church, walking those first tenuous steps together. During that time I introduced her to as many people as possible, initiating conversations on her behalf and trying to bridge her to others who could be her friend.

A church full of people committed to this kind of ministry will have no problem making singles (and all other new people) feel welcomed. At the very least, it must happen within each adult Bible class, but, truthfully, many new people never make the trip from the sanctuary to the classroom. If we don't catch them in the larger group, we may not catch them at all.

> *We aren't looking for Bible studies or formal instruction sessions—we are looking for friends who will, perhaps without even realizing it, share their lives and their expertise with us.*

"But Wendy," you protest, "my friendship platter is already over-flowing. I can't spread myself any thinner by adding all these new best friends!" From personal experience, I don't think you have to worry too much. Of the dozens of people I tried to bridge, only one is really a "best friend" today. The goal of bridging is to move them from you to a place of belonging in the church.

"But Wendy," you protest again, "I'm really not very outgoing; I just don't think I could do this." I didn't think I could either—remember how I hide in the church kitchen to avoid small talk? The only thing that makes it easier is realizing that new people are often even more uncomfortable than I am. So I step out of my comfort zone to help them enter one of their own.

Building Bridges: From "Old" to Young

Several years ago, I sat on a panel for a ladies' event at my church. The topic for discussion was mentoring and discipleship, two millennial buzzwords. Speaking for the single women in the church, I told the group how my peers and I hunger to learn the "secrets" of living from older women. We aren't looking for Bible studies or formal instruction sessions—we are looking for friends who will, perhaps without even realizing it, share their lives and their expertise with us. Many of the skills that are second nature to the church's mature members are unknown to a younger generation. And while cross-generational relationship building is not a need that's unique to singles, it is definitely one area in which the church can communicate to singles that they are an integral part of the Family.

This dynamic between older and younger is crucial to passing on the faith, a task that requires more than transmitting a set of Scriptural facts. It requires living the faith. Fred Wevodau of the Navigators says of this process, "Many have never seen someone whose life demonstrates that Christianity is desirable, let alone doable. They're waiting for living examples of kingdom life that will call forth the best in them."[9]

> *For many singles, stepping inside the church doors means sacrificing an identity they enjoy outside the church. . . . singles often find that they are second-class citizens who don't fit into the mainstream of church life.*

It sounds good on paper, but how do we initiate and foster these relationships in the church? Gradually, say those who have done it. And with balance. Overhauling your entire ministry to make it all intergenerational is probably not a good idea. Pastor Ben Freudenburg says the church needs both age-specific and cross-generational ministries: "Age-specific ministries, like the traditional Sunday school, children's church, and adult Bible studies, are great for teaching the stories and concepts of the faith. Age-integrated ministries, however, teach us how to incorporate those truths into relationships. There needs to be a place for both."[10]

Sarah Snelling has been on the younger end of a couple of mentoring relationships, and her expectations affirm that what the younger generation needs most is not someone to adopt them as a project, but to love them as a friend. Be authentic with me, spend time with me, help me look in the mirror, keep my confidence, pray with me, offer me grace, encourage my spiritual growth.[11] These are the makings of friendship, and mentoring the singles in your church can be as simple as that.

Caught in the Middle

For many singles, stepping inside the church doors means sacrificing an identity they enjoy outside the church. In their careers, they likely stand on equal footing with all other employees and are valued for the significant contributions they make to an organization—marital status is inconsequential. In society singles even enjoy an elevated status, carrying a culturally granted license to pursue whatever their hearts desire simply because they don't have the limitations of marriage and family. But when they come to church, singles often find that they are second-class citizens who don't fit into the mainstream of church life.

What's a single to do? Culture says, "'Grab what you can get in your career, get your needs met, and enjoy life.' [And the church says], 'Love your spouse and raise your children wisely.' When those are the two messages, the Christian single is caught in between and so struggles alone, finding the silence deafening."[12]

If the church is going to love singles, it will have to expand its message to include the burgeoning number of Christians and not-yet-Christians who fall in this silent middle ground. This will happen as the church identifies ways it alienates singles, determines to change, and commits to nurturing friendships with singles. Singles will beat a path to the door of a church like this because they'll know it's home.

chapter eleven

Loving the Church

When my sister Suzy graduated from high school without plans to attend a Christian college, one of her teachers told her she wouldn't get married if she didn't go where the fish were. Ironically, two years later she "went where the fish were," spent four years there without catching one, returned home, and married someone who had been swimming in a local pond all along.

I've been where all the fish are for most of my life—Christian school, Christian college, good-sized church, Christian work environments, and seminary—but still, few bites and no catch. Several years ago some friends suggested I attend singles events at a larger fishpond down the road. I could have—it's been done successfully before. I don't have a problem with singles putting themselves in places where they can meet potential spouses, but I made the personal choice not to participate in other singles groups for several reasons, one of which was the fact that my schedule of church involvement was already quite full. Trying to fit another church's events into my life at that point was ridiculous unless I planned to add three more days to my week or eliminate some of my church responsibilities. Possible consequence? I'm still single. Definite consequence? My local church was on the receiving end of 100 percent of Wendy Widder. I loved that body of believers and did whatever I could to meet its needs.

The greatest needs of that church weren't swelling attendance rolls, better facilities, or more qualified staff members. Its needs were the same as they are for every church in every community around the world, regardless of size, location, or annual budget. From Singapore to Sandusky, the church needs its members to live the transformed life of the believer. It needs its members to take the truths of God's Word and the values of the kingdom and live them on two fronts—in the church and in the culture.

In a previous chapter we tried to make sense of singleness in the greater plan of God by asking what singleness brings to the church theologically. We determined that singleness completes the full-orbed picture of God's love by illustrating the inclusive nature of God's love—there's always room for one more—whereas marriage pictures the exclusive nature of God's love. We also highlighted how celibate singleness can help the church keep a proper perspective on the overriding purpose of sexuality—rather than merely driving us toward sexual activity, it is an aspect of God's image that provides a constant reminder that we are created to need Someone and "someones" outside ourselves.

Singleness *means* all these things, but what should Christian singles *do?* In this chapter, we will ask how singles can live in a way that meets the church's need to have transformed members living the message in the community and taking it to the culture.

Looking Inward: Kingdom Life in the Church Community

Living the values of the kingdom within the church community can happen as singles incorporate three practices. First, we must season our speech with grace, refusing to adopt language patterns of the culture around us. Second, we must commit ourselves to a local body of believers. And finally, we must serve with the best of who we are and what we have.

Special Seasoning

According to a 2002 survey by the research group Public Agenda, rudeness among Americans is getting worse. This is not a news flash to those of us who get ankle exercise driving in rush hour traffic, skim entire magazines in grocery store "express" lanes, or try to order hamburgers without onions and mustard during the lunch rush.

> *It is true that there's a misaligned focus on the family in the church, and it's true that singles have sometimes been treated as second-class citizens. However, we have not therefore been victimized and licensed to "speak the truth in love"—minus some of the truth and all of the love.*

However, it appears we not only have an abrasive edge, but we also have someone or something to blame for it. Those surveyed offered several explanations for the rudeness trend, including overcrowding in public places, increasingly busy lives, and the American icon who manages to appear everywhere—Elvis (a woman in Texas cited The King's pelvic gyrations as the first step down the slippery slope of shockingly rude behavior).[1] We justify our bad manners by assuming the role of victim: we've been abused by government, families, and even innocent bystanders. We are quick to notice—and advertise—the ways we've been "mistreated" and slow to admit our own shortcomings.

I am chagrined to find this habit in myself and saddened to see how much company I have in the church. Pew-bound preachers, the Sunday morning equivalent of the Sunday afternoon armchair quarterback, flourish in our churches. From a distance, they see everything wrong in the ministry and they know exactly how it ought to be different—but all they ever do about it is verbally lacerate the people who actually play.

Many singles fit the category of pew-bound preachers. It is true that there's a misaligned focus on the family in the church, and it's true that singles have sometimes been treated as second-class citizens. However, we have not therefore been victimized and licensed to "speak the truth in love"—minus some of the truth and all of the love.

Many singles in the Christian community have a militant edge that they wield against the greater Christian community at any opportunity. They talk more like the church is the enemy instead of the body, not realizing that instead of winning they are wounding. Cynicism and criticism only serve to mutilate the body to which they belong. We, singles and the church, are on the same team—the kingdom team. Our goal is, or ought to be, the same—extending the values of the kingdom in our reaches of the world.

I do not mean to underestimate the pain many singles have experienced at the hands of the church. Many have prayed, hoped, and worked for change, only to see none. But if we can't come up with up a different kind of response to offenses than the rude ones everybody else in the world uses, we have absorbed the attitude of a culture that says, "Me first! I'm the one with the rights here, and I expect to be treated accordingly."

I am not suggesting that offenses should be ignored, but Scripture is clear on how we deal with them (and nowhere does it include cynicism). We approach one another with love—*not* behaving rudely. We think no evil, keep no record of wrongs, always hope, trust, and persevere. We look for the good and accept our part of the bad. We build up, encourage, and look to make the other better. We recognize that every issue has two sides—and more often than not, neither is the "right" one.

Loving one another is a choice, a choice we demonstrate in the way we speak to and about each other. When I love someone, I take up my concerns with her face-to-face and work toward reconciliation. When I love someone, I speak well of him, even though he's given me cause not to. Love means granting the other person the dignity of the benefit of the doubt. When, as a single, I choose to love the church, it means I don't highlight its shortcomings, but instead I season my words and opinions with generous amounts of grace. I speak well of and defend the body for I am part of it.

Committed: Bumps, Satellites, or Faithful Members

When it comes to levels of involvement in the church, singles generally fall into one of three categories—they are bumps on the log, satellites in the city, or faithful in the ministry.

> *It's possible to be an active member—and even a leader—of a singles ministry, and still be a bump on the church log.*

Experts say the average church operates according to the "80–20 principle"—80 percent of the work is done by 20 percent of the people. The rest of the people can be classified as "bumps on the church log." I have no trouble believing this statistic if the car washes my singles group held are any indication of what happens in churchwide ministry. On a good day, twenty singles would show up at or around the designated time to help run a free car wash for the community. The day before the wash, however, one of us would restock the soap and rag supply, inspect the condition of the signs, and double-check the church calendar for a clear parking lot. An hour before the wash, two of us would set up the signs, round up the hoses, and ready the washing supplies. Then during the wash, a handful of us would actually wash cars. After the event, two or three of us (usually the same two or three) would reel in the hoses, take down the signs, launder the rags, and clean up water tracks in the building—while the majority of the group made plans to regroup for the evening. An evening activity after an afternoon car wash was always an incomprehensibility to me—all I ever wanted to do was take my aching, soggy self home to a warm shower, dry clothes, and a comfortable couch where I would watch something like golf until I dropped off in an exhausted sleep. Am I just a party pooper? I can be—but being part of the twenty percent can make you, well, pooped.

Hopefully the church will create an environment where more than twenty percent of singles will feel welcomed to participate in the life of the church, but even then, it can't force them. Singles must also take initiative. For those who are part of a singles ministry—and perhaps even part of the twenty percent carrying the load of the singles ministry—you must be wise with your time. Are you so absorbed with your singles group, your extension of the larger body, that you don't know the rest of the body? It's possible to be an active member—and even a leader—of a singles ministry, and still be a bump on the church log.

Integration with the whole body must always be a priority. When the nursery sign-up sheets come around, sign up. When the maintenance crew hosts a workday, show up. When people are needed to build props for the Easter drama, arrange your schedule so you can help. Consider yourself first a member of the church, and then of the singles group.*

If your church doesn't have a singles group, much of the same applies. Sign up and show up. Ask yourself if you stopped attending next week, what gaps would be left in the ministry. If your only answer is that the back pew would have room for one more, then you are a bump on the church log. Take some initiative, as hard as it can be, to make yourself an active member of the Family.

> By refusing to "marry" one church, you miss the richness of a monogamous relationship that endures through better or worse, richer or poorer, in sickness and health.

Some singles, however, are too involved . . . in churches all over town. They scout the best activities offered by local churches and get in on as many of them as possible with as little commitment as possible. I call these people satellite singles because they revolve around several churches but never really become an integral part of one. They can also be appropriately labeled smorgasbord singles—they attend a Bible study with one church, play volleyball at another, participate in worship nights at another, join the missions trip at another, and go to Six Flags with still another. They heap their plates full of favorites and manage to avoid what they find distasteful.

Don't misunderstand me: there's nothing inherently wrong with taking advantage of opportunities offered by various churches and pursuing avenues that will introduce you to potential mates, but if it

---

* If your singles group is so large that it's a mini-congregation, I realize that getting to know the "rest" of the church is an overwhelming (and impossible) suggestion. In such a situation, let me challenge you to find ways that your singles group can get involved in larger church activities, making yourselves available to know and be known by more than just singles.

keeps you from being a fully committed member of *one* local body, then you have a problem. You may think you're getting the best of all worlds, but in reality you cheat yourself much like a philandering man cheats himself out of the enduring rewards of commitment. By refusing to "marry" one church, you miss the richness of a monogamous relationship that endures through better or worse, richer or poorer, in sickness and health.

The philandering man, however, doesn't only cheat himself. He hurts the women he woos by reaping the benefits of their bodies without really investing in their whole selves. By not committing to one local church, you cheat the churches you quasi-attend, taking advantage of their best without getting your hands dirty in the worst. You get the paycheck where you haven't done any work. And perhaps still worse, you cheat the church out of the best of *you*—your gifts, your time, your faithful service, and all the rewards that can result from a long-term relationship with *you*.

If singles are going to meet the church's needs, we must commit to a local body of believers where we can wholeheartedly invest ourselves, trading our bump or satellite status for unblinking loyalty and faithful service. D. J. Burke observes what happens when singles do this: "Singles who do participate in our church life and find a surrogate family in the church often form a core of the most loyal attenders, givers and servers within the framework of the congregation."[2] Singles love the church by committing ourselves to its survival—and "thrival."

Serve with Who and What We Are

Love lavishes. It is not doled out when things become desperate. It is not measured sparingly. Love gives the best of everything within its power to give. When I love the church, I give it the best of who I am and what I have, surrendering my abilities and gifts for its benefit and utilizing my resources and time to advance its cause. I recognize that everything I have is a gift from God, and I am just a steward.

Each of us brings a unique package of abilities and resources to the church. We are undeniably diverse people, a fact intended to work for the benefit of the body. When Paul declared our Christian unity in Galatians 3:28—"There is neither Jew nor Greek, there is neither slave nor free, there is neither male nor female; for you are all one in Christ Jesus."—he abolished divisions among us but had no intention of erasing the diversity that characterizes us. Robert Banks in his book about Paul's concept of community notes that the differences among us— such as rich and poor, married and single, male and female—"provide a springboard for *helpful service* within the community from which all may benefit."[3] Our distinctiveness creates openings for unique service to one another. Banks cites the New Testament examples of Gaius and Nympha who used their wealth to benefit the entire community by providing meeting places in their homes for the church (Rom. 16:23; Col. 4:15).

Like every other member of the church, singles have spiritual gifts that can benefit the body—gifts like teaching, serving, and administrating. These gifts should be put to use where the church needs them. However, single friends, don't expect the church to automatically recognize your giftedness. And don't wait for them to come to you. Volunteer in areas of particular interest to you, but be careful not to hastily dismiss needs that may not be of special interest to you. Love means pitching in where help is needed, whether or not it's your area of "giftedness."

In addition to these kinds of gifts, many singles also have resources unique to and even resulting from their singleness. Again, the circumstances and causes of singleness vary dramatically, but speaking strictly from my current life situation as a thirty-something single with no children, I have a certain freedom of time and money that eludes my close-in-age friends who are raising children. Before all my single friends jump down my throat for perpetuating the myth that singles have all the time and money in the world, let me clarify. Most of the singles I know are not sitting around waiting for mold to grow in their showers so they have something to do, and neither are they weighing the advantages of rearranging their stock portfolios—again. In fact, my single friends are the ones who are rarely home when I call looking for someone to do a "no-budget outing" with me.

> *When we are bound by schedules and finances,*
> *sometimes—as in my case—it has been by*
> *choice. And sometimes it's because we have*
> *voluntarily overcommitted ourselves or we've*
> *been unable to say no when asked to*
> *participate.*

I have more on my plate to do than I can feasibly accomplish, and I wonder if I'll ever be able to get ahead financially. But, ironically, in my situation these are both true *because* of my singleness. I made the choice to drop everything, quit two good jobs, and move out of state because I wanted to pursue a graduate degree that, frankly, was more related to my favorite hobby than to the career path I was on. My "free time" during this phase of my life is devoted to readin', writin', and research, while my "free money" is channeled into the business office of the fine institution I attend. At other times in my single life, my "free money" has bought me travel experiences, paid off a car loan, and allowed me to save some of the money that's now funding my educational goals. I realize this is not the case for all singles—and especially for single women. The majority of us never anticipated having to figure out a way to support ourselves by competing in the dog-eat-dog world—and we never wanted to. It isn't by "choice" that many singles work long hours and obtain higher degrees; it's required to survive.

For some singles, however, it is true that we are freer than we want to admit. When we are bound by schedules and finances, sometimes—as in my case—it has been by choice. And sometimes it's because we have voluntarily overcommitted ourselves or we've been unable to say no when asked to participate.*

---

* Life circumstances change, and as singles and their married friends grow older, it seems the tables turn in this regard. Singles are still putting in their nine-to-five workdays (at least—and more when married coworkers take advantage of the "free time" of singles), while many married friends are acquiring the freedoms of empty nesting. In the midst of full days, many singles are also called upon to care for aging parents, a burden that is immensely heavy to carry alone. The point of my illustrations is not to make universal statements about the resources that accompany the single life, but rather to highlight the principle of stewardship and issue a call for singles to make a serious assessment of how they are stewarding whatever resources God has given them.

As for money, singles without children have a one-to-one ratio of people making and costing money in their households. In a home with children, one or two people make the money to cover the costs of living for the entire household. Children are expensive. The lower end of statistics indicates that rearing a child to the age of eighteen can cost $120,000.[4] One hundred twenty thousand dollars in my budget over a lifetime will buy a lot of things my married friends will have to forego.

Single friends with no kids, the reality for some of us at certain phases of our career paths is that our lives are less encumbered. If and when we find this to be the case in our lives, we bring a unique resource to the ministry of the local church. How does the church benefit because I can have more flexibility in my schedule? How is the ministry enhanced because I have more discretionary income? How are the marriages of my friends in the church strengthened because of my gifts? The answers to these questions will be as unique as we are— joining missions trips, counseling at camp, running special errands, taking the late shift for the cleaning crew.[*5]

For many, such "freedom" is a great gift that we know how to lavish on ourselves, but I challenge you as I challenge myself—our churches need us to love them with the best of who we are and what we have.[**]

Remember the Christmas Eve service I attended alone? By anyone's standards, it should have qualified as a dreadful event for me. I had

---

* I am indebted to my longtime friend, Julie Sanders, for sharing several ways singles in the church have loved the church by supporting her marriage and family. We've compiled a list of ideas that are included at length in the endnotes for this chapter because Julie's insights as a married friend, pastor's wife, and missionary add great breadth to this issue.

** The whole area of finances provides a beautiful illustration of the opportunity to serve each other in love. When the church loves singles, it removes barriers that communicate to them that they are not equally valued. I suggested in the previous chapter that the church avoid offering discounts for couples to attend special events. However, hopefully as singles learn to love the church, we will use our resources to meet needs within the body. Perhaps the best solution is sensitivity on both sides—the church removes the barriers that alienate singles (i.e., discounts for couples), and singles offer what they have to provide for the needs of the church (i.e., if possible, I pay my cost and then anonymously help pay for a couple that couldn't otherwise attend).

given up my seat twice, been insulted by a longtime member, and settled for a chair in the lobby. At the conclusion of the service, masses of people poured out of the sanctuary into a madhouse of family reunions. Without any family present, I could have easily slipped out the door unnoticed and gone home. No one would have blamed me.

Instead, on a night when my freedom from family constraints could have been cause for discouragement and even depression, I chose to love the church by giving the gift of that freedom. I chose to serve people with my singleness, beginning with the two seats I gave up for the benefit of two families. Later as the crowds exited the building, most of them in family groupings, I noticed that no one was standing at the door to thank people for coming and wish them a merry Christmas. They all had people to collect and parties to attend. I didn't, so I put on my coat and stationed myself at the frigid exterior doors where I offered people a warm smile, a handshake, and sincere appreciation for their presence before they went out into the wintry night.

> Christian singles who are fully-functioning members of the body of Christ are positioned to provide a clear picture of the alternative single life to a generation of singles who have feasted on a steady diet of "Friends," "Seinfeld," and "Sex and the City"—and still find life lacking.

I don't tell this story to extol my virtues. On another night, I might have left in tears—it's happened before. Somehow, though, on that particular evening, the enabling grace of God prompted me to joyfully serve the Family, to give what little I had to benefit the body. I had a gift to give, and while I still wish I'd been invited to sit with someone, love meant I didn't hold that against anyone. Love meant I still found a way to serve, even when I had an apparently good reason not to.

Showing love within the church community requires that singles offer the increasingly rare gift of gracious and supportive speech. It demands that they commit themselves to loving a local body of believers, giving the best of who they are to that church. Meeting the needs of the church, however, takes more than focusing *in* on a body of believers. The church accomplishes its mission and grows as its members also focus *out* on the culture, taking the transforming message of the kingdom to their unique corners in the culture.

Looking Outward: Living the Kingdom in the Culture

Christian singles who are fully-functioning members of the body of Christ are positioned to provide a clear picture of the alternative single life to a generation of singles who have feasted on a steady diet of "Friends," "Seinfeld," and "Sex and the City"—and still find life lacking. While it's true that most of us will marry at some point, the road we travel to get there is an important one. We can show our love for the church by demonstrating clearly to the singles culture outside the church what it means to follow Christ. In chapter 8, we looked at how Christian singles can live with a purpose outside ourselves, rather than merely getting all we can out of life. In the remainder of this chapter, then, we will venture into territory that dominates the singles landscape, both secular and Christian—male-female relationships. How do Christian singles approach the dating scene in a way that demonstrates values of the kingdom to a culture gone astray?

The Dating Game

When Joshua Harris wrote his best-selling book *I Kissed Dating Goodbye,* he started a maelstrom of controversy over the issue of dating among Christians. Harris's book is based on the idea that the modern dating system has little Christian about it, but instead provides a sugarcoated means for self-gratification while actually causing harm to brothers and sisters in the body of Christ. Verbal reviews of Harris's book in my circles ranged somewhere between enthusiastic support to suggestions that he was crazy.

> *"If I were relying strictly on the models of relationship-building I see in Scripture . . . I would either be waiting for God to create a wife for me out of my rib or expecting my parents to select for me a comely bride from among the other families in our subdivision."*—Rob Marus

Regardless of what you think of Harris's ideas, he was right to raise questions long ignored by Christians. What should relationships between unmarried men and women with potential interests beyond friendship look like? Is anything wrong with the way we do relationships now? If Christ's redemption includes all of life—and it does—it must include dating relationships, so how do we as agents of His redemption reclaim this area of singleness for His glory?

We have traditionally mimicked cultural patterns for male-female relationships without even blinking, but, as believers approaching any cultural issue, we ought to begin by asking what God has to say. When we've discovered what the Bible says about dating relationships, we can evaluate how the current situation aligns with His standard and determine what, if anything, has gone wrong. Finally, we can discern ways to redeem it.

Dating, Scriptural Style

So, what does the Bible say about dating relationships? Not much. In his critique of several books about dating from a supposedly biblical perspective, Rob Marus concluded that Scripture affirms no dating methods: "If I were relying strictly on the models of relationship-building I see in Scripture . . . I would either be waiting for God to create a wife for me out of my rib or expecting my parents to select for me a comely bride from among the other families in our subdivision."[6]

Does this mean the Bible teaches we shouldn't date? Does it mean we can date whomever and however we want? Why doesn't God answer questions like this more clearly? I had a seminary professor who was fond of saying that when Scripture doesn't have answers we aren't asking the right questions. (Actually, what he said is that we're asking dumb questions!) God has given us more than enough information about *all* relationships to establish some principles about dating, but, as is often the case with Scripture, the answers can only be found when we stop looking through our concordances and start looking at the whole Story.

People are prone to think the Bible is a book of rules, but they are wrong. From beginning to end, the Bible is a book about relationships. The Story begins with God making people with whom He could have a relationship, and who could enjoy among themselves the same kind of relationship God himself had been enjoying forever. When these created people rejected this divine plan in Genesis 3, God began His pursuit to reestablish a relationship with them (and us)—a pursuit that continues through Revelation 22.

> If God's goal was to reach as many people as possible with news about Jesus, He should have sent Him into a world more like the one we know.

The framework for His pursuit was the nation of Israel, a people He redeemed from slavery in Egypt and covenanted with to be their God. Along with this covenant came a detailed set of guidelines for their relationships with each other. On a rainy Saturday, make a pot of coffee and curl up with the Hebrew Torah, God's law for His chosen people. A careful read through these first five books of the Bible may take you all day and a couple pots of coffee (Leviticus isn't exactly Dr. Seuss), but you can't read it and not be struck by (at least) two things: God cared very much how His people approached their relationship with Him, and He cared very much how they treated each other.

It should come as no surprise that these two elements are integrally related—in fact, the second one is dependent on the first one. Pause in your reading when you get to Exodus 20, the Ten Commandments. Have you ever noticed how these famous commands are arranged? The first four are about our relationship with God, and the last six are about our relationships with others. The order is no mistake: without the first four, trying to keep the last six is an exercise in futility.

Two thousand years after Exodus 20, God once again made clear His desire for relationships when Jesus appeared on the scene. Have you ever wondered why Jesus didn't come in an era when information could travel around the globe in seconds via the Internet or satellite TV? Or when news could be printed and distributed with an ease scribes would have happily given both arms for? If God's goal was to reach as many people as possible with news about Jesus, He should have sent Him into a world more like the one we know. How much more quickly the message could have been spread!

> *Being in right relationships with people (dating or otherwise) is dependent on being in a right relationship with God.*

Instead, Jesus entered a time when news traveled by foot and books were copied one letter at a time. He entered a place more like West Virginia than Washington, D.C., and while He had the ability to amass large crowds with His miraculous deeds and His peculiar teaching, Jesus spent most of His time with a group of twelve men. It is obvious that Jesus valued relationships with people over mass promotion of His message—relationships with people who would have relationships with people who would have relationships with people all the way to you.

When asked by an astute student of Jewish law to prioritize God's commands (and the lawyer meant more than the ten we know), Jesus summarized the entire Torah in two commands: love God and love your neighbor. Again, notice the order. The entire Story hinges on relationships, first with God through Christ and then with others. Relationships are as integral to the working out of God's plan as wheels are to the driving of a car.

Thus, we can state our first biblical principle about relationships: *being in right relationships with people (dating or otherwise) is dependent on being in a right relationship with God.*

When we are in right relationship with God, everything else in life can be seen in its proper perspective. A perpetual recognition of my sinfulness and God's grace fits me with glasses through which I see others—I am not, as every marketer would have me believe, number one. I am one among billions. My worth as a human being is the same as that of the vagrant who digs through garbage dumps in every major world city. My value is equal to that of the Filipino farmer trapped in a fight for survival against nature and economics. I am inherently worth no more than a terrorist conspiring the demise of life as we know it.

> *Whatever you want men to do to you, do also to them, for this is the Law and the Prophets.*
> *(Matthew 7:12)*

When my relationship with God brings me to these uncomfortable thoughts regularly, I better understand the discomfort of those who first heard Jesus tell the story of the Good Samaritan. "Samaritan" to Jewish ears was synonymous with "scoundrel," and yet Jesus said the man was a neighbor and therefore should be loved in the way they loved themselves.

A glimpse of ourselves and of God compels us to meet the needs of others just as we would meet our own. (This kind of compulsion properly practiced would likely do away with the overabundance of canned peas at food drives. In their place would appear more bags of Oreos, sour cream and onion potato chips, and Coke.) Do we truly see others with the same value we ascribe to ourselves? If my own perspective is any indication of the rest of the world, I'd have to admit that often people are either in the way or serve as potential means to an end.

The second principle for relationships can be summarized the way Scripture says it, word for word: *"Whatever you want men to do to you, do also to them, for this is the Law and the Prophets"* (Matt. 7:12). We call this principle the Golden Rule, and even though we've all learned the words, it's impossible to practice unless we see one another with the same value we see ourselves.

> *Believers build up and edify one another in Christ*
> *that we may each become more like Him.*

While the second principle is a fundamental response we should have toward all humanity based on our shared physical life and mutual parentage in Adam, the third principle is a response we should have toward our brothers and sisters in Christ based on our shared life in the Spirit and our shared Father.

The author of Hebrews states our responsibilities to each other in the body of Christ: "Let us consider one another in order to stir up love and good works, not forsaking the assembling of ourselves together, as is the manner of some, but exhorting one another, and so much the more as you see the Day approaching" (10:24–25). As believers, it's not just a good idea to help each other grow in Christ; it's required. We are called and commissioned to help each other grow through gracious exhortation and loving encouragement. Where there is sin or error, we (after checking for planks in our own eyes) help our brothers or sisters remove the specks from their eyes. Where there is defeat or pain, we share the weight of discouragement and offer the gift of perspective. Where there is ignorance or confusion, we come alongside bearing truth. We care for the body by giving up our rights and desires to serve the best interests of the other members. The third principle, then, is this:

Believers build up and edify one another in Christ that we may each become more like Him.

Measuring the Modern Dating System

I don't need to describe the modern dating system for you—you've either experienced it or seen it on the screen. But perhaps you've never evaluated it by God's standard. Let's work briefly through each of the preceding relationship principles and see how dating measures up.

Being in right relationships with people is dependent on being in a right relationship with God. Single friend, if you have never transferred your allegiance to God in every area of life as the Gospel demands, then your relationships are straw houses waiting for a few huffs and puffs. Even if you manage to hold a relationship together, you will never enjoy the depths of genuine intimacy unless both you and the other person are rightly related to God.

> If you are thinking, "I'll take care of this marriage thing and then I'll get things right between me and God," you are only fooling yourself—and possibly your future spouse.

If you are entrusting your life and future to God, currently choosing to do things His way every day, then any notion of an intimate relationship with someone who doesn't share this commitment is ridiculous. It's logically impossible, regardless of what you think you have in common. You are in the kingdom of light; they are in the kingdom of darkness. You are spiritually alive; they are spiritually dead. You are free; they are enslaved. You can see; they are blind. You serve God; and no matter how nice they are, they serve Satan. What did you say you had in common?

Perhaps you made a decision to follow Christ at some point in your life, but your Bible has grown dusty, your attendance at church is optional, and your checkbook register hasn't seen the name of your church in eons. May I gently suggest that dating isn't for you until you get the most important relationship in your life back on track? If you are thinking, "I'll take care of this marriage thing and then I'll get things right between me and God," you are only fooling yourself—and possibly your future spouse.

"Wendy," you might be saying, "you're taking this whole dating thing a little too seriously. I just date for fun. I don't intend to marry the person—we just go out because it's something to do." Sometimes this is the case. Like you, I've had friends over the years that I've gone out with for fun (or because it stinks to go to weddings alone) and neither of us has been weighing the long-term possibilities of proposing or accepting marriage.

However, the principle of *doing unto others as we would have them do unto us* requires that we take even casual relationships more seriously. Sometimes we say, "I just date for fun," and assume that since we've given our disclaimer, we can plow ahead regardless of what the other person might be thinking. Dating "just for fun" can become a license to use other people for our pleasure. I suspect, although I can't statistically confirm it, that this license works primarily against women since we are the ones who are more likely ready and looking for a long-term relationship. To compound this problem, women are also experts at interpreting (or misinterpreting) men's behavior—and then we analyze it to death, often with other "experts," until we're nearly ready to schedule a wedding photographer.

> *Too many Christians approach dating with the same bottom line philosophy as their unredeemed friends: "What's in it for me?"*

Treating one another as we'd like to be treated requires that we examine our motives for dating. In chapter three we looked extensively at the effects of sin on relationships, and discovered that we want to pursue identity, acceptance, value, and intimacy in our relationships with people when only God can meet these needs for us. Expecting another person to provide what is lacking in our lives is mistreatment of that person—he or she can never measure up.

The Golden Rule also requires that we refuse to exploit the differences between the way men and women operate. Knowing that women are unable to divorce the physical and the verbal from the emotional ought to dictate what men say and what they do with their hands on a date. Knowing that men are aroused by sight ought to dictate what a woman wears on a date (and anywhere else for that matter). Treating each other the way we want to be treated demands that we respect and protect the unique features of each other.

Believers build up and edify one another in Christ that we may each become more like Him. Too many Christians approach dating with the same bottom line philosophy as their unredeemed friends: "What's in it for me?" Dating that isn't built on biblical relationship principles can be a dangerous crucible for rejection. Dating allows—nay, encourages—us to test people, judging their success or failure as a date and evaluating whether there is possibility for any future personal benefit. If they fail this unofficial test, we reject them (unofficially, of course, but everyone knows what happened when the phone doesn't ring again) and move on to greener pastures. If we are not careful, we end up playing the field and leaving it scattered with discarded, wounded people.

How Can We Fix It? Asking the Better Question

Dating "Christianly" doesn't mean avoiding questions related to personal satisfaction. For example, it's important to ask, Do I enjoy this person's company enough to be in it until death do us part? and Can I live with that annoying habit every day for the rest of my life?

"What's in it for me?" has its place even in a Christian dating relationship, but the more important question to ask about a potential relationship is, "What's in it for God?" Do we share each other's goals to the extent that the kingdom of God will march farther faster because we are together and not apart?

You may wrinkle your nose at this approach and think me the most unromantic person you've ever read on the subject (and be quite sure you have the answer to the oft-asked question, "So, why isn't Wendy married?"), but the truth is that a husband and wife will spend much more time struggling in the trenches against life than they will floating on cloud nine. Before we walk the aisle, we'd better be sure we're at least fighting for the same ground.

I've had friends ask me recently if I'm still interested in marriage, and my answer is still "yes," but it's a much more qualified "yes" than it was fifteen years ago. When I was a carefree (although I didn't know it then) college student, the field of potential spouses was much wider open than it is now. Since then, God has kept me enrolled in His school, giving me an education I neither knew I needed nor went looking for. This God-ordained education has honed my qualifications for kingdom work to the extent that I couldn't marry someone I may have been able to marry then. It would be poor stewardship of what God has spent fifteen years developing. We each receive a different education in God's school, but the question "What's in it for God?" runs across the curriculum. It must be the question that dominates our desire for relationships.

And even then, rejection will happen. God-fearing couples in pursuit of the same goals break up. Dating "Christianly" does not eliminate the pain that's worse, as a friend of mine says, than getting your arm ripped off. Rejection is an unavoidable aspect of two people trying to figure out if they better serve the kingdom as two or one. But if we are more attuned to why we date, it is likely we will date fewer people—lessening the number of rejections that occur. And if we carefully follow God's principles for relationships, we will all be better equipped to wrestle through the pain rejection brings—and we'll find ourselves in a network of people who can walk the dark miles with us. Our responsibility to members of the body requires that we do more than go out with people for our own enjoyment. It requires that we are continually asking, "How can I help this person become what God intended? If I say or do such-and-such, will it help or hurt them?"

How Can We Fix It? Raising the Bar

It appears that the way many Christian singles approach dating is virtually indistinguishable from the way unbelieving singles do. Knowing what principles God has established for relationships, how then can Christian singles redeem the dating game?

The fastest way for Christian singles to get away from "what's in it for me" relationships that our culture promotes is to raise the sexual bar a lot higher, in both dating relationships and entertainment choices.

> *Calculating how much we can get from each other before we've gone "too far" is like figuring out how to cross the piranha infested Amazon River on lily pads when a boat is waiting.*

Who decided that holding hands and kissing is normal for two people who barely know each other? Is my body really a gift I'm entitled to give for the sensual pleasure of someone other than my husband? We have fallen prey to the cultural notion that dating should include an active and growing physical relationship—it's the "spark" that keeps the flame going. Frankly, for a majority of couples that flame turns into a raging fire that burns them before they reach their wedding day.

Who are we fooling? We slowly remove barricades and think when the dam breaks, we'll be able to hold it back. We ask questions like "How far is too far?" which in my professor's words is a dumb question. If you must answer the question, I suppose the best answer is that it depends on where you want to go. Scripture has established the standard for relationships, and calculating how much we can get from each other before we've gone "too far" is like figuring out how to cross the piranha infested Amazon River on lily pads when a boat is waiting. If we align our desires with God's, treat others as we want to be treated, and concentrate on building up siblings in Christ, this problem will never enter our experience.

> *We play with sin (at least in our minds, which according to Jesus is no different than actually doing it) and call it fun—or worse, normal.*

My personal (and unpopular) opinion based on these relationship principles is that any physical affection that's inappropriate between me and my biological brother is also inappropriate between me and a brother-in-Christ to whom I've made no commitment. I am not interested in establishing legalistic guidelines, but I am very concerned about stewarding the gifts of my emotional wholeness and sexual purity. Sexual desires awakened prematurely—that is, before God says they can be satisfied in marriage—don't go back to sleep.

This kind of perspective removes, or at least relaxes, the tension of physical expectations that generally accompanies male-female relationships. It allows Christian singles to relate to people as friends and fellow human beings, not just as males or females, and it serves as a powerful witness to a sex-obsessed culture that we are more than just sex objects.

If I haven't stepped on your toes yet, you might want to tuck them in now. As Christian singles we also do ourselves no favors in the redemptive fight against sexual obsession when we drink it in through movies and television. Instead of just trying to combat it in the "real world" of relationships, we invite sexual obsession into our "virtual world" when it becomes our means of entertainment. We play with sin (at least in our minds, which according to Jesus is no different than actually doing it) and call it fun—or worse, normal. As singles committed to celibacy, this form of entertainment is like taking a starving man through a buffet line and then grabbing his plate just before he can eat.

Watching television and going to movie theaters are not sins, but they are mental battlegrounds between the opposing values of the kingdom and the values of the world. Yet often we mindlessly absorb whatever Hollywood hit comes our way. When was the last time you turned off the television or left the theater because you chose to fight the battle for your mind?

When the dating and entertainment practices of Christian singles are dictated by the values of the kingdom, they will glow in the darkness of cultural corruption, shining in corners of the world currently without the Light.

Conclusion

If singles are genuine followers of Christ, we have no choice but to love the church. It is not optional according to Scripture. Instead, the Bible is clear that it is impossible to have a personal relationship with Jesus, the Head, and not also be an active part of His body, the Church.

Because of our singleness, we have unique opportunities to demonstrate love by meeting the needs of the church—its needs to have all members living the values of the kingdom both inward to the community of believers and outward to the culture. The question Christian singles must answer (if not for themselves now, then certainly before God on a future day) is not *will* we love the church, but *how* will we love the church.

stage five

UNTIL DEATH DO US PART

I'd been dreaming about my wedding since I was a little girl, but for the first time in my life, I could see the groom's face clearly. The winsome smile and dancing eyes of Alex filled my future, and I could hardly believe that so much of what I'd longed for finally seemed to be coming true. Alex was more than I had hoped for in a husband, and I was thrilled with the prospect of joining my life with his in a perfect partnership.

We had known from its surprise beginning that if our re-lationship was to make it, we had some miles to travel, some storms to weather, and some obstacles to overcome. At times the distance, dark clouds, and roadblocks seemed overwhelm-ing, but traveling it together was reward enough to make us keep going.

Until the following summer. Alex had just made a major life decision that would take him out of town indefinitely, and we had lots of things to work through before he left. I wasn't stupid—the years ahead would be incredibly difficult. But I knew we could make it. We were, after all, a perfect match.

I had gained such depth of conviction from Alex. In all our problem solving to that point, he had been the solid rock, more certain of our relationship than nearly anything else. The uncertainties and timidity I had wrestled with during the previous year were long gone, chased away by his boyish confidence and repeated assurances. Regardless of the obstacles that had always been in our way and the immense odds that had always been stacked against us, Alex was like a buoy on stormy waters, never losing his sense of who we were and where we were headed. Until this night.

As we talked, I knew Alex was keeping something back. The dread slowly rose in my heart as I probed for the missing information, and I fought to keep it from overwhelming me. When Alex's uncertainties finally surfaced, I lost the battle and despair washed over me in waves. How could he *be uncertain? He had always been sure.*

With our relationship writhing between us, I managed to give him my words of affirmation. I suppose I hoped that my confidence and commitment would magically go back to where it had come from in the first place. No matter what lay ahead—and it was certain to be demanding—I was committed. I was absolutely prepared to hunker down and see it through the distance and the time. But—only if he still wanted to.

The Alex I knew would have jumped right in and wholeheartedly said to count him in; he was there, no matter what. Instead, an Alex I didn't know paused. Silence. The silence of a stranger, a person that from that moment I could never again be sure I knew. His silence was a fist that leveled a solid blow at my stomach, knocking the hope out of me. When he finally started to talk, trying to put his knife-like words in the least painful arrangement possible, it was already too late. The horror of his silence had turned a year of sweet memories into cackling ghouls that would haunt my every waking moment for months to come.

As he labored painstakingly through feelings he'd carefully hidden for weeks, my mind shut him out and my heart groped in a thousand directions reaching for an explanation that would make sense of the silence. But there was none.

During the long days ahead, I asked myself over and over how this could have happened. How does a perfect match get unmatched? If we had been so right for each other, what could have gone so wrong? Somewhere between fits of anger and floods of tears, I began to understand that perfection isn't just the way things are. Perfection is what things become when we devote ourselves to accomplishing a goal. Olympic champions and virtuoso musicians aren't born that way. They achieve perfection after days, months, and years of discipline, practice, and commitment. Relationships work in much the same way. Alex and I may have had the makings of a perfect match, but actually becoming one would have required discipline, practice, and commitment—every day until death parted us.

Years later I can look back on this relationship and be glad it didn't work, although I still believe it could have. The fact that it didn't reminds me that relationships are fragile treasures, always subject to the commitment and sacrifice of those involved. These treasures are works in progress, and only those who make continual choices to love will reap the rewards of a truly perfect match.

chapter twelve

Going the Distance

Sometimes I believe the thesis of this book, and sometimes I'm not so sure I do. As I've worked through the process of studying, thinking, and writing, I've talked to myself a lot about this uncertainty, and at times I've thought I might be going crazy for some of my Tevye-like "Unheard of! Absurd!" conclusions. On one end of the conversational spectrum, I wonder if I've made this all up just because I need to feel better about being single. Perhaps I'm just trying to convince myself that my unmarried life is okay, and the more people I can get to believe me, the better it will be.

On the other end of my thoughts is the confidence that God's Word stands behind me on this issue. It *is* okay to be single—more than okay, in fact—and I'm not just trying to create some sort of coping technique to deal with the "disaster" of singleness.

Scattered between these two perspectives are uncertainties about whether anyone else will be convinced. Maybe I've got this whole thing wrong and the majority's opinion that marriage is better is the right one after all.

One evening when I had someone beside myself to talk to, I shared these disconcerting thoughts with an astute friend. I told him that sometimes I feel like a hypocrite because I'm writing about the value of singleness, but given the right opportunity I'd leave it all behind. Not only do I have a God-given desire to be someone's helpmate, but quite honestly, sometimes the marriage grass looks greener than what I'm standing on. The pull of the majority is powerful.

Kelly shook his head in disagreement and surprised me with his response. "Wen, that's really an advantage to what you're trying to say." Puzzled, and thinking perhaps I had company in my craziness, I asked him to explain. "The fact that you know what Scripture says (singleness is absolutely okay) and the fact that you are still so swayed by your own cultural conditioning (marriage is better) makes the point perfectly. That's exactly the problem. The church says it knows what the Bible says, but generally it still operates under cultural norms. You grew up with the Bible *and* cultural expectations, and the result is great tension in what you know, what you want, and what you do. You are trying to honestly sort it out and help others see it too. That's not hypocritical."*

I either need more friends like this or I need to spend more time with Kelly. Maybe next time we talk, he can explain to me how having a really messy bedroom is an advantage. Or how having a perilously low bank account or an aversion to exercise could be advantageous. If he does, I'm not sure I'll believe him, but when it comes to singleness and the church, I think he's right. My struggle to understand and value singleness according to what the Bible says is only a small-scale picture of what's happening in the evangelical community—or what needs to happen.

I hope by now you are at least convinced that we have some rethinking to do as a Christian community. With the best of intentions, we have focused so intently on marriage and the family—against the very real cultural demise of the family—that we have elevated it to an almost idolatrous level. And we have failed to understand the value and biblical role of singles in our midst.

At the same time, singles also have some rethinking to do. We have bought into the cultural lie that screams it's all about us, and we bring this attitude to the church where we are unceasingly disappointed. Perhaps unawares, we have become nearly indistinguish-

---

* Neither Kelly nor I were denying the fact that wanting to be married is a perfectly natural human desire. It's the way God originally intended things to be, and this alone is a valid reason for wanting to be married. We were, instead, processing our views of the *value* of marriage as compared with the *value* of singleness based on cultural—and Christian—assumptions.

able from our cultural counterparts, fulfilling our desires in much the same way they do.

We, singles and the church, have misunderstood and mistreated one another. And biblically, we have both been wrong. The Church is the Family where all believers belong, whether or not they have a spouse. It is the place where every believer ought to be a fully engaged member.

As I suggested in the Introduction, this is not something singles can fix, and it's not something the church can fix. It's something *we* must fix. Everyone who is part of the Family of God is part of the solution.

> *The perfect match between singles and the church will only be the product of a love that bears all things, believes all things, hopes all things, endures all things—every day until death parts us or Jesus comes.*

It is my sincere prayer that singles and church leaders will start the groundswell of God-fearing people who've caught the vision for what we, the Church of Jesus Christ, can—and must—become together for the glory of God. If this book can be a tool for you to share the truth with others in your churches, it will have accomplished its goal.

It is also my earnest desire that the increasingly visible demographic group of Christian singles will commit to living the values of the kingdom with renewed fervor, becoming a powerful witness to the wholeness found in Christ, the genuine community in the Church, and the transforming nature of God's grace.

Singles and the church have the makings of a perfect match, but perfect matches don't just happen. They develop over time as both sides commit to love the other with a willingness to forgive past offenses, weather future hurts, and remain unflinchingly faithful. The perfect match between singles and the church will only be the product of a love that bears all things, believes all things, hopes all things, endures all things—every day until death parts us or Jesus comes.

Paul's View of Singleness in 1 Corinthians 7

Paul's views on marriage and singleness have received extensive attention throughout the history of the church. While these topics appear in 1 Corinthians 7, the passage was not written as Paul's treatise on sex, marriage, divorce, remarriage, celibacy, and singleness. He was responding to one church with particular questions and issues, and he tailored his answers accordingly. If chapter 7 answers modern marriage/singleness questions, it only does so "through the back door." Modern people tend to demand answers to questions that Paul himself was not answering.

Our primary concern here is singleness, so we will especially draw together the strands of Paul's thinking on the subject, keeping in mind the larger context in which those thoughts are found.

The Corinthian Context

The Church

Paul founded the Corinthian church during his second missionary journey. Some Jewish Christians were in the church, but the majority of converts in Corinth were Gentiles who lived immersed in an idolatrous culture. There is good evidence that Paul wrote 1 Corinthians while he was in Ephesus (ca. 54–55). In this letter, Paul is writing to people he has not seen for a few years, and some of them apparently think he is never coming back. From a physical and an emotional distance, he confronts serious problems and teaches basics that the community does not understand well.[1]

Paul's task is difficult. There is internal strife in the Corinthian church, but the primary conflict he must address is between the church and its founder—Paul himself.[2] The epistle contains two main sections. First, in 1:10 through 6:20, Paul responds to problems that have been reported to him. Second, in 7:1 through 16:12, he responds to questions contained in a letter from the Corinthians.[3] Romans 7 must be understand within its role as the opening of this second section. In this second section, each new response to a specific question is introduced by περὶ δὲ, which can be translated "Now concerning. . . ." This construction signals the start of new topics in 7:1, 25; 8:1; 12:1; and 16:1, 12.

Erroneous Beliefs Within the Church

The Corinthians' problems were rooted in their understanding of what it means to be "spiritual" (πνευματικός).[4] For some, an "overrealized eschatology" warped their thinking. The experience of ecstatic utterance or *glossolalia* may have prompted them to believe that their being had become like that of the angels. If they spoke "as the angels," then they would exist like the angels—apart from sexuality. These Corinthians believed that they had begun to live in their spiritual bodies and could now "slough off the [physical] body."[5] To be "spiritual" meant adopting a lifestyle of asceticism. Abstaining from sex within marriage, divorcing if such celibacy could not be maintained, and denying marriage to "virgins" made perfect sense within this lifestyle.[6]

In 1 Corinthians 7, the flow of Paul's argument must be considered against the backdrop of this heresy, in which asceticism was made a goal or even a requirement of Christian life.[7]

The Passage: 1 Corinthians 7:1–40

In this second primary section of the epistle that begins in chapter 7, Anthony Thiselton notes that the tone has changed from Paul's confrontation of incest, litigation, and immorality in general. Now "the key point . . . is Paul's pastoral sensitivity to grey areas of difficulty."[8] Gordon Fee notes, however, that this is not a "friendly exchange, in which the new believers in Corinth are asking spiritual advice of their mentor in the Lord, [but instead] they were taking exception to his position on point after point. In light of their own theology of spirit, with heavy emphasis on 'wisdom' and 'knowledge,' they have answered Paul with a kind of 'Why can't we?' attitude."[9]

Fee's three subdivisions of chapter 7 take seriously the περὶ δὲ constructions in the chapter. In this organization, Paul's thoughts can be divided: (1) to the married (introduced by περὶ δὲ; vv. 1–16); (2) the guiding principle (vv. 17–24); (3) about the "virgins" (introduced by περὶ δὲ; vv. 25–40). Since the second section is not introduced by περὶ δὲ, some scholars view these verses as a digression. Fee sees it as not only illustrative, but as integral to Paul's argument.[10]

Hinges of the Passage

The interpretation of Paul's thought in this chapter hinges on two key exegetical questions: "Who said it?" and "Who's who?" Addressing these issues at this point will make it easier later to handle the specifics of the passage.

Who Said It?

The first exegetical question arises five words into the passage with the statement "καλὸν ἀνθρώπῳ γυναικὸς μὴ ἅπτεσθαι"—usually translated "it is good for a man not to touch a woman," a euphemism for having sexual intercourse.[11]

The "notorious crux"[12] of this entire passage is whether Paul here makes a statement ("It is good. . . .") that he intends to modify and clarify or if he is repeating a slogan that had currency within the church of Corinth. Yet another possibility is that this is a form of question ("Is it good . . . ?"). Antoinette Clark Wire notes that the construction of 7:1 "suggests that Paul is not answering questions, but questioning answers."[13] In recent discussions of 1 Corinthians 7, a consensus has favored the interpretation that Paul wanted to modify a Corinthian slogan.

The question is not *whether* Paul preferred celibacy in the context of his culture. He makes that preference clear throughout the chapter (7:7–8, 33–35). The issue is the reason *why* he favored celibacy. He did not advocate sexual asceticism within the marriage relationship—as some Corinthians surely did—and neither did he view marriage as a lesser lifestyle.

The consensus that 7:1b quotes a Corinthian slogan is based upon the fact that the structure of 7:1b is similar to that where Paul definitely seems to be quoting other slogans in the Corinthian correspondence (8:1, 8, and perhaps vv. 5–6). Also, the content and the style of this passage is similar to that found in 8:1, 6.[14] In these other instances, the Corinthians "had chosen the superior . . . and more dangerous course of action. . . . The Corinthians' attitudes towards idol meat and marital intercourse are entirely consistent."[15] Careful comparison of 7:1 to 8:1, 8 does present compelling evidence that these are parallel points. Paul does seem to be repeating a Corinthian slogan. He proceeds to expound a nuanced analysis of its teaching.

Who's Who?

The second major exegetical issue that plagues the entire passage is "Who's who?" Paul uses a variety of terms to refer to groups of married and unmarried people (possibly different groups, but not necessarily). It is no small feat to properly identify and then avoid confusing these varied groups. Paul essentially has in mind forms of χήρα, ἄγαμος, and παρθένος.

Χήρα is used throughout the New Testament, and there is little dispute that it means "widow." Here it occurs in the plural (χήραις, "widows").

Ἄγαμος is used only in this chapter in the Greek New Testament, so its meaning is more obscure. Literally the word refers to those who are the opposite of the married (γάμος). It first appears in chapter 7 in the masculine/neuter plural in conjunction with the widows (v. 8). Traditionally this word has been understood to refer to all categories of people who are unmarried, and especially to those who have never been married. This would mean that Paul uses a generic term and then adds the special category of widows. However, Fee doubts that "unmarried" can be equated with "virgins"—the never-married—here (see below). In verse 2, Paul already has advised the unmarried to get married, so Fee wonders why he would repeat the counsel here and in verses 25 to 38.[16]

W. F. Orr points out that ἀγάμοις in verse 8 is masculine while χήραις is feminine. A pattern of balanced pairs prevails throughout this section. He further notes (from Liddell and Scott's *Greek-English Lexicon*) that ἄγαμος is the word generally used in Greek for a widower.[17] Being a widow in antiquity created special problems for women, so most cultures had a specific word to identify widowed women. However, these cultures did not necessarily have a word for widowers.[18] While Greek does have a word for widowers, "it appears seldom to have been used, and never in the *koine* period, in which ἄγαμος served in its place."[19]

That Paul takes up the question of those not-yet-married later in verse 25 makes a plausible case that he refers to "widower" and "widow" in verses 8 and 9.[20] Because Paul balances his references to husbands and wives throughout the chapter, doing so in this context is most natural.[21] Additionally, in verse 11 the word refers to a woman separated from her husband, and in verse 34 it is a term of contrast to those never married. These usages indicate that Paul employed ἄγαμος to refer to "demarried" people—those who had once been married but no longer had a spouse.[22]

Παρθένος is equated with virginity in the lexical authority *BDAG*, while the Louw and Nida lexicon relates the term to anyone who is unmarried. Paul himself uses the word only in his Corinthian correspondence, in 1 Corinthians 7 and 2 Corinthians 11:2. In chapter 7, it first appears after the second περὶ δὲ construction (v. 25). Thiselton summarizes the perspective on παρθένων:

[virgins] accurately renders παρθένων. But while *virgins* may

not jar in 1611 or 1881 (AV/KJV and RV) the word today belongs usually to medical discourse or to sexual discourse with
prior value-judgments. Yet REB's *the unmarried* does not (as
it needs to do) exclude widowed and separated partners, whom
Paul addresses elsewhere in this chapter. We dissent from
Moffatt's overnarrow *unmarried women*. Either *those who have
not married* or **those who have not yet married** seems best
for modern English and public reading. The former matches
the Greek more closely, but the latter reflects the Greek-in-
context more clearly.[23]

Since virgins are mentioned three times in the latter section (vv.
25–40), whatever group is in view with the word, Fee believes that it
must be the same group throughout this passage since Paul uses it
without qualifying distinction.[24] Citing similarities in structure between the two περὶ δὲ sections, Fee chooses to identify the "virgins" as
those—men or women—who are betrothed to be married and are
uncertain whether they should proceed, given the Corinthian teaching quoted in verse 1 that "it is good to be unmarried."[25]

It is also possible, although unlikely, that Paul could have been referring to couples in a "spiritual marriage," men and women who lived together but did not engage in sexual activity. While this practice was most
prevalent from the second to the fifth centuries, it is at least plausible that
the ascetically minded Corinthians practiced spiritual marriages as well.[26]

Verses 36 through 38 throw another difficulty into the interpretation, prompting the King James and New American Standard transla-
tions to identify the παρθένον as virgin daughters, an interpretation
largely bypassed by scholars today.

Section-by-Section Analysis

7:1–16—To the Married

Verses 1 through 7 address those who were married and had been
driven by an ascetic ideal to deprive one another of sexual relations.

In verse 7, while Paul does affirm the good of celibacy and his preference for it under certain conditions, he does not recommend that
married people live celibate lives. They may refrain from intercourse
only for a short time for the purpose of prayer (v. 5). The demonstra-
tive του"το that begins verse 6 does not refer to marriage, but to temporary abstinence.[27] This celibacy is a "concession" mutually agreed
upon by husband and wife (v. 6).

Because of immorality (v. 2)—possibly the scandalous activity of
chapter 6 where married Christian men were going to temple prostitutes because their spouses were ascetically minded[28]—married partners should give each other full conjugal rights: each man should have
(ἐχέτω) his own wife, and each wife should have (ἐχέτω) her own
husband (v. 2). This comprises an idiom that usually means "to 'have
sexually' (Exod. 2:1; Deut. 28:30; Isa. 13:16) or simply to be married
or to be in continuing sexual relations with a man or woman (see esp.
5:1 and 7:29; cf. Mark 6:18; John 4:18)."[29] Paul is not saying that everyone should marry because of rampant immorality, but rather that
those who are married should "have" their spouse in sexual terms.
Paul refutes the Corinthians' ascetic slogan in reference to married
people.

Verse 7 summarizes Paul's comments in the preceding verses. Celibacy is not for those who are married; it is for those with the χάρισμα
to live a celibate life.[30] In his context, Paul wishes all could be as he is
(celibate), but he refuses to place either celibacy or marriage on a higher
spiritual plane as the Corinthians did. This gracious enabling for celibacy does "not refer to singleness as such (after all, many who are
'celibate' in this sense wish they were otherwise), but to that singular
gift of freedom from the desire or need of sexual fulfillment that made
it possible for [one] to live without marriage in the first place."[31] Paul
will later address those who may not necessarily have this particular
χάρισμα but would do well to choose celibacy for other reasons (vv.
25–38).

Paul shifts topics slightly in verses 8 and 9 to address the ἄγαμοις
("widowers"—see above) and the widows. Yet both the placement and
content of verses 8 and 9 are troublesome. Its position in the text is

unclear, and its message seems to be that "marriage is a grudging condescension to those who burn with sexual passion and cannot be continent."[32] Although these verses begin a new paragraph in the Greek New Testament, their content seems more directly related to Paul's comment about celibacy in verse 7 than to his comments about divorce that begin in verse 10.[33] However, Fee notes that the parallel construction of verses 8, 10, and 12—a connective δὲ ("now") with a first-person singular verb of speech or command and the audience addressed in the dative—"suggests that Paul is taking up a series of situations to which he will apply the general rule, 'Stay as you are.'"[34]

In traditional thought, "Paul ranks marriage as little more than a remedy for a strong sex drive which cannot be controlled."[35] This position is primarily based on the phrase translated "but if they cannot exercise self-control. . . ." Michael Barré, however, says this translation is unwarranted and misleading because of the absence of a verb such as δύνασθαι or ἰσχύειν to imply an ability or inability to control oneself. Furthermore, the verb ἐγκρατεύεσθαι does not mean "to have the *gift* of continence." Rather, it "clearly refers to the practice of abstinence from something in itself morally neutral. . . . What is essential is that the athlete [I Cor. 9:25] *exercise* self-restraint in all things; whether he has a natural disposition or 'gift' for doing so is entirely beside the point."[36] Paul is not addressing those who are unable to control themselves, and he is not—contrary to the common view of the text—offering marriage as an alternative to lust for hormone-crazed youths. Instead, marriage is "the proper alternative for those who are already consumed by that desire and are sinning."[37]

In verses 10 through 16, Paul addresses the issue of divorce within Christian and mixed-faith marriages. Although the issue of singleness relates indirectly to this issue, divorce involves complex exegetical issues that we cannot delve into here.

7:17–24—The Guiding Principle

This section may appear to be a digression from Paul's flow of thought, but Fee contends that Paul here is driving home the central point of the entire chapter. Paul's message to the Corinthians is that singleness or sexual asceticism does not elevate spiritual status:

> Under the rubric, "It is good not to have relations with a woman," they were seeking to change their present status, apparently because as believers they saw this as conforming to the more spiritual existence they had already attained. Thus they saw one's status with regard to marriage/celibacy as having *religious* significance and sought change because of it. Under the theme of "call" Paul seeks to put their "spirituality" into a radically different perspective. They should remain in whatever social setting they were at the time of their call since God's call to be in Christ (cf. 1:9) transcends such settings as to make them essentially irrelevant. That is, the call *to* Christ has created such a change in one's essential relationship (with God) that one does not need to seek change in other relationships (with people). These latter are transformed and given new meaning by the former. Thus one is no better off in one condition than in the other.[38]

Paul's ultimate concern is not that they either retain or abandon their social status, but "that they *recognize* it as the proper one in which to live out God's call."[39] He wants them to stop trying to change their lives to gain some spiritual leverage, and instead live as God's called people. On one hand, Paul did not care whether the Corinthians were married, single, slave, free, circumcised, or uncircumcised. On the other hand, he did not care if the unmarried got married (exceptions aside) or the slave became free. It was all irrelevant, since one could live out a spiritual calling as a transformed person in any of these social categories. Social settings merely create backdrops for godly living. They do not define spirituality.

These illustrations are sandwiched between Paul's answers to issues about marriage, providing the controlling motif of his response: "'Do not seek a change in status.' This occurs in every subsection (vv. 2, 8, 10, 11, 12–16, 26–27, 37, 40) and is the singular theme of the paragraph that ties the two sections together (vv. 17–24)."[40]

7:25–40—About the "Virgins"

Paul has addressed Corinthians who are married, widowed, separated, considering separation, and in a mixed marriage of believer to unbeliever. Now he considers those who are "virgins." Given the nature of the entire chapter, it is logical to assume that the Corinthian slogan from verse 1 was used to place betrothed couples in a dilemma. If it was "more spiritual" for a husband and wife to practice celibacy, then should an engaged couple marry at all? Thus, Paul is speaking to a particular class of people—those who have set a course toward marriage and now are confronted with the ascetic ideal.

Interestingly, this portion of the passage is laced with qualifiers: "I think" (v. 36); "I am sparing you" (v. 28); "I wish" (v. 32); "I say this for your own good" (v. 35); "let him do as he wishes" (v. 36); "he shall do well" (v. 37). The imperatives that do appear "merely reiterate the stance of vv. 17–24, and as elsewhere are immediately qualified. Whatever else," notes Fee, "this is not your standard Paul."[41] While Paul's opinion is trustworthy, he is being careful not to bind the lives of his hearers with commands in the matter of deciding whether to marry. This would support the proposition that Paul believes marital status is essentially irrelevant for matters of spirituality. Paul is offering advice and direction through sticky gray areas.

Paul agrees with the Corinthians that it is good to remain single (vv. 26–27), but he qualifies this with the affirmation that it is also perfectly acceptable to marry. For practical reasons, singleness/celibacy is preferable in certain contexts, but he does not employ the χάρισμα language of verse 7. In view of the "present distress" (v. 26), he is trying to spare the Corinthians and help them remain free from the concerns/anxiety that accompany marriage (vv. 32–35). He urges celibacy/singleness for both pastoral and eschatological reasons. Eschatologically, the present world is passing away. Pastorally, caring for a spouse and family in distressful times increases the potential for suffering.[42]

Paul does not elaborate on what he means by the "present distress" (ἐνεστῶσαν ἀνάγκην). It might very well have involved multiple layers of meaning—something already present in the lives of Corinthian Christians and the unknown distresses of eschatological events to come.[43] Of immediate distresses, scholars suggest three ideas: First, Paul later mentions some who were weak, sick, and dying (11:30), indicating that some misfortune had befallen the community. Second, Paul could be referring to the end of the world. Third, a famine might have been wreaking havoc in Corinth.[44]

Whatever the immediate circumstances were that prompted Paul's concern to spare the Corinthians the added responsibilities of marriage, his pastoral empathy cannot be mistaken. He counsels the choice of singleness to alleviate the potential for greater distress.

In verses 36 through 38, Paul will restate from verses 25 through 28, that it is good for virgins to remain as they are, with the definite understanding that those who choose to marry commit no sin. Verses 29 through 35 provide further explanation for these parallel statements. Paul first gives attention to the "shortened time" (v. 29), and the passing nature of the earthly order. Ben Witherington notes that Paul does not say time is "short," but that it is "shortened," presumably by the Christ-event that is now past: "He does not speak of a future crisis, but rather of a present necessity. He does not say that the world will pass away, but that it is already doing so."[45] Everything that others are absorbed in, the Christians are free from since they look forward with an eternal perspective.

It is because "the Corinthians were very status-conscious people [that] Paul injects a dose of eschatology, which relativizes the importance of *all* social status."[46] Marriage belongs to the present scheme of things that is already on its way out. For that matter, asceticism also belongs to the order that is passing away. Paul returns to this theme that circumstances are irrelevant for the believer, who is called to live out God's calling in the midst of various circumstances.

Paul then turns to the idea of anxiety—μεριμνάω—in verses 32 through 34. Cognates of this word appear six times in three verses. He wants them to be ἀμερίμνους—free from concern, an infinitive/adjectival construction that has "to do with a state of being, not with 'cares' as such."[47] Paul wants all the Christians to be this way—married or unmarried. Since circumstances do not determine existence, believers do not have to be anxious about things in the passing order. Both married and unmarried have concerns, but the verb μέριμνα can be read "positively, meaning to 'care for' (12:25; Phil. 2:20),"[48] and William Isley notes that "it is better to see both states as divine vocations, taking μέριμνα positively all four times in this section."[49] Everyone who lives in this passing order has things to care for, but a married person has the added division of interests as he or she must attend to the needs of a spouse and family. The difference between marriage and singleness is not that one has cares and the other does not. The difference is that those who are married are "pulled in two directions"[50] as they care for the needs of a spouse.

In spite of his contextual preference for singleness, Paul cannot be more clear that marriage is an entirely acceptable option as well—in contradiction to the Corinthians' overblown asceticism. He "is urging on them a wholly different worldview. Because of the 'present distress' and 'shortened time,' the betrothed may wish to remain single; but being single or married in itself is not the crucial question. Either is all right, he has said and will say again; what is important is that in either situation one live 'as if not,' that is, without one's relationship to the world as the determining factor."[51]

Verse 35 serves as a transition statement, summarizing Paul's argument and setting the stage for his reiteration of what he began in verse 25. He intends his words for their benefit and to promote what is seemly. In verses 36 through 38, he returns to the problem facing betrothed couples and specifically speaks to possible "unseemliness" attached to their situation.

The appearance of the hapax legomena ὑπέρακμος in verse 36 has multiplied the difficulty of understanding this passage. The traditional interpretation has posited the scenario that Paul here speaks to a father who must determine what to do when his virgin daughter is mature enough to marry. Exegetical difficulties seem to favor a betrothed couple or a man and woman in a "spiritual marriage" (see above discussion of παρθένων) who really want to marry each other. Paul tells them that the choice is theirs.

Paul concludes his treatment of marriage in chapter 7 by returning to an affirmation of the permanence of marriage and his preference for singleness (vv. 39–40).

Conclusion

It is ironic that most modern Christians come to this passage from a perspective that is precisely the opposite of that in the Corinthian church. The Corinthians in question elevated celibacy/singleness above marriage for spiritual reasons, and Paul had to convince them that marriage was just as acceptable a choice. The prevailing Protestant perspective elevates marriage above celibacy/singleness. It is no wonder, then, that we read Paul's comments with confusion. A further element in the confusion is that Paul was writing in a very specific context, far removed from what we understand today. Those in Corinth (and others) who were single were, for the most part, alone by choice. In today's culture, most singles are alone more by providence than personal choice.

It seems that if we really took 1 Corinthians 7 seriously, we would have to work much harder to balance our view of the good of *marriage,* and we would understand that most of the questions we ask of the chapter are not neatly answered, if in fact they are addressed at all.[52]

Bibliography

Barré, Michael L. "To Marry or to Burn: πυροῦσθαι in 1 Cor 7:9." *Catholic Biblical Quarterly* 36 (1974): 193–202.

Brown, Colin, ed. *New International Dictionary of New Testament Theology.* 4 vols. Grand Rapids: Zondervan, 1975–1985.

Cartlidge, David R. "1 Corinthians 7 as a Foundation for a Christian Sex Ethic." *Journal of Religion* 55 (1975): 220–34.

Cha, Jung-Sik. "The Ascetic Virgins in 1 Corinthians 7:25–38." *Asia Journal of Theology* 12 (April 1998): 89–117.

Danker, Frederick W., ed. *A Greek-English Lexicon of the New Testament and Other Early Christian Literature.* 3d rev. ed. Chicago: University of Chicago Press, 2000.

Dawes, Gregory W. "'But If You Can Gain Your Freedom' (1 Corinthians 7:17–24)." *Catholic Biblical Quarterly* 52 (October 1990): 681–97.

Elliott, J. K. "Paul's Teaching on Marriage in 1 Corinthians: Some Problems Considered." *New Testament Studies* 19 (1972–73): 219–25.

Fee, Gordon D. "1 Corinthians 7:1 in the NIV." *Journal of the Evangelical Theological Society* 23 (December 1980): 307–14.

———. *The First Epistle to the Corinthians.* The New International Commentary on the New Testament. Grand Rapids: Eerdmans, 1987.

———. "Toward a Theology of 1 Corinthians." In *Pauline Theology, Volume 2: 1 & 2 Corinthians.* Edited by David M. Hay. Minneapolis: Fortress, 1993.

Furnish, Victor Paul. "Theology in 1 Corinthians." In *Pauline Theology, Volume 2: 1 & 2 Corinthians.* Edited by David M. Hay. Minneapolis: Fortress, 1993.

Garland, David E. "The Christian's Posture Toward Marriage and Celibacy: 1 Corinthians 7." *Review and Expositor* 80 (2001): 351–62.

Greenfield, Guy. "Paul and the Eschatological Marriage." *Southwestern Journal of Theology* 26, no. 1 (fall 1983): 32–48.

Hafemann, S. J. "Corinthians, Letters to the." In *Dictionary of Paul and His Letters.* Edited by Gerald F. Hawthorne, Ralph P. Martin, and Daniel G. Reed. Downers Grove, Ill.: InterVarsity, 1993.

Isley, William L. "A Spirituality for Missionaries." *Missiology* 27 (July 1999): 299–309.

Keener, C. S. "Marriage." In *Dictionary of New Testament Background.* Edited by Craig A. Evans and Stanley E. Porter. Downers Grove, Ill.: InterVarsity, 2000.

Kistemaker, Simon J. *Exposition to the First Epistle to the Corinthians.* New Testament Commentary. Grand Rapids: Baker, 1993.

Laney, J. Carl. "Paul and the Permanence of Marriage in 1 Corinthians 7." *Journal of the Evangelical Theological Society* 25 (September 1982): 283–94.

Laughery, G. J. "Paul: Anti-Marriage? Anti-sex? Ascetic? A Dialogue with 1 Corinthians 7:1–40." *Evangelical Quarterly* 69 (April 1997): 109–28.

Louw, Johannes P., and Eugene A. Nida. *Greek-English Lexicon of the New Testament: Based on Semantic Domains.* New York: United Bible Society, 1988, 1989.

MacDonald, Margaret Y. "Women Holy in Body and Spirit: The Social Setting of 1 Corinthians 7." *New Testament Studies* 36 (1990): 161–81.

Orr, W. F. "Paul's Treatment of Marriage in 1 Corinthians 7." *Pittsburgh Perspective* 8 (1967): 5–22.

Poirier, John C., and Joseph Frankovic. "Celibacy and Charism in 1 Cor 7:5–7." *Harvard Theological Review* 89 (January 1996): 1–18.

Thiselton, Anthony C. *The First Epistle to the Corinthians: A Commentary on the Greek Text.* The New International Greek Testament Commentary. Grand Rapids: Eerdmans, 2000.

von Allmen, Jean-Jacques. *Pauline Teaching on Marriage.* London: Faith, 1963.

Wimbush, Vincent L. *Paul: The Worldly Ascetic: Response to the World and Self-Understanding According to 1 Corinthians 7.* Macon: Mercer University Press, 1987.

Wire, Antoinette Clark. *The Corinthian Women Prophets: A Reconstruction Through Paul's Rhetoric.* Minneapolis: Fortress, 1990.

Witherington, Ben, III. *Conflict and Community in Corinth: A Socio-Rhetorical Commentary on 1 and 2 Corinthians.* Grand Rapids: Eerdmans, 1995.

Wright, D. F. "Sexuality, Sexual Ethics." In *Dictionary of Paul and His Letters.* Edited by Gerald F. Hawthorne, Ralph P. Martin, and Daniel G. Reed. Downers Grove, Ill.: InterVarsity, 1993.

Endnotes

Introduction

1. Martin Luther, *Commentary on 1 Corinthians 7*, vol. 28 of *Luther's Works*, ed. Hilton C. Oswald, trans. Edward Sittler (St. Louis: Concordia, 1973), 11.
2. Tim Stafford, *Sexual Chaos: Charting a Course Through Turbulent Times* (Downers Grove, Ill.: InterVarsity, 1989), 153. This quote does not reflect Tim Stafford's view; he is stating what he perceives the church's view to be.

Chapter 1: An Unlikely Pair

1. Margaret Feinberg, "A Singular Mission Field," *Christianity Today*, 6 June 2001, 33.
2. Rich Hurst (Director of Strategic Adult Ministry Resources for Cook Communications and a twenty-year vet of singles ministry) quoted in Margaret Feinberg, "A Singular Mission Field," *Christianity Today*, 6 June 2001, 33.
3. Mary Jo Weaver, "Single Blessedness," *Commonweal*, 26 October 1979, 588–91; quoted in Rodney Clapp, *Families at the Crossroads*, (Downers Grove, Ill.: InterVarsity, 1983), 12.
4. Rodney Clapp, *Families at the Crossroads*, 89.
5. Barna Research Online, "Church Demographics," 2000; http://www.barna.org/cgi-bin/PageCategory.asp?CategoryID=11.
6. Dennis Franck uses this expression in his article, "Single Adults: A Population Group Too Large to Ignore," *Enrichment Journal*, summer 2000 (http://enrichmentjournal.ag.org/enrichmentjournal/

200003/030_too_large.cfm). He defines single adults as "unmarried adults, eighteen years of age or older, who happen to be single by chance, change, or choice (whether theirs or someone else's). They fall into one or more of the following categories: never married; formerly married (divorced); widowed; single parent; separated (the separated person is legally married but living a single lifestyle)."

7. Shelton Smith, ed., "Questions Answered by Dr. Smith," *The Sword of the Lord,* 17 August 2001, 4.
8. Gilbert Bilezikian, "Why Single Adults Often Feel Excluded from the 'Church Team,'" *S.A.M. Journal,* January–February 1998, 10.

Chapter 3: Singles

1. Larry Crabb, *Connecting: A Radical New Vision* (Nashville: Word, 1997), 57.

Chapter 4: The Church

1. A restored relationship with God is possible when you understand and accept yourself:
   a. What's true about God: He is holy and cannot tolerate sin. He is just and must punish sin (Rom. 6:23).
   b. What's true about you: You are sinful and unable to do anything to gain God's favor (Isa. 64:6; Rom. 3:23; Titus 3:5).
   c. What's true about you and God: You are separated from God forever because of your sin. BUT . . . God loves His creation and has provided a way for people to have a relationship with Him. That way is Jesus.
   d. What's true about Jesus: Jesus lived a perfect life and took your sin on Himself in His death, satisfying the punishment that God required. He rose again and is alive in heaven today, providing the only way for people to have a restored relationship with God (Acts 4:12).

Just knowing and believing all these things to be true does not restore your relationship with God—even Satan believes. You must confess to God that you are a sinner and in need of the salvation His Son, Jesus, offers. You must give up trusting in your own goodness to save yourself and trust Him instead. This is what genuine faith in God is all about. When you do this, God makes you a new person (2 Cor. 5:17). He restores your relationship with Him and joins you to all other people who have believed in Him through the ages. You are part of the Church! Now you will want to live in a way that pleases Him.

Chapter 5: A Picture of Perfect Singleness

1. Rodney Clapp, *Families at the Crossroads* (Downers Grove, Ill.: InterVarsity, 1983), 70.
2. Rabbi Eleazar, in the Talmud, *Yebamoth* 63a; cited in Leon Morris, *The First Epistle of Paul to the Corinthians* (Downers Grove, Ill.: InterVarsity, 1958; reprint, Grand Rapids: Eerdmans, 1985), 104.
3. Raba and Rabbi Ishmael, Talmud, *Kiddushin* 29b; cited in Morris, *First Epistle of Paul to the Corinthians,* 104.
4. Albert Y. Hsu, *Singles at the Crossroads* (Downers Grove, Ill.: InterVarsity, 1997), 34.

Chapter 6: The Rest of the Story

1. David Ashton, "Did He Come to Start a Kingdom and Get Stuck with a Church Instead?" *Light and Life,* January–February 2002, 54.
2. Ibid., 55.
3. Rodney Clapp, *Families at the Crossroads* (Downers Grove, Ill.: InterVarsity, 1983), 80.
4. Ibid., 78.
5. Ibid., 68.
6. Ibid., 75–76.

Chapter 7: Making Sense of Church

1. Michelle Wirth Fellman, "Teens Clique for God," *Science and Spirit,* January–February 2002, 18.
2. Wayne A. Grudem, *The First Epistle General of Peter,* vol. 17 of

Tyndale New Testament Commentaries (Grand Rapids: Eerdmans, 1988), 99–100.

3. Bob Garfield, "Top 100 Advertising Campaigns of the Century," 2 April 2002; http://www.adage.com/century/campaigns.html.
4. Augustine, *City of God*, ed. Vernon J. Bourke, trans. Gerald G. Walsh et al. (New York: Image Books, 1958), 268.
5. John R. W. Stott, *The Cross of Christ* (Downers Grove, Ill.: InterVarsity, 1986) 255.

Chapter 8: Making Sense of Singleness

1. Tamala M. Edwards, "Flying Solo," *Time Magazine,* 28 August 2000, 47–48.
2. Ibid., 48.
3. Catherine Fitzpatrick, "Me First," *JSOnline/Milwaukee Journal Sentinel,* 5 November 2000; www.jsonline.com.
4. Albert Y. Hsu, "The Myth of Singleness," *Singles at the Crossroads* (Downers Grove, Ill.: InterVarsity, 1997), 48–62.
5. Ibid.
6. Guy Greenfield, "Paul and the Eschatological Marriage," *Southwestern Journal of Theology* 26 (fall 1983): 44.
7. I am indebted to the writings of Stanley Grenz, Roy Bell, and Tim Stafford for thoughts about how singleness demonstrates the inclusive nature of God's love.
8. Stanley Grenz and Roy Bell, *Betrayal of Trust: Sexual Misconduct in the Pastorate* (Downers Grove, Ill.: InterVarsity, 1995), 71.
9. Ibid., 65.
10. Augustine, *The Confessions* bk. 1; http://www.ccel.org/a/augustine/confessions/confessions_enchiridion.txt.

Chapter 9: Loves Me, Loves Me Not

1. John Ortberg, *Love Beyond Reason: Moving God's Love from Your Head to Your Heart* (Grand Rapids: Zondervan, 1998). Pandy's story is told in chapter 1, pages 11–26.
2. Ibid., 18.

3. Robert E. Webber, *Ancient-Future Faith: Rethinking Evangelicalism for a Postmodern World* (Grand Rapids: Baker, 1999), 80.
4. Larry Mercer, "What Does Caring Look Like?" *Moody,* January–February 2002, 18.
5. Mary Louise Schumacher, "The Mideast's Forgotten People," *Milwaukee Journal Sentinel,* 22 October 2000, 3 (L).

Chapter 10: Loving Singles
1. Diane Langberg, "Does Single Have to Mean Alone?" *Urban Mission,* December 1996, 9.
2. Lauren F. Winner, "Solitary Refinement," *Christianity Today,* 11 June 2001, 32.
3. Langberg, "Does Single Have to Mean Alone?" 8.
4. Camerin Courtney, "What Single Women Wish You Knew," *Today's Christian Woman,* May–June 2002, 50–51.
5. Langberg, "Does Single Have to Mean Alone?" 12.
6. Winner, "Solitary Refinement," 26.
7. D. J. Burke, "Singleness As a Christian Lifestyle, 1," *Review and Expositor* 74 (winter 1977): 78.
8. Walter Wangerin Jr., *Mourning into Dancing* (Grand Rapids: Zondervan, 1992), 91–92.
9. Fred Wevodau, "From Generation to Generation," *Discipleship Journal,* May–June 2002, 34.
10. Ben Freudenburg, quoted in "Connecting the Generations," by Drew Zahn, *Leadership,* spring 2002, 39.
11. Sarah Snelling, "When Starbucks Meets Sanka," *Discipleship Journal,* May–June 2002, 55–58.
12. Langberg, "Does Single Have to Mean Alone?" 12.

Chapter 11: Loving the Church
1. "Survey Finds Rudeness Is Getting Worse," CNN.com, 3 April 2002.
2. D. J. Burke, "Singleness As a Christian Lifestyle, 1," *Review and Expositor* 74 (winter 1977): 79.

3. Robert Banks, *Paul's Idea of Community: The Early House Churches in Their Historical Setting* (Grand Rapids: Eerdmans, 1980) 130.

4. MSN Money web site, 14 June 2003; http://moneycentral. msn.com/articles/family/kids/tlkidscost.asp.

5. The following ideas of how singles can love their married friends were compiled with the help of my longtime friend Julie Sanders. Julie's thoughts, while flowing out of a stage in her life when she is raising young children, are also based on numerous friendships she and her husband have with singles. Circumstances will vary for other married and single friends, but the principle is the same: What are *we* doing to encourage and build up our married friends in *their* unique circumstances? We want and need them to do the same for us, as chapter 10 discusses in a very practical way. Taken out of context, this list may appear to refute everything I've claimed in this book about the equality of marriage and singleness. Taken in context, however, it demonstrates some practical ideas for singles who want to serve the body of Christ with the best of who they are and what they have.

   a. *Baby-sit*—On several occasions, I have volunteered to baby-sit for the children of my married friends just to give them a break. It provides them a much-appreciated opportunity to have a real date together and it gives me the delightful chance to spend time with their kids—a privilege I don't take lightly. As families, they have welcomed me into their homes on so many occasions, and I have grown to know and love their children. Among other things, I believe my service is a means by which my married friends can give their relationships a boost, their kids can benefit from interaction with me (I hope!), and I am given a greater appreciation for what my friends' lives are like.

   b. *Flex with life's stages*—Julie and I were best friends in college, but life changed drastically after we graduated. We moved a significant distance apart. She got married and I am still single. Her life as a pastor's wife and mother of two young children kept her from being able to make the eight-hour trip to visit me, so I always traveled to visit her. I could have resented this, but I chose to value our friendship above the inconvenience. As we matured in our friendship, I realized how much it meant to Julie that I flexed for her, knowing her constraints and valuing her friendship more than the potential frustrations. When I did visit, our time together was squeezed in around the needs of toddlers and infants, and again, Julie appreciated that I understood her limitations during a frazzled phase of life.

c. *Make it to meaningful events*—When Julie and her husband were being commissioned for missionary service, I made the trip to be there. When another out-of-town married girlfriend turned thirty, I made arrangements with her husband and flew there to surprise her with a day trip—just the two of us. When another couple's baby girl was born, I made the trip to the hospital to share the earliest hours of joy. I certainly don't make it to everything, but I do want my married friends to know that when something significant is happening in their lives, it's significant to me too—just as I hope they will do for me. Sometimes being there means going alone, and like many of you, I don't always relish going solo. But I do it—because it's not about me. My presence is important to them—and to me because I've chosen to make myself part of their lives.

d. *Guard their marriage*—I have a single friend who had an affair with his best friend's wife. I'm sure there was enough blame to go around, but regardless of what the couple should have done to protect their marriage, I was angry with my friend for not doing *his* part as a single to protect the marriage of his friends.

It can be a delicate thing for singles to befriend both a husband and a wife. In the church context, if I have ministry interaction with a married person of the opposite sex and we become good friends, I make it my job to do what I can to cultivate a friendship with the friend's spouse. I want her to know I'm her friend—not a threat. If I'm talking with her husband about a subject that might exclude her for an extended period of time, I need to switch topics to draw her in. Some "singles humor" is off-limits in the company of married friends—I don't want to go anywhere near sexual references, innuendo, or otherwise flirtatious behavior when her husband is around. I can't control what happens within their marriage, but I can carefully guard what part I play in their relationship.

e. *Look for ways to help.* Julie shares this story: "When our family had been in the Philippines just a short time, but long enough to be overwhelmed and feeling the sudden isolation, the first person to contact us was a single missionary woman. She wanted to meet us ALL for lunch. She suggested a place and time, and we agreed. Though the location was crowded and noisy, and our son was 'challenging' as he encountered the foreign environment, she was flexible and easy going. She arrived with a bag of activities for the kids, small things that communicated that she had prepared for us, thought about us, and wanted to let us belong to her. Her personality and age and status may not have been a natural fit, but her extension of herself as another believer overcame us with her love to us. Her wise and appropriate extension of herself as a friend to all of us set a beautiful stage of freedom for us in our relationship. She had made it so comfortable, so encouraging, and such a blessing. Her freedom as a single was a sweet gift she gave to us that day."

f. *Include them in same-sex outings*—It's not always possible for my married girlfriends to get away, but I know it means a lot to them when I exert the effort to include them in "girls-only" outings. Just because they're married doesn't mean they don't need time with girlfriends—and as Julie has often reminded me, perhaps they need them more. It's easy as a single to assume because my friends have husbands, their social lives are cared for. Not true.

g. *Notice when they are going solo*—I know what it's like to sit by myself in church, go to a wedding alone, and attend formal events without a date. Most of my married friends are out of practice in this area, and when I notice that a situation calls for it, I try to "make it a date." I've heard many pastors' wives talk about sitting alone in church or going to Sunday school alone—and rather than thinking, "Yeah, now they know what it's like to be single," I want my response to be, "I know how it feels, and I can help ease the difficulty—for *both* of us!"

For the following additional suggestions, I am indebted to my editor, Robin, for her thoughtful contributions to how singles can help encourage their childless married friends or those whose nests are empty. If these precious people do not have a strong network of friends within the church, they (like singles) can also be "at risk" in a family-focused church.

h. *Make them part of the church family*—Look around before Sunday services and other church activities. If you spot older couples sitting alone, go join them and strike up a conversation! Give them a special invite to future church events and tell them you'll keep an eye out for them, so they'll know someone is noticing whether they're around or not.

i. *Share interests*—Do some detective work to find out what special interests your older married acquaintances may have, and then look for ways to get involved alongside them. Some examples might be pets, music, theater, sporting events, or local history.

j. *Take advantage of their experience*—Humble yourself and ask their advice in situations—practical or spiritual—you may be struggling with. They can be a wellspring of knowledge in a wide variety of areas. They may even be willing to assist in projects or tasks in which you have no background, like sewing, cooking, or car maintenance. On a spiritual level, they also may have faced the difficulties you are dealing with and so can offer empathy. Your load may be lightened and they will feel valued.

k. *Include them in celebrations*—When the occasion is appropriate, include older marrieds in special celebrations, like apartment- or housewarming parties; graduation, new job, or promotion parties; or events you may be hosting for younger married friends. Take pictures of them enjoying themselves and give them copies.

l. *Be sensitive to basic needs*—Take note of the special circumstances your older married friends may be in and look for opportunities to help out. If one is having health problems, the burden of care on the other may be great. Providing rides to the doctor, picking up some things at the store, or stopping by with snacks or take-out will relieve some of the strain on the caregiver.

m. *Holidays*—Empty-nesters whose children or relatives can't be with them during holidays will appreciate some extra attention at those times. It's hard to squeeze out more time during busy seasons but it's worth the investment, especially if you're away from your own family.

6. Rob Marus, "Kissing Nonsense Good-bye," *Christianity Today,* 11 June 2001, 47–48.

Appendix: Paul's View of Singleness in 1 Corinthians 7

1. Ben Witherington III, *Conflict and Community in Corinth: A Socio-Rhetorical Commentary on 1 and 2 Corinthians* (Grand Rapids: Eerdmans, 1995), 73.

2. Gordon Fee, *The First Epistle to the Corinthians,* New International Commentary on the New Testament (hereafter NICNT; Grand Rapids: Eerdmans, 1987), 6.

3. S. J. Hafemann, "Corinthians, Letters to the," in *Dictionary of Paul and His Letters*, ed. G. F. Hawthorne and R. P. Martin (Downers Grove, Ill.: InterVarsity, 1993).

4. Fee, *First Epistle to the Corinthians*, NICNT, 6.

5. Gordon Fee, "Toward a Theology of 1 Corinthians," in *Pauline Theology, Volume 2: 1 & 2 Corinthians*, ed. David M. Hay (Minneapolis: Fortress, 1993), 38.

6. Gordon Fee, "1 Corinthians in the NIV," *Journal of the Evangelical Theological Society* 23 (December 1980): 313. Fee cites Paul's attack against the Corinthians' position in chapter 15 where they deny not only a future resurrection, but the bodily nature of it. "Who needs it?" seems to be their point of view.

7. David R. Cartlidge, "1 Corinthians 7 as a Foundation for a Christian Sex Ethic," *Journal of Religion* 55 (1975): 224.

8. Anthony C. Thiselton, *The First Epistle to the Corinthians*, New International Greek Testament Commentary (hereafter NIGTC; Grand Rapids: Eerdmans, 2000), 483.

9. Fee, *First Epistle to the Corinthians*, NICNT, 266–67.

10. Ibid., 270–357.

11. Gordon Fee deals extensively with this verse as translated in the NIV in his article, "1 Corinthians 7:1 in the NIV," 307–14.

12. Thiselton, *First Epistle to the Corinthians*, NIGTC, 498.

13. Antoinette Clark Wire, *The Corinthian Women Prophets: A Reconstruction Through Paul's Rhetoric* (Minneapolis: Fortress, 1990), 80.

14. Thiselton, *First Epistle to the Corinthians*, NIGTC, 499.

15. J. C. Hurd, *Origin of 1 Corinthians* (London: SPCK, 1965; 2d ed. Macon, Ga.: Mercer University Press, 1983), 164, 165.

16. Fee, *First Epistle to the Corinthians*, NICNT, 287.

17. W. F. Orr, "Paul's Treatment of Marriage in 1 Corinthians 7," *Pittsburgh Perspective* 8 (1967): 5–22.

18. Fee, *First Epistle to the Corinthians*, NICNT, 287.

19. Ibid, 287–88.

20. Fee, "1 Corinthians 7:1 in NIV," 310.

21. Antoinette Clark Wire notes that throughout this chapter, Paul

uses "rhetoric of equality or justice. Paul goes far beyond what is required in Greek to make the point that men and women have the same responsibilities toward each other. Ten times an instruction is rephrased twice, once for the male in relation to the female, and once for the female in relation to the male" (*Corinthian Women Prophets,* 79).

22. Fee, *First Epistle to the Corinthians,* NICNT, 288.
23. Thiselton, *First Epistle to the Corinthians,* NIGTC, 571 (emphasis Thiselton's).
24. Fee, *First Epistle to the Corinthians,* NICNT, 323.
25. Ibid.
26. Ibid., 327.
27. Simon J. Kistemaker, *Exposition to the First Epistle to the Corinthians,* New Testament Commentary (hereafter NTC; Grand Rapids: Baker, 1993), 214.
28. Fee, "1 Corinthians 7:1 in the NIV," 311. Fee also argues that because the πόρνη in 6:12–20 are female prostitutes, it is entirely possible that the wives were responsible for the Corinthian slogan in 7:1—on the one hand they elevated celibacy and at the same time they urged their husbands to go to the temple prostitutes for "free sex" since they hadn't yet attained the eschatological maturity with regard to their bodily appetites (314).
29. Fee, *First Epistle to the Corinthians,* NICNT, 278.
30. John C. Poirier and Joseph Frankovic challenge the notion that Paul equates his "gift" with celibacy. "One . . . might legitimately ask whether Paul in fact refers to celibacy as a χάρισμα or if perhaps he subsumes celibacy under the obligations attending his own χάρισμα. That is, does Paul's prophetic self-understanding call for a celibate lifestyle that he would like to impose upon others but finds that he cannot, since they do not have the χάρισμα of prophecy? The most obvious point in favor of the latter interpretation is that nowhere else does Paul call celibacy a χάρισμ, whereas he calls prophecy a χάρισμ in several places" ("Celibacy and *Charism* in 1 Cor 7:5–7," *Harvard Theological Review* 89 [January 1996]: 6).

ENDNOTES

249

31. Fee, *First Epistle to the Corinthians*, NICNT, 284.
32. Ibid., 286.
33. *New American Standard Bible*, King James Version, and *New King James Version* identify the first section as verses 1–9. The *New International Version* and *New Living Bible* form a paragraph with verses 8–9, but allow the entire chapter to fall under the heading "Marriage."
34. Fee, *First Epistle to the Corinthians*, NICNT, 286.
35. Thiselton, *First Epistle to the Corinthians*, NIGTC, 516–17.
36. Michael L. Barré, "To Marry or to Burn: πυροῦσθαι in 1 Cor 7:9," *Catholic Biblical Quarterly* 36 (1974): 199–200.
37. Fee, *First Epistle to the Corinthians*, NICNT, 289.
38. Ibid., 307 (emphasis Fee's).
39. Ibid., 309.
40. Ibid., 268.
41. Ibid., 324.
42. William L. Isley Jr., "A Spirituality for Missionaries," *Missiology* 27 (July 1999): 306.
43. Thiselton, *First Epistle to the Corinthians*, NIGTC, 573.
44. Kistemaker, *Exposition to the First Epistle to the Corinthians*, NTC, 238.
45. Witherington, *Conflict and Community in Corinth*, 179.
46. Ibid.
47. Fee, *First Epistle to the Corinthians*, NICNT, 343.
48. Ibid., 344.
49. Isley, "Spirituality for Missionaries," 300.
50. Thiselton, *First Epistle to the Corinthians*, NIGTC, 588.
51. Fee, *First Epistle to the Corinthians*, NICNT, 341.
52. For example, this entire paper has focused on Paul's theology of singleness, but this chapter does not even mention the most common category of "singles" today—the never-married/not-engaged. He addresses widowed, separated, divorced, and engaged. Our quest for neat answers does not always find what it's looking for!

Resources for Additional Study

Theology of Singleness and Sexuality

Clapp, Rodney. *Families at the Crossroads.* Downers Grove, Ill.: InterVarsity, 1993. Chapter 3, "The Superiority of Singleness" is one of the finest treatments of singleness I've ever read, but the entire book is a worthwhile read as it relates to the idolatry of the family and the role of the church.

Grenz, Stanley. *Sexual Ethics: A Biblical Perspective.* Dallas: Word, 1990. Chapters 9 and 10 deal specifically with singleness.

Grenz, Stanley, and Roy Bell. "Misconduct as Betrayal of a Sexual Trust." Chapter 3 in *Betrayal of Trust: Sexual Misconduct in the Pastorate.* Downers Grove, Ill.: InterVarsity, 1995. Includes an excellent theology of sexuality—for both singleness and marriage.

Hsu, Albert Y. *Singles at the Crossroads: A Fresh Perspective on Christian Singleness.* Downers Grove, Ill.: InterVarsity, 1997. A must-read for singles *and* church leaders.

Norris, Kathleen. "Celibate Passion," *The Christian Century* 113 (20–27 March 1996): 331–34.

Stafford, Tim. *Sexual Chaos: Charting a Course Through Turbulent Times.* Downers Grove, Ill.: InterVarsity, 1989.

Stagg, Frank. "Biblical Perspectives on the Single Person," *Review and Expositor,* winter 1977, 5–19.

Singles Statistics, Trends, and Implications for Church Leaders

Barna, George, ed. *Single Adults.* Glendale, Calif.: Barna Research Group, 2002.

Franck, Dennis. "Single Adults: A Population Group Too Large to Ignore,"

Enrichment Journal, summer 2000. This issue of *Enrichment* contains several good articles about singleness.

Koons, Carolyn, and Michael Anthony. *Single Adult Passages: Uncharted Territories.* Grand Rapids: Baker, 1991. This book is older and out of print, but it's worth trying to find a used copy.

Single Life—Contentment and Wholeness— Resources for Singles

There's an endless supply of books for singles, and more coming out every day. My list is very limited since, generally, singles know where to find books about singleness and because the focus of *A Match Made in Heaven* is not how to live the single life.

Demoss, Nancy Leigh. *Singled Out for God.* Buchanan, Mich.: Life Action Ministries, 1998.

Elliot, Elisabeth. *Passion and Purity.* 2d ed. Grand Rapids: Revell, 2002.

Fagerstrom, Doug, ed. *Single to Single: Daily Devotions by and for Single Adults.* Grand Rapids: Kregel, 2000.

Smith, Lori. *The Single Truth: Challenging the Misconceptions of Singleness with God's Consuming Truth.* Shippensburg, Pa.: Treasure House, 2002.

Whelchel, Mary S. *Common Mistakes Singles Make.* Grand Rapids: Revell, 1999.

Widder, Wendy. *Living Whole Without a Better Half.* Grand Rapids: Kregel, 2000.

Singles in the Church

Albaum, Thomas G. "Double Doors for Singles Ministry," *Leadership Journal,* winter 1991, 84–88. This article provides a helpful and practical perspective on getting singles in the door of the church.

Burke, D. J. "Singleness as a Christian Lifestyle, 1," *Review and Expositor* 74 (winter 1977): 75–80.

Courtney, Camerin. "What Single Women Wish You Knew," *Today's Christian Woman,* May–June 2002, 50–51.

Fagerstrom, Douglas L. *Baker Handbook of Single Adult Ministry.* Grand Rapids: Baker, 1997.

Fortosis, Steve G. "Perspectives on Community: Young Singles in the Congregation," *Christian Education Journal* 10, no. 1 (1989): 39–50.

Langberg, Diane. "Does Single Have to Mean Alone?" *Urban Mission,* December 1996, 6–15.

Marus, Rob. "Kissing Nonsense Good-bye," *Christianity Today,* 11 June 2001, 46–48.

McInerney, Virginia. *Single, Not Separate: How to Make the Church a Family.* Lake Mary, Fla.: Charisma House, 2003. The first half of this book deals with issues singles may face in general, but the second half offers valuable suggestions for integrating singles into the Family.

Sell, Charles M. "Developing Ministries to Singles and Families in Transition." Chapter 26 in *Family Ministry.* 2d ed. Grand Rapids: Zondervan, 1995.

Smith, Jerie. "Models and Ministry with Singles," *Word and World* 5, no. 4 (1985): 405–13.

Winner, Lauren F. "Solitary Refinement," *Christianity Today,* 11 June 2001, 30–36.

Community in the Church

Banks, Robert. *Paul's Idea of Community: The Early Church Houses in Their Historical Setting.* Grand Rapids: Eerdmans, 1980.

Crabb, Larry. *Connecting: A Radical New Vision.* Nashville: Word, 1997.

Johnson, Jan. "Welcoming Strangers," *Moody,* January–February 2002, 22–25.

Lupton, J. Daniel, and Elizabeth Cody Newenhuyse. "Do You Feel Connected at Church?" *Moody,* January–February 2002, 12–15.

Mercer, Larry and Annie. "What Does Caring Look Like?" *Moody,* January–February 2002, 16–18.

Rowell, Ed. "When Your Church Lets You Down," *Moody,* January–February 2002, 26–30.

Smith-Morris, Jennifer. "My First Sunday at Your Church," *Leadership Journal,* summer 2001, 45–46.

Tabb, Mark A. "Getting It Right," *Moody,* January–February 2002, 19–21.

Webber, Robert E. *Ancient-Future Faith: Rethinking Evangelicalism for a Postmodern World.* Grand Rapids: Baker, 1999.

Intergenerational Relationships

Snelling, Sarah. "When Starbucks Meets Sanka," *Discipleship Journal*, May–June 2002, 55–58.

Wevodau, Fred. "From Generation to Generation," *Discipleship Journal*, May–June 2002, 32–39.

Zahn, Drew. "Connecting the Generations," *Leadership*, spring 2002, 37–42. Besides having valuable information about intergenerational ministry, this article also includes a listing of other resources for connecting the generations in your church.

Resources for ongoing information about singles ministry:

S.A.M. Journal (Strategic Adult Ministries Journal) is published six times a year by Cook Communications Ministries. Some information is available on Cook's Website: http://www.cookministries.com

www.singlesmall.com

Also by Wendy Widder

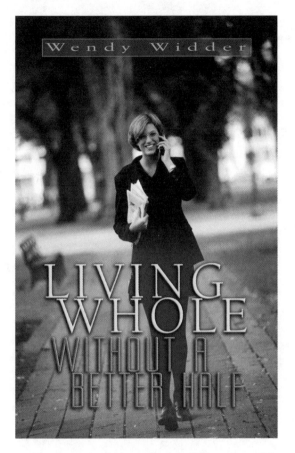

Living Whole Without a Better Half
0-8254-4111-0

An unabashed celebration of the wholeness of single life lived within the will of God. Using the lessons of Bible characters, Wendy shows singles how to find abundance in life instead of letting it slip away while waiting for marriage.

"A refreshing approach. It's easy and fun to read. I give it an A+."

—Gary M. Gray, publisher and editor
Living Solo Magazine